Europe, 1648–1815

Other Volumes Available from Oxford University Press

The Ancient Mediterranean World (*forthcoming*)
Robin W. Winks and Susan Mattern-Parks

Medieval Europe and the World: From Late Antiquity to
Modernity, 400–1500 (*forthcoming*)
Robin W. Winks and Teofilo Ruiz

Europe in a Wider World, 1350–1650
Robin W. Winks and Lee Palmer Wandel

Europe, 1815–1914 (*forthcoming*)
Robin W. Winks and Joan Neuberger

Europe, 1890–1945: Crisis and Conflict
Robin W. Winks and R. J. Q. Adams

Europe, 1945 to the Present: A Global Perspective
(*forthcoming*)
Robin W. Winks and John E. Talbott

Look for these titles on our website: www.oup-usa.org

Europe

1648–1815

From the Old Regime to the Age of Revolution

Robin W. Winks
Yale University

Thomas E. Kaiser
University of Arkansas at Little Rock

New York   Oxford
OXFORD UNIVERSITY PRESS
2004

Oxford University Press

Oxford   New York
Auckland   Bangkok   Buenos Aires   Cape Town   Chennai
Dar es Salaam   Delhi   Hong Kong   Istanbul   Karachi   Kolkata
Kuala Lumpur   Madrid   Melbourne   Mexico City   Mumbai
Nairobi   São Paulo   Shanghai   Taipei   Tokyo   Toronto

Published by Oxford University Press, Inc.
198 Madison Avenue, New York, New York, 10016
http://www.oup-usa.org

Oxford is a registered trademark of Oxford University Press

Library of Congress Cataloging-in-Publication Data
Winks, Robin W.
    Europe, 1648–1815: from the old regime to the age of revolution / Robin W. Winks,
Thomas E. Kaiser.
    p. cm.
    Includes bibliographical references.
    ISBN-13 978-0-19-515446-7 (pbk)

    1. Europe—History—1648–1789. 2. Europe—History—1789–1815. 3.
Revolutions—Europe—History—18th century. 4. Europe—Economic conditions—18th
century. 5. Europe—Economic conditions—19th century. 6. Europe—Intellectual life—18th
century. 7. Europe—Intellectual life—19th century. 8. France—History—1789–1815. I.
Kaiser, Thomas. II. Title.

D273 .W53 2004
940.2'5—dc21   2002038184

Contents

Maps

Preface

The Value of History

History is a series of arguments to be debated, not a body of data to be recorded or a set of facts to be memorized. Thus controversy in historical interpretation—over what an event actually means, over what really happened at an occurrence called "an event," over how best to generalize about the event—is at the heart of its value. Of course history teaches us about ourselves. Of course it teaches us to understand and to entertain a proper respect for our collective past. Of course it transmits to us specific skills—how to ask questions, how to seek out answers, how to think logically, cogently, lucidly, purposefully. Of course it is, or ought to be, a pleasure. But we also discover something fundamental about a people in what they choose to argue over in their past. When a society suppresses portions of its past record, that society (or its leadership) tells us something about itself. When a society seeks to alter how the record is presented, well-proven facts notwithstanding, we learn how history can be distorted to political ends.

Who controls history, and how it is written, controls the past, and who controls the past controls the present. Those who would close off historical controversy with the argument either that we know all that we need to know about a subject, or that what we know is so irrefutably correct that anyone who attacks the conventional wisdom about the subject must have destructive purposes in mind, is in the end intent upon destroying the very value of history itself—that value being that history teaches us to argue productively with each other.

Obviously, then, history is a social necessity. It gives us our identity. It helps us to find our bearings in an ever more complex present, providing us with a navigator's chart by which we may to some degree orient ourselves. When we ask who we are, and how it is that we are so, we learn skepticism and acquire the beginnings of critical judgment. Along with a sense of narrative, history also provides us with tools for explanation and analysis. It helps us to find the particular example, to see the uniqueness in a past age or past event, while also helping us to see how the particular and the unique contribute to the general. History thus shows us humanity at work and play, in society, changing through time. By letting us experience other lifestyles, history shows us the values of both subjectivity and objectivity—those twin conditions of our individual view of the world in which we live, conditions between which we constantly, and usually almost without knowing it, move. Thus, history is both a form of truth and a matter of opinion, and the close study of history should help us to distinguish between the two. It is important to make such distinctions, for as Sir Walter Raleigh wrote, "It is not truth but opinion that can travel the world without a passport." Far too often what we read, see, and hear and believe to be the truth—in our newspapers, on our television sets, from our friends—is opinion, not fact.

History is an activity. That activity asks specific questions as a means of arriving at general questions. A textbook such as this is concerned overwhelmingly with general questions, even though at times it must ask specific questions or present specific facts as a means of stalking the general. The great philosopher Karl Jaspers once remarked, "Who I am and where I belong, I first learned to know from the mirror of history." It is this mirror that any honest book must reflect.

To speak of "civilization" (of which this book is a history) is at once to plunge into controversy, so that our very first words illustrate why some people are so fearful of the study of history. To speak of "Western civilization" is even more restrictive, too limited in the eyes of some historians. Yet if we are to understand history as a process, we must approach it through a sense of place: our continuity, our standards, our process. Still, we must recognize an inherent bias in such a term as "Western civilization," indeed, two inherent biases: first, that we know what it means to be "civilized" and have attained that stature; and second, that the West as a whole is a single unitary civilization. This second bias is made plain when we recognize that most scholars and virtually all college courses refer not to "Eastern civilization" but to "the civilizations of the East"—a terminology that suggests that while the West is a unity, the East is not. These are conventional phrases, buried in Western perception of reality, just as our common geographical references show a Western bias. The Near East or the Far East are, after all, "near" or "far" only in reference to a geographical location focused on western Europe. The Japanese do not refer to London as being in the far West or Los Angeles as being in the far East, although both references would be correct, if they saw the world as though they stood at its center. Although this text will accept these conventional phrases, precisely because they are traditionally embedded in our Western languages, one of the uses of history—and of the writing of a book such as this one—is to alert us to the biases buried in our language, even when necessity requires that we continue to use its conventional forms of shorthand.

But if we are to speak of civilization, we must have, at the outset, some definition of what we mean by "being civilized." Hundreds of books have been written on this subject. The average person often means only that others, the "noncivilized," speak a different language and practice alien customs. The Chinese customarily referred to all foreigners as barbarians, and the ancient Greeks spoke of those who could not communicate in Greek as *bar-bar*—those who do not speak our tongue. Yet today the ability to communicate in more than one language is one hallmark of a "civilized" person. Thus definitions of civilization, at least as used by those who think little about the meaning of their words, obviously change.

For our purposes, however, we must have a somewhat more exacting definition of the term, since it guides and shapes any book that attempts to cover the entire sweep of Western history. Anthropologists, sociologists, historians, and others may reasonably differ as to whether, for example, there is a separate American civilization that stands apart from, say, a British or Italian civilization, or whether these civilizations are simply particular variants on one larger entity, with only that larger entity—the West—entitled to be called "a civilization." Such an argument is of no major importance here, although it is instructive that it should occur. Rather, what is needed is a definition sufficiently clear to be used throughout the narrative and analysis to follow. This working definition, therefore, will hold that "civilization" involves the presence of several (although not necessarily all) of the following conditions within a society or group of interdependent societies:

1. There will be some form of government by which people administer to their political needs and responsibilities.
2. There will be some development of urban society, that is, of city life, so that the culture is not nomadic, dispersed, and thus unable to leave significant and surviving physical remnants of its presence.
3. Human beings will have become toolmakers, able through the use of metals to transform, however modestly, their physical environment, and thus their social and economic environment as well.
4. Some degree of specialization of function will have begun, usually at the workplace, so that pride, place, and purpose work together as cohesive elements in the society.
5. Social classes will have emerged, whether antagonistic to or sustaining of one another.
6. A form of literacy will have developed, so that group may communicate with group and, more importantly, generation with generation in writing.
7. There will be a concept of leisure time—that life is not solely for the workplace or for the assigned class function or specialization—so that, for example, art may develop beyond (although not excluding) mere decoration and sports beyond mere competition.
8. There will be a concept of a higher being, although not necessarily through organized religion, by which a people may take themselves outside themselves to explain events and find purpose.
9. There will be a concept of time, by which the society links itself to a past and to the presumption of a future.
10. There will have developed a faculty for criticism. This faculty need not be the rationalism of the West, or intuition, or any specific religious or political mechanism, but it must exist, so that the society may contemplate change from within, rather than awaiting attack (and possible destruction) from without.

A common Western bias is to measure "progress" through technological change and to suggest that societies that show (at least until quite recently in historical time) little dramatic technological change are not civilized. In truth, neither a written record nor dramatic technological changes are essential to being civilized, although both are no doubt present in societies we would call civilized. Perhaps, as we study history, we ought to remember all three of the elements inherent in historical action as recorded by the English critic John Ruskin: "Great nations write their autobiographies in three manuscripts, the book of their deeds, the book of their words, and the book of their art."

The issue here is not whether we "learn from the past." Most often we do not, at least at the simple-minded level; we do not, as a nation, decide upon a course of action in diplomacy, for example, simply because a somewhat similar course in the past worked. We are wise enough to know that circumstances alter cases and that new knowledge brings new duties. Of course individuals "learn from the past"; the victim of a mugging takes precautions in the future. To dignify such an experience as "a lesson of history," however, is to turn mere individual growth from child into adult into history when, at most, such growth is a personal experience in biography.

We also sometimes learn the "wrong lessons" from history. Virtually anyone who wishes to argue passionately for a specific course of future action can find a lesson from the past that will convince the gullible that history repeats itself and therefore that the past is a map to the future. No serious historian argues this, however. General patterns may, and sometimes do, repeat themselves, but specific chains of events do not. Unlike those subjects that operate at the very highest level of generalization (political science, theology, science), history simply does not believe in ironclad laws. But history is not solely a series of unrelated events. There are general patterns, clusters of causes, intermediate levels of generalization that prove true. Thus, history works at a level uncomfortable to many: above the specific, below the absolute.

If complex problems never present themselves twice in the same or even in recognizably similar form—if, to borrow a frequent image from the military world, generals always prepare for the last war instead of the next one—then does the study of history offer society any help in solving its problems? The answer surely is yes—but only in a limited way. History offers a rich collection of clinical reports on human behavior in various situations—individual and collective, political, economic, military, social, cultural—that tell us in detail how the human race has conducted its affairs and that suggest ways of handling similar problems in the present. President Harry S. Truman's secretary of state, a former chief of staff, General George Marshall, once remarked that nobody could think about the problems of the 1950s who had not reflected upon the fall of Athens in the fifth century b.c. He was referring to the extraordinary history of the war between Athens and Sparta written just after it was over by Thucydides, an Athenian who fought in the war. There were no nuclear weapons, no telecommunications, no guns or gunpowder in the fifth century b.c. , and the logistics of war were altogether primitive, yet twenty-three hundred years later one of the most distinguished leaders of American military and political affairs found Thucydides indispensable to his thinking.

History, then, can only approximate the range of human behavior, with some indication of its extremes and averages. It can, although not perfectly, show how and within what limits human behavior changes. This last point is especially important for the social scientist, the economist, the sociologist, the executive, the journalist, or the diplomat. History provides materials that even an inspiring leader—a prophet, a reformer, a politician—would do well to master before seeking to lead us into new ways. For it can tell us something about what human material can and cannot stand, just as science and technology can tell engineers what stresses metals can tolerate. History can provide an awareness of the depth of time and space that should check the optimism and the overconfidence of the reformer. For example, we may wish to protect the environment in which we live—to eliminate acid rain, to cleanse our rivers, to protect our wildlife, to preserve our majestic natural scenery. History may show us that most peoples have failed to do so, and it may provide us with some guidance on how to avoid the mistakes of the past. But history will also show that there are substantial differences of public and private opinion over how best to protect our environment, that there are many people who do not believe such protection is necessary, or that there are people who accept the need for protection but are equally convinced that lower levels of protection must be traded off for higher levels of productivity from our natural resources. History can provide the setting by which we may understand differing opinions, but recourse to history will not get the legislation passed, make the angry happy, make the future clean and safe. History will not define river pollution, although it can provide us with statistics from the past for comparative measurement. The definition will arise from the politics of today and our judgments about tomorrow. History is for the long and at times for the intermediate run, but seldom for the short run.

So, if we are willing to accept a "relevance" that is more difficult to see at first than the immediate applicability of science and more remote than direct action, we will have to admit that history is "relevant." It may not actually build the highway or clear the slum, but it can give enormous help to those who wish to do so. And failure to take it into account may lead to failure in the sphere of action.

But history is also fun, at least for those who enjoy giving their curiosity free reign. Whether it is historical gossip we prefer (how many lovers did Catherine the Great of Russia actually take in a given year, and how much political influence did their activity in the imperial bedroom give them?), the details of historical investigation (how does it happen that the actual treasures found in a buried Viking ship correspond to those described in an Anglo-Saxon poetic account of a ship-burial?), more complex questions of cause and effect (how influential have the writings of revolutionary intellectuals been upon the course of actual revolutions?), the relationships between politics and economics (how far does the rise and decline of Spanish power in modern times depend upon the supply of gold and silver from New World colonies?), or cultural problems (why did western Europe choose to revive classical Greek and Roman art and literature instead of turning to some altogether new experiment?), those who enjoy history will read almost greedily to discover what they want to know. Having discovered it, they may want to know how we know what we have learned, and may want to turn to those sources closest in time to the persons and questions concerned—to the original words of the participants. To read about Socrates, Columbus, or Churchill is fun; to read their own words, to visit with them as it were, is even more so. To see them in context is important; to see how we have taken their thoughts and woven them to purposes of our own is at least equally important. Readers will find the path across the mine-studded fields of history helped just a little by extracts from these voices—voices of the past but also of the present. They can also be helped by chronologies, bibliographies, pictures, maps—devices through which historians share their sense of fun and immediacy with a reader.

In the end, to know the past is to know ourselves—not entirely, not enough, but a little better. History can help us to achieve some grace and elegance of action, some cogency and completion of thought, some harmony and tolerance in human relationships. Most of all, history can give us a sense of excitement, a personal zest for watching and perhaps participating in the events around us that will, one day, be history too.

History is a narrative, a story; history is concerned foremost with major themes, even as it recognizes the significance of many fascinating digressions. Because history is largely about how and why people behave as they do, it is also about patterns of thought and belief. Ultimately, history is about what people believe to be true. To this extent, virtually all history is intellectual history, for the perceived meaning of a specific treaty, battle, or scientific discovery lies in what those involved in it and those who came after thought was most significant about it. History makes it clear that we may die, as we may live, as a result of what someone believes to be quite true in the relatively remote past.

We cannot each be our own historian. In everyday life we may reconstruct our personal past, acting as detectives for our motivations and attitudes. But formal history is a much more rigorous study. History may give us some very small capacity to predict the future. More certainly, it should help us arrange the causes for given events into meaningful patterns. History also should help us to be tolerant of the historical views of others, even as it helps to shape our own convictions. History must help us sort out the important from the less important, the relevant from the irrelevant, so that we do not fall prey to those who propose simple-minded solutions to vastly complex human problems. We must not yield to the temptation to blame one group or individual for our problems, and yet we must not fail to defend our convictions with vigor.

To recognize, indeed to celebrate, the value of all civilizations is essential to the civilized life itself. To understand that we see all civilizations through the prism of our specific historical past—for which we feel affection, in which we may feel comfortable and secure, and by which we interpret all else that we encounter—is simply to recognize that we too are the products of history. That is why we must study history and ask our own questions in our own way. For if we ask no questions of our past, there may be no questions to ask of our future.

Robin W. Winks

Introduction

Europe, 1648–1815

"Order and Progress" is the motto emblazoned on the flag of Brazil, but these words could just as well introduce the history of Europe from 1648 to 1815. This history may be envisioned as the product of two successive movements, each having as its central goal the achievement of one or the other of these general objectives.

In the period from 1648 until about 1750, European elites engaged in a desperate effort to restore order, after experiencing wrenching changes during the previous century that caused many to fear that society was quickly dissolving into chaos. In the realm of religious practice, the experimentation of the late Middle Ages and the Reformation had forced Europeans—from the top of the social ladder to the bottom—to choose sides in a bitter and bloody Catholic/Protestant conflict. By 1648 that conflict had yielded a stalemate neither side wanted. From this time forward, both parties would have to learn to live with "heretics" or face the prospect of endless warfare at home and abroad. Regarding the economy and society, a powerful capitalist movement originating in the Middle Ages had begun to dissolve old social ties in the countryside, leading to the near disappearance of serfdom in western Europe and to the formation of a larger merchant class in the cities. Easier access to foreign markets, abetted by better forms of transportation, was encouraging economic specialization and the growth of a money-based economy, which provided new opportunities for enrichment. But these changes also threatened to erode long-standing ways of life. Rich bourgeois were pushing to move into the more privileged classes, aristocrats saw their privileges under threat, and peasants became more dependent on the ever-changing market for their livelihood. Politically, Europe was facing the emergence of a system of medium-sized states designed, above all, as machines of war. Siphoning off ever-increasing amounts of wealth generated by the larger economy, early modern states were still in the throes of a "military revolution" that engaged them in ever costlier conflicts with as yet badly disciplined armies. As the scale of war increased, so did its theaters expand, forcing kings and their ministers to develop foreign policies embracing the Continent. Internally, the monarchical state bulked larger and larger, attempting to make its power "absolute," that is, effectively unchallengeable. Although intended to pacify society, this dynastic power-grab had touched off a wave of revolts that was only cresting in 1648. Intellectually, the Scientific Revolution had begun to corrode old certainties about the universe, just as the exploration and plundering of the New World had revealed the existence of peoples, cultures, and even continents unknown two centuries earlier.

Coping with all these changes was the task of European power-brokers who blended new instruments of power and new symbols of authority with traditional ones. The result was an arrangement of power structures and ideologies historians have called the "Old Regime." Although the Old Regime could take significantly different forms in different national contexts, European elites from the mid-seventeenth through the mid-eighteenth centuries were struggling with many of the same projects. Religious splintering was countered by the stiffening of religious orthodoxies, including Protestantism, and fresh efforts were made to convert dissenters forcibly. Global commercialization evoked policies of "mercantilism," whereby princes sought to regulate and divert the anarchic flow of goods, labor, and money in ways that benefited themselves and the nations they governed. National states struggled to discipline more effectively the large, unruly armies they had generated, while developing balance-of-power strategies to stabilize international relations. Bureaucracies and patronage systems arose. Their purpose was not to break the power of the nobility, who were gradually disbanding their armies in the face of unassailable competition from the king's military machine, but to incorporate the nobles as partners in the expanding national state and thereby reinvigorate the structure of privilege. "Divine-right" ideologies were elaborated to shore up the authority of kings. States developed complex censorship procedures to police expression, while courts and royal academies laid down the guidelines for politically correct forms of art, science, and even elite speech, dress, and written language. In short, European rulers launched a major effort to strengthen the hierarchy and to close ranks against the sources of division and instability.

Monolithic and unmovable as these strengthened institutions appeared, the Old Regime was shot through with compromises and contradictions that undermined it in the end, and by 1750 the search for order began to give way to a search for progress. Paradoxically, this occurred largely because of the Old Regime's many successes. By ending the sense of crisis, the Old Regime gradually made its authoritarian features seem less necessary. After 1750, Europeans felt freer to criticize the failures and inefficiencies of the Old Regime in a movement known as the "Enlightenment." In a calmer age, the heavy-handed methods used by the Old Regime became increasingly resented, as the face of "absolutism" blended with that of "despotism," a regime characterized by an absence of laws. Armies became more disciplined over the eighteenth century, and the balance-of-power techniques developed during the Renaissance still worked well enough to prevent the domination of any single nation. Yet balance-of-power policies also promoted aggression abroad, since territorial conquest by one leading state invited other states to gobble up territory elsewhere. Thus kings in eastern Europe carved up weak states such as Poland, while western Europeans competed to build vast, far-flung colonial empires in the Americas on the backs of imported African slaves. The result was a string of wars, which, if not as disastrous to European civilian populations as the Thirty Years' War was, were nonetheless costly enough to put enormous financial pressures on all European states. The impulse for reform, for "progress," generally thus arose not only from a change of intellectual atmosphere, but also from the needs of state operations.

At the same time that states were straining to streamline their bureaucracies and enhance their revenues, Europe was unknowingly moving toward the Industrial Revolution. This transformation of production methods was the result of increasing demand generated by a growing population, better transportation, more efficient agriculture, sufficient investment capital, and a will to apply the principles of the new science to production. Although the impact of the Industrial Revolution would only be felt in the nineteenth century, the factors that led to it already were raising living standards in the eighteenth, as evidenced by a still larger middle class, the growth in demand for modestly priced manufactured products that made life more comfortable, and rising rates of literacy. The mass-marketing of high culture via the proliferation of books and newspapers, concerts, and artistic exhibitions helped expand the political and artistic publics. "Public opinion," a vague and threatening force to leaders for a long time, was now gaining so much authority that even princes and kings believed they had to respect it, at least in their rhetoric.

These developments influenced all European nations, but none as dramatically as France, which in 1789 experienced the most explosive and far-reaching political and social revolution of the early modern period. Sweeping away many of the instruments of power and privilege of the Old Regime, the French Revolution laid down the foundations for modern political society, including equality before the law, democracy, and constitutional government. The impact of this revolution transcended the borders of France, as many of its institutions and ideas were carried to the four corners of Europe by Napoleon, thus giving birth to a modern age in which the search for order and progress would have to begin once again.

ONE

The Problem of Divine-Right Monarchy

The Peace of Westphalia in 1648 ended the Thirty Years' War but also marked the end of an epoch in European history. It ended the Age of the Reformation and Counter-Reformation, when wars were both religious and dynastic in motivation, and the chief threats to a stable international balance came from the Catholic Habsburgs and from the militant Protestants of Germany, the Netherlands, and Scandinavia. After 1648 religion, although continuing to be a major source of friction in France and the British Isles, ceased to be a significant international issue elsewhere. In western Europe, most international conflicts centered on efforts to contain French expansion into surrounding territories. For seventy-two years (1643–1714) France was under a single monarch, Louis XIV, who inherited the throne when only four.

Louis was the embodiment of the early modern form of royal absolutism—monarchy by divine right—and he was the personification of royal pride, elegance, and luxury. To the French, Louis XIV was *le grand monarque.* His long reign brought to an end *le grand siècle,* that great century (begun under Cardinal Richelieu in the twenty years before Louis's accession) that was marked by the international triumph of French arms and French diplomacy and, still more, of French ways of writing, building, dressing, eating— the whole style of life of the upper classes in France, which called itself *la grande nation.*

While French culture went from triumph to triumph, Louis XIV's bid for political hegemony was ultimately checked. Among Louis's most resolute opponents during his last two wars was England. After playing a relatively minor role in European affairs for more than a century, England emerged as a first-rank power by the end of Louis's reign. England's success abroad was partly the result of its success in settling domestic conflicts that resulted from the collision between the forces of the Stuart monarchy and High Church Anglicanism, on the one hand, and those of Parliament and the Puritans, on the other. The final settlement, after decades of violence and change, was a compromise weighted in favor of the parliamentary side, with one English king executed and another forced into exile. While France appeared stable, England was racked by revolution and insecurity.

The stabilization of England and France resulted from efforts to resolve a broad range of problems that in varying ways and to varying degrees swept the Continent. Religious dissent, civil conflicts, declining economic growth, and social dislocations caused by war were among the most common sources of difficulty. One answer to these disturbing tendencies was the growth of the national state. Although they reached distinctively different constitutional settlements, the national states of France and England, like those of other countries, managed to impose more law and order at the end of the seventeenth century than they had at the beginning. Feeding off expanded government revenues and heavier government borrowing, larger and more disciplined armies pacified the countryside and cities more effectively. The state offered pensions, privileges, honors, and government jobs, most notably in the expanded military, to social elites in order to discourage aristocratic rebellions. The seventeenth century may as rightly be considered the age of aristocracy as it can the age of kings.

Culture in seventeenth-century Europe was also slowly transformed. These changes occurred partly in response to the needs and interests of the state and of the upper classes, who sought to strengthen their privileged status by adopting lifestyles and intellectual pursuits that marked them off from the rest of the population, most of it still illiterate. Royal courts, especially the French court, elaborated new codes of aristocratic etiquette and provided showcases for the arts. The state also patronized the new science through the establishment of major scientific academies. Many of the seventeenth century's greatest thinkers—Bacon, Descartes, Newton, Leibniz—worked for Europe's princes and kings. Whatever the disadvantages of this state sponsorship, historians have found this period so rich in intellectual creativity that they have called it the "century of genius."

Bourbon France

In 1610 the capable and popular Henry IV was assassinated in the prime of his career by a madman who was believed at the time to be working for the Jesuits—a charge for which there is no proof. The new king, Louis XIII (r. 1610–1643), was nine years old; the queen mother, Marie de Medici, served as regent but showed little political skill. Her Italian favorites and French nobles, Catholic and Huguenot alike, carried on a hectic competition that threatened to undo all that Henry IV had accomplished. During these troubles the French representative body, the Estates General, met in 1614 for what was destined to be its last session until 1789. Significantly, the meeting was paralyzed by tensions between the noble deputies of the second estate and the bourgeois of the third. Meanwhile, Louis XIII, although barely into his teens, tried to assert his personal authority and reduce the role of his mother. Poorly educated, sickly, masochistic, and subject to depression, Louis needed expert help.

Louis XIII and Richelieu, 1610–1643

Louis was fortunate in securing the assistance of the remarkably talented duc de Richelieu (1585–1642), who was an efficient administrator as bishop of the remote diocese of Autun. Tiring of provincial life, Richelieu moved to Paris and showed unscrupulous skill in political maneuvering during the confused days of the regency. He emerged as the conciliator between the king and his mother and was rewarded, first, by being made a cardinal and then, in 1624, with selection by Louis as his chief minister. While the king maintained a lively interest in affairs of state, Richelieu was the virtual ruler of France for the next eighteen years. Although ruthless enough to be a Machiavellian, Richelieu firmly believed his policies were in accordance with his Christian faith.

Richelieu had four goals for the France of Louis XIII: to eliminate the Huguenots as an effective political force; to remind the nobles that they were subordinate to the king; to make all of France conscious of a sense of national greatness; and, through these measures, to make the monarchy truly rather than only theoretically absolute. *Raison d'état* made the ruin of the Huguenots the first priority, for the political privileges they had received by the Edict of Nantes made them a major obstacle to the creation of a centralized state. The hundred fortified towns they governed, chiefly in the southwest, were a state within the state, a hundred centers of potential rebellion. Alarmed, the Huguenots rebelled. The fall of La Rochelle, their chief stronghold, in 1628 and Richelieu's unexpectedly humane approach—by which the political and military clauses of the Edict of Nantes were revoked while partial religious toleration continued—helped Richelieu neutralize the Huguenots.

The siege of La Rochelle was prolonged because France had no navy worthy of the name. Over the next ten years Richelieu created a fleet of warships for the Atlantic and a squadron of galleys manned by European slaves for the Mediterranean. Meanwhile, he guided France expertly through the Thirty Years' War, committing French resources only when concrete gains seemed possible and ensuring favorable publicity by supplying exaggerated accounts of French victories to the *Gazette de France*.

Next Richelieu tried to humble the nobles, with only partial success, by ordering the destruction of some of their fortresses and forbidding private duels. More effective was his use of royal officials called "intendants," who neither inherited nor bought their offices, to keep in check nobles and officeholders of doubtful loyalty. These officials had existed earlier but had performed only minor functions; now they were given greatly increased powers over justice, the police, and taxation.

Richelieu made possible *la grande nation* of Louis XIV by building a centralized state. But this state was hardly "bureaucratic" in the modern sense, since the vast majority of state officers bought their offices from the state, which thereby acquired badly needed revenue and a certain amount of loyalty. The disadvantage of this system of "venality" to the state was that ministers could not impose quality controls on most of their personnel, nor could they fire incompetent officials without paying these officials back for their offices—a luxury the state could almost never afford. Moreover, Richelieu did little to remedy the chronic fiscal weakness of the government, particularly the corruption in tax collection and the recurrent deficits. His concentration on *raison d'état* led him to take a callous view of the subjects on whose loyal performance of their duties the strength of the state depended. He believed that the masses were best kept docile through hard work, that leisure led to mischief, and that the common people ought to take pride in the splendors of the monarchy, in the accomplishments of French literary culture, and in victories over the monarch's enemies. Individual hardship, especially among the lower classes, was to be accepted in the interests of national glory. Such acceptance is a common ingredient of nationalism.

Mazarin

The deaths of Richelieu in 1642 and Louis XIII in 1643, the accession of another child king, and the regency of the hated queen mother, Anne of Austria (actually a Habsburg from Spain, where the dynasty was called the house of Austria), all seemed to threaten a repetition of the crisis that had followed the death of Henry IV. The new crisis was dealt with by the new chief minister, Jules Mazarin (1602–1661), a Sicilian who had been picked and schooled by Richelieu himself and was exceptionally close to Anne. Mazarin, too, was a cardinal (although not a priest, as Richelieu had been) and a supreme exponent of *raison d'état*. Mazarin also was careless about the finances of France, and like Richelieu, he amassed an immense personal fortune during his career. He antagonized both branches of the French aristocracy: the nobles of the sword, descendants of feudal magnates, and the nobles of the robe (the reference is to the gowns worn by judges and other officials), descendants of commoners who had bought their way into government office. The former resented being excluded from the regency by a foreigner; the latter, who had invested heavily in government securities, particularly disliked Mazarin's casual way of borrowing money to meet war expenses and then neglecting to pay the interest owed to the state office-holders.

In 1648 discontent boiled over in the *Fronde* (named for the slingshot used by Parisian children to hurl pellets at the rich in their carriages), one of several mid-century uprisings in Europe. Some of the rioting involved the rural peasantry and the common people of Paris, impoverished by the economic depression accompanying the final campaigns of the Thirty Years' War and deeply affected by the peak famine years of 1648–1651. But the Fronde was essentially a revolt of the nobles, led first by the judges of the Parlement of Paris, a stronghold of the nobles of the robe, and then, after the Peace of Westphalia, by aristocratic officers returned from the Thirty Years' War. Various "princes of the blood" (relatives of the royal family) confusingly intervened with private armies. Although Mazarin twice had to flee France and go into exile, and although the royal troops had to lay siege to Paris, and despite concessions Mazarin felt forced to make, the end result of what was in reality two revolts in one—of the Parlement and of the nobles—was to weaken both. The

This illustration from Abraham Bosse's "Le Palais Royal" (1640) provides a good picture of French fashions and tastes. Bosse (1602–1676) took a particular interest in etchings that showed how the upper middle class dressed. Furniture also evolved in new styles to accommodate the new clothing. (New York Public Library Picture Collection)

Fronde prepared the way for the personal rule of Louis XIV, with the mass of ordinary citizens in Paris supporting the queen and her son when they returned in triumph in October 1652. Essentially, the Fronde failed because it had no real roots in the countryside, not even in the rising middle classes of the provincial cities. Rather, it was essentially a struggle for power, pitting Mazarin and his new bureaucracy against the two privileged groups of nobles, each of which distrusted the other. All Mazarin had to do was to apply the old Roman maxim, "Divide and rule."

Louis XIV, 1643–1714

When Mazarin died in 1661, Louis XIV began his personal rule. He had been badly frightened during the Fronde when rioters had broken into his bedroom, and he was determined to suppress any challenge to his authority, by persuasion and guile if possible, and by force if necessary. In 1660 he married a Spanish princess for political reasons. After a succession of mistresses, he married one of them in 1685, Madame de Maintenon, a devout former

Few official portraits from this period have survived. The only ones fully authenticated are those of Louis XIII and Richelieu. Philippe de Champaigne (1602–1674) often depicted Richelieu, and in this triple portrait he sought to emphasize the rationalism of the age. (National Gallery, London)

Huguenot who was the governess of his illegitimate children. She did much to assure dignified piety at court for the rest of his reign.

Louis XIV, the Sun King, succeeded as *le grand monarque* because by education, temperament, and physique he was ideally suited to the role. He had admirable self-discipline, patience, and staying power. He never lost his temper in public and went through long daily council meetings and elaborate ceremonials with unwearied attention and even enjoyment, to which his conspicuous lack of a sense of humor may have contributed. He had an iron physical constitution, which enabled him to withstand a rigorous schedule, made him indifferent to heat and to cold, and allowed him to survive both a lifetime of gross overeating and the crude medical treatment of the day.

He was five feet five inches tall (a fairly impressive height for that day) and added to his stature by shoes with high red heels. Even as a youth he was determined to "be perfect in all things" and to fail at nothing. To provide a suitable setting for the Sun King, to neutralize the high nobility politically by isolating it in the ceaseless ceremonies and petty intrigues of court life, and also to prevent a repetition of the rioters' intrusion into his bedroom in Paris, he moved the capital from Paris to Versailles, a dozen miles away. There, between 1668 and 1711, he built a vast palace more than a third of a mile long, set in an immense formal garden that demonstrated control over nature, a garden with fourteen hundred fountains supplied by water that had to be pumped up from the River Seine at great expense. Versailles housed, mainly in cramped, uncomfortable, and unsanitary quarters, a court of ten thousand, including dependents and servants of all sorts. This was self-conscious government by spectacle, and it would be copied by every monarch who could afford it—and some who could not.

Divine-Right Monarchy

The much admired and imitated French state, of which Versailles was the symbol and Louis XIV the embodiment, is also the best historical example of divine-right monarchy. Perhaps Louis never actually said, "L'état c'est moi" ("I am the state"), but the phrase clearly summarizes his convictions about his role. In theory, Louis was the representative of God on earth—or at least in France. He was not elected by the French, nor did he acquire his throne by force of arms; rather, he was born to a position God had planned for the legitimate male heir of Hugh Capet, who had been king of France in the tenth century. As God's agent his word was final, for to challenge it would be to challenge the structure of God's universe; disobedience was a religious as well as a political offense. Thus the origins of divine right were a logical extension of Gallicanism, which sought to limit papal intervention in the French church to purely doctrinal matters.

In some ways the theory that justified divine-right monarchy looked back to the Middle Ages, to the view that right decisions in government are not arrived at by experiment and discussion but by "finding" the authoritative answer provided for in God's scheme of things. In other ways the theory was "modern" or forward looking, in that it derived from expectations about national loyalties and the growth of a sense of nationalism. Henry IV, Richelieu, and Louis XIV sought to fuse all of the inhabitants of France into a single national unit. But nationalism in this period was primarily an affair of elites, whose opinion alone counted in the affairs of state. Thus although the court and the French Academy produced a refined French to replace the hodgepodge of local dialectics spoken by the nobility, there is no evidence that Louis XIV cared which language his peasants spoke. Still, the king's ministers did attempt to set the king up as the symbol of common Frenchness. The king collected taxes, raised armies, and touched the lives of his subjects in a hundred ways. The French had to believe that the king had a right to do all this, and that he was doing it for them rather than to them.

Divine-right monarchy, with its corollary of unquestioning obedience on the part of subjects, was thus one ingredient in the growth of the modern centralized nation-state. It was an institution that appealed to old theological ideas, such as the biblical admonition to obey the powers that be, for "the powers that be are ordained of God." But it was also inspired by the newer ideas of binding people together in a productive, efficient, and secure state. Naturally, in practice the institution did not wholly correspond to theories about it. Louis XIV was not the French state, and his rule was not absolute in any true sense of that word. He simply did not have the physical means to control in detail everything his subjects did; but his policies could touch their daily lives by bringing relative prosperity or hardship, peace or war. And Louis XIV could endeavor, in the majesty of his person, to act out the theories of those, like Bishop Jacques Bossuet (1627–1704), who provided the intellectual foundations for a universal history that justified divine-right arguments.

Increasingly, the chief opposition to such ideas came not from the various faiths but from the nobles, so that in both France and England the seventeenth century brought a crisis to the aristocracy. The degree to which the nobility was integrated into the new state machinery was of crucial importance in the development of modern Europe. In Habsburg Spain and in the Habsburg lands of central Europe, the old nobility generally accepted the new strength of the Crown but maintained many of their privileges and all of their old pride of status. In Prussia they were more successfully integrated into the new order, becoming servants of the Crown, yet with a social status that set them well above bourgeois bureaucrats. In England the nobility achieved a unique compromise with the Crown. In France the nobles of the sword were deprived of most major political functions, but they were allowed to retain social and economic privileges and important roles as officers in the king's army.

The process of reducing the power of the old French nobility in national political life had begun as early as the twelfth century and had been much hastened by the religious and civil wars of the sixteenth century. An important part of the nobility, perhaps nearly half, had become Protestant, in large part from sheer opposition to the Crown, during the late sixteenth century, although many soon reconverted to Catholicism. Under Richelieu and Louis XIV the process was completed by the increasing use of commoners to run the government, from the great ministers of state, through the intendants, down to local administrators and judges. These commoners were usually elevated to the nobility of the robe, which did not at first have the social prestige of the nobility of the sword. But the Fronde had shown that these new nobles could not be counted upon as loyal supporters of the Crown, and among the old nobles they aroused contemptuous envy. Although at times the nobles were able to work together, they posed no serious threat to the Crown under Louis XIV.

Nor did the church. Under Louis XIV the French clergy continued to possess important privileges; they were not subject to royal taxation; they contributed a voluntary grant of money that they voted in their own assembly. Carefully the Crown fostered the evolution of a national Gallican church, firmly Catholic although controlled by the monarchy. The Gallican union of throne and altar reached a high point in 1682, when an assembly of French clerics drew up the Declaration of Gallican Liberties, asserting in effect that the "rules and customs admitted by France and the Gallican church" were

The Palace of Versailles, outside Paris, grew to immense proportions. Built for Louis XIV, the Sun King, construction took forty-three years, from 1668 to 1711. The central portion was the work of Louis LeVau (1612–1670), and, later, the gardens were laid out by André Le Nôtre (1613–1700). This early picture from the museum at Versailles shows the original chateau in its more modest 1668 dimensions. (Réunion des Musées Nationaux/Art Resource, NY)

just as important as the traditional authority of the papacy. Louis XIV thereupon took as the goal of his religious policy the application of a French motto—un roi, une loi, une foi (one king, one law, one faith).

Where Richelieu had attacked only the political privileges of the Huguenots, Louis attacked their fundamental right of toleration and finally revoked the Edict of Nantes in 1685. Fifty thousand Huguenot families fled abroad, notably to Prussia, Holland, the Dutch colony in southern Africa, England, and British North America. The practical skills and the intellectual abilities of the refugees strengthened the lands that received them, and the departure of industrious workers and thousands of veteran sailors, soldiers, and officers weakened France. Some Huguenots remained in France, worshiping secretly despite persecution. Others fled abroad to Protestant countries, where they contributed to a flow of propaganda leveled against Louis XIV.

Within the Catholic church itself, Louis attempted to repress two movements of which he disapproved. Both groups saw themselves as countering the Counter-Reformation while remaining within the Catholic church. The Quietists, a group of religious enthusiasts led by Madame Jeanne Marie Guyon (1648–1717), sought a more mystical and emotional faith and believed

*Louis XIV was sixty-three and at the height of his power when Hyacinthe Rigaud
(1659–1743) painted this strikingly posed portrait. In the background Rigaud has invoked
memories of another great empire, Rome, while showing Louis's strength and sense of elegance in the flowing robe, the great ceremonial sword of office, and the coiffed wig. This portrait hangs in the Louvre in Paris.   (Réunion des Musées Nationaux/Art Resource, NY)*

in direct inspiration from God and perfect union with him, so that a priesthood was not needed; but their tendency to exhibitionism and self-
righteousness, and their zeal for publicity, belied their name and offended the
king's sense of propriety. The Jansenists, sometimes called the Puritans of the
Catholic church, were a high-minded group whose most distinguished
spokesman was the scientist and philosopher Blaise Pascal (1622–1662).
Named for Cornelius Jansen (1585–1638), bishop of Ypres, the Jansenists took
an almost Calvinistic stand on predestination. They stressed the need to obey
God rather than man, no matter how exalted the position of the particular
man might be. They therefore questioned the authority of both king and pope

and attacked the pope's agents, the Jesuits. At the end of his reign, Louis responded to Jansenism with ever-increasing fury. In 1709, he razed a Jansenist stronghold at Port-Royal, and in 1713 he elicited from Rome the bull *Unigenitus*, which condemned Jansenist principles allegedly contained in a theological treatise. Of all the poisoned legacies Louis left behind him, *Unigenitus* was perhaps the most deadly. For the next half-century, political controversy over *Unigenitus* would erupt again and again. Jansenist resistance to its imposition by the monarchy would eventually corrode the very foundations of the French monarchy.

The Royal Administration

Of course, in a land as large and complex as France, even the tireless Louis could do no more than exercise general supervision. At Versailles he had three long conferences weekly with his ministers, who headed departments of war, finance, foreign affairs, and the interior. The king kept this top administrative level on an intimate scale; he usually had only four ministers at one time and gave them virtually permanent tenure. Jean Colbert (1619–1683) served as controller general for eighteen years; Michel Le Tellier (1603–1685) was secretary of state for the army for thirty-four years, a post later entrusted to his son, who had been ennobled as the marquis de Louvois (1639–1691). All told, only sixteen ministers held office during the fifty-four years of Louis's personal reign. Yet in practice the royal administration was full of difficulties and contradictions. There were many conflicting jurisdictions, survivals of feudalism. The thirty key provincial administrators, the intendants, were agents of the Crown, but many of them exercised considerable initiative on their own, despite being moved about from one administrative unit to another.

A particularly important potential for trouble existed in the parlements, the supreme courts of appeal in the various provinces. The Parlement of Paris enjoyed special prestige and power from its place in the capital and from the size of its territorial jurisdiction—almost half of France. The judges who staffed these courts headed the nobility of the robe, owned their offices, and could not be removed by the king. Besides the usual work of a court of appeals, the parlements also had to register royal edicts before they went into force. They thus claimed the right to refuse an edict if they thought it not in accord with the higher law of the land. Although this claim negated theoretical royal absolutism, Louis got around it in his own lifetime by using another old institution, the *lit de justice* (literally, "bed of justice"), in which he summoned the Parlement of Paris before him in a formal session and ordered the justices to register a royal edict. In this way, for instance, he enforced measures against Jansenism, which was strong among the judges. But the parlements were also to continue to plague his eighteenth-century successors.

Mercantilism and Colbert. Divine-right monarchy was not peculiarly French, of course, nor was the mercantilism practiced by the France of Louis

XIV. But like divine-right rule, mercantilism flourished most characteristically under the Sun King. Mercantilism was central to the early modern effort to construct strong, efficient political units. The mercantilists aimed to make their nation as self-sustaining as possible, as independent as possible of the need to import goods from other nations, which were its rivals and potential enemies. The mercantilists held that production within a nation should provide all the necessities of life for a hard-working population and also provide the power needed to fight and win wars. They believed that these goals required planning and control from above, including control of the guilds. But they did not believe, as free-trade economists would later argue, that people should be free to do whatever they thought would enrich themselves. Instead, the mercantilists would channel the national economic effort by protective tariffs, by government subsidies, by grants of monopolies, by industries run directly by the government, and by scientific and applied research.

The mercantilists viewed overseas possessions as a particularly important part of France, which should be run from the homeland by a strong government. Many foodstuffs and raw materials were more easily available overseas than in Europe. Colonies therefore should be encouraged to provide necessities, so that the mother country need not import them from competitors. In return, the mother country would supply industrial goods to the colonies and have a monopoly over colonial trade. This mercantilistic approach to colonies was followed not only by France and Spain but by the less absolutist governments of England and Holland.

The great French practitioner of mercantilism was Colbert, who had served his apprenticeship under Mazarin and advanced rapidly to become controller general early in the personal reign of Louis. He never quite attained the supremacy reached by Richelieu and Mazarin; he was the collaborator, never the master, of Louis XIV, since other great ministers, especially Louvois for military affairs, stood in the way of his supremacy. Yet Colbert was influential in all matters affecting the French economy, most interested in foreign trade and in the colonies and therefore in the merchant marine and in the navy. His hand was in everything: in invention, in technological education, in designing and building ships, in attracting foreign experts to settle in France.

Among the industries Colbert fostered were the processing of sugar, chocolate, and tobacco from the colonies; the production of military goods by iron foundries and textile mills; and the manufacture of the luxuries for which the French soon became famous. The fifteenth-century Gobelins tapestry enterprise in Paris was taken over by the state and its output expanded to include elegant furniture, for which the king was a major customer. Glassblowers and lace makers were lured away from Venice, despite strenuous efforts by the Venetian republic to keep their valuable techniques secret. In a blow against French competitors, Colbert imposed heavy tariffs on some Dutch and English products. To promote trade with the colonies and also with the Baltic and the Mediterranean, he financed trading companies, of which only the French India Company eventually succeeded.

At home, Colbert encouraged reforestation, so that iron foundries could have abundant supplies of charcoal (then essential for smelting); he also promoted the planting of mulberry trees to nourish the silkworms vital to textile output. He even attempted—vainly, as it turned out—to control quality by ordering that defective goods be prominently exhibited in public, along with the name of the offending producer, and that the culprit be exhibited for a third offense. He also endeavored, again for the most part in vain, to break down the barriers to internal free trade, such as provincial and municipal tariffs or local restrictions on the shipment of grain to other parts of France. He did, however, successfully sponsor the construction of important roads and canals—the Canal du Midi, linking the Atlantic port of Bordeaux with the Mediterranean port of Narbonne, reduced transport charges between the two seas by three-fourths and was described as the greatest engineering feat since Roman days.

It is not clear how much Colbert's policies helped or hindered the growth of the French economy. The later seventeenth century was not an age of great economic expansion generally in Europe, nor was it a period of economic boom in France. English economic growth, partly stimulated by relatively large increases of population, was markedly greater. England introduced new methods of power machinery and concentrated on large-scale production of inexpensive goods, while France clung to the policies set by Colbert, favoring relatively small-scale production of luxuries and other consumer goods. But the difference between French and English industry was also a difference in the focus of national energies; while for the time, England focused inward, France, like Spain before it, spent an exceptional proportion of its national product on war.

French Expansion

France was the real victor in the Thirty Years' War, acquiring lands on its northeastern frontier. In a postscript to the main conflict, it continued fighting with Spain until the Treaty of the Pyrenees in 1659, securing additional territories. Prospering economically, France was ready for further expansion when the young and ambitious Louis XIV began his personal rule in 1661. Louis hoped to complete the gains of 1648 and 1659 and secure France's frontiers along the Rhine and the Alps. As his sense of confidence grew, he waged a mercantilist war against France's major economic competitors, Holland and England. Certainly, Louis delighted in exerting French pressure in foreign affairs, and he was perfectly willing to wreak military terror on his enemies. He frequently had himself praised for his ability to make his enemies tremble, and he so gloried in his violent conquests that he commissioned and prominently displayed many works of art celebrating them. Yet it is important not to misconstrue these bellicose tendencies. However much it may offend modern sensibilities, gaining glory through conquest was more respectable in Louis's age, and if other kings did not match Louis in this regard, it was only because they lacked his resources. There is no evidence that Louis consciously sought to build a "universal monarchy" in Europe, as his many enemies alleged. And while he was fascinated by and instinctively drawn to war, Louis also sought to spread French influence abroad by nonmilitary means—chiefly through the spread of French language and culture.

Louis XIV and his talented experts fashioned splendid instruments to support this aggressive foreign policy. In 1661 half a dozen men made up the whole ministry of foreign affairs; half a century later it had a large staff of clerks, archivists, coders (and decoders) of secret messages, secret agents, and great lords and prelates who lent their dignity to important embassies. The growth of the French army was still more impressive, from a peacetime force of twenty thousand to a wartime one almost twenty times larger. Louis and his lieutenants almost revolutionized the character of France's fighting forces. At the ministry of war the father and son team of Le Tellier and Louvois grouped regiments in brigades under a general to bring them under closer control. They also introduced two new ranks of officer, major and lieutenant colonel, to give more opportunity to talented commoners; these new commissions were awarded only for merit and were not available for purchase, like the ranks of colonel or captain. Supplies were more abundant, pay was more regular, and an effort was made to weed out the lazy. The inspector general of infantry, Jean Martinet (d. 1672), was so rigorous in drilling and discipline that his name added a word to the modern vocabulary. The armies showed particular strength in artillery, engineering, and siege techniques, all important in the days when armies moved ponderously and did much fighting in the waterlogged Low Countries. The French boasted an engineer of genius, Marshal de Vauban (1633–1707), of whom it was said that a town he besieged was indefensible and a town he defended was impregnable. And although military medical services remained crude and sketchy, a large veterans' hospital, the Hôtel des Invalides, was built in Paris.

The First Two Wars of Louis XIV.   The main thrust of this vast effort was northeast, toward the Low Countries and Germany. Louis XIV sought also to secure Spain as a French satellite with a French ruler. Finally, French commitments overseas in North America and in India drove him to attempt, against English and Dutch rivals, to establish a great French empire outside Europe.

The first war of Louis XIV was a minor one, with Spain, and it ended quickly with the peace of Aix-la-Chapelle in 1668. Furious at the Dutch because of their economic ascendancy, their Calvinism, and their republicanism, Louis resolved to teach them a lesson for entering into an alliance with England and Sweden against him. He bought off Sweden and England, and in 1672 French forces invaded Holland. The terrified Dutch turned to the youthful William III of Orange (1650–1702), great-grandson of the martyred hero of Dutch independence, William the Silent. But the French advance was halted only by the extreme measure of opening the dikes.

Thereupon, Spain, the Holy Roman Empire, and Brandenburg-Prussia joined against France and her allies. French diplomacy separated this ineffective coalition at the six treaties of Nijmegen (Nimwegen) in 1678–1679.

Holland was left intact at the cost of promising to remain neutral, and the French gave up Colbert's tariff on Dutch goods; Spain ceded to France the Franche Comté (Free Country of Burgundy), part of the Habsburgs' Burgundian inheritance, plus some towns in Belgium; Prussia, which had defeated Louis's ally, Sweden, at Fehrbellin (1675), was nonetheless obliged by French pressure to return Swedish lands in Germany. The power and prestige of France were now at their peak, as rulers all over Europe, and in particular the host of minor German princes, tried to copy the standards of Versailles.

The Last Two Wars. But in the last three decades of Louis's reign most of his assets were consumed. Not content with the prestige he had won in his first two wars, Louis took on most of the Western world in what looked like an effort to destroy the independence of Holland and most of western Germany and to bring the Iberian peninsula under a French ruler. As a prelude to new military aggression special courts, "chambers of reunion," were set up by the French in the early 1680s to tidy up the loose ends of the peace settlements of the past generation. And there were loose ends aplenty on the northern and eastern frontiers of France, a zone of political fragmentation and confused feudal remnants, many of which were technically within the Holy Roman Empire. After examining the documents in disputed cases, the chambers of reunion "reunited" many strategic bits of land to territories controlled by France. In this way the former free city of Strasbourg, the chief town of Alsace, passed under French control.

Continued French nibbling at western Germany and Louis's assertion of a dynastic claim to most of the lands of the German elector Palatine set off the third of his wars, the War of the League of Augsburg, 1688–1697. This league against Louis was put together by his old foe, William of Orange, who after 1688 shared the throne of England with his wife Mary, daughter of James II. Thereafter England was thoroughly against Louis. The League also included Spain, the Holy Roman Empire, and Savoy, which was threatened by Louis's tactics of "reunion." The English won a great naval victory at Cape La Hogue in 1692, but William was repeatedly defeated on land in the Low Countries, although never decisively crushed. In Ireland, French (and thus Catholic) attempts to restore the deposed English king, James II, were foiled at the battle of the Boyne in 1690. France and England also exchanged blows in India, the West Indies, and North America, where the colonists called the conflict King William's War. The Treaty of Ryswick ended the war in a peace without victory, although Louis did have to give up part of his territorial gains.

In 1701 Louis XIV took a step that led to his last and greatest conflict, the War of the Spanish Succession (1701–1714). Charles II, the Habsburg king of Spain and Louis's brother-in-law, had died in 1700 without a direct heir. For years diplomats had been striving to arrange a succession that would avoid putting on the throne either a French Bourbon or an Austrian Habsburg. Although they had agreed on a Bavarian prince, he had died in 1699, and plans were made to partition the Spanish inheritance between Habsburgs and Bourbons. Charles II left his lands intact to Philip of Anjou, grandson of Louis XIV. Louis accepted on behalf of Philip, even though he had signed the

treaty of partition. This threat to the balance of power was neatly summarized in the remark a gloating Frenchman is supposed to have made, "There
are no longer any Pyrenees." England, Holland, Savoy, the Holy Roman
Empire, and many German states formed the Grand Alliance to preserve a
separate Spain.

In the bloody war that followed, the French were gradually worn down. In
North America they lost Nova Scotia to the English, and in Europe they were
beaten by the allies in four major battles, beginning with Blenheim in 1704
and concluding with Malplaquet in 1709. The allied armies were commanded
by two great generals, the French-born Prince Eugene of Savoy (1663–1736)
and the English John Churchill (1650–1722), first duke of Marlborough. But
the French were not annihilated, and Malplaquet cost the allies twenty thousand casualties, at least as many as the French suffered. By scraping the bottom of the barrel for men and money, the French still managed to keep armies
in the field.

Moreover, the Grand Alliance was weakening. The English, following their
policy of keeping any single Continental power from attaining too strong a
position, were almost as anxious to prevent the union of Austria and Spain
under a Habsburg as to prevent the union of France and Spain under a Bourbon. At home they faced a possible disputed succession to the throne, and the
mercantile classes were sick of a war that was injuring trade and seemed
unlikely to bring any compensating gains. In 1710 the pro-peace party won a
parliamentary majority and began negotiations that culminated in a series of
treaties at Utrecht in 1713.

Utrecht was a typical balance-of-power peace, which contained France
without humiliating it. France lost Newfoundland, Nova Scotia, and the
Hudson Bay territories to England, while preserving Quebec, Louisiana, and
its Caribbean islands. In a sense Louis gained what he had gone to war over,
for Philip of Anjou was formally recognized as King Philip V of Spain and
secured the Spanish lands overseas. However, the French and Spanish
crowns were never to be held by the same person, so the allies, too, had won
their point. Furthermore, England took from Spain the Mediterranean island
of Minorca and the great Rock of Gibraltar guarding the Atlantic entrance to
the Mediterranean. The English also gained the *asiento*, the right to supply
slaves to the Spanish colonies—a right that also gave them opportunities for
smuggling. The Austrian Habsburgs were compensated with Belgium and
the former Spanish possessions of Milan and Naples. In Belgium—now the
Austrian Netherlands—the Dutch were granted the right to garrison certain
fortified towns, "barrier fortresses," for better defense against possible
French aggression. For faithfulness to the Grand Alliance, the duke of Savoy
was eventually rewarded with Sardinia and the title of king. The elector of
Brandenburg was also rewarded with a royal title, king *in* (not *of*) Prussia,
which lay outside the Holy Roman Empire.

Yet the rivalry between France and England for empire overseas was undi-
minished. After Utrecht, in India, as in North America, each nation would
continue to try to oust the other from land and trade. In Europe the Dutch did

not feel secure against the French, and the Austrian Habsburg emperor, Charles VI (1711–1740), never gave up hope of becoming "Charles III" of Spain. The distribution of Italian lands satisfied no one, Italian or outsider, and the next two decades were filled with acrimonious negotiations over Italy. In short, the peace was fatally flawed.

French Aggression

Proponents of the view that Europe underwent a severe crisis during the seventeenth century can find much evidence in the horrors resulting from Louis XIV's aggressions. The total cost of his wars in human lives and economic resources was very great, especially in the deliberate French devastation of the German Palatinate during the War of the League of Augsburg. The battle of Malplaquet, which left forty thousand men wounded, dying, or dead in an area of ten square miles, was not surpassed in bloodshed until Napoleon's Russian campaign a century later. There was also much suffering behind the lines, notably in the great famine that struck France in 1693–1694. And the year of Malplaquet, 1709, was one of the grimmest in modern French history, as bitter cold, crop failures, famine, skyrocketing prices, and relentless government efforts to stave off bankruptcy by collecting more taxes caused almost universal misery. The Parisians complained bitterly in a mock paternoster: "Our Father which art at Versailles, thy name is hallowed no more, thy kingdom is great no more, thy will is no longer done on earth or on the waters. Give us this day thy bread which on all sides we lack."[*]

Louis set himself up as a champion of Catholicism, especially after the revocation of the Edict of Nantes in 1685, and William of Orange was hailed as a Protestant champion. Yet Louis, unlike his predecessor in aggression, Philip II of Spain, had no real hope of stamping out Protestantism among the Dutch. William's victory at the Boyne brought new hardship to Irish Catholics, and in England and New England the French were hated because they were Catholics. In the end, however, the Grand Alliance against Louis was a complex mixture of Catholic and Protestant in which religion played a comparatively minor role. Louis XIV had achieved no permanent stability for Europe or France, and his authority would die with him; his funeral procession was mocked as it passed through the streets of Paris, although he remained a figure of veneration to the rural masses who made up the majority of France.

Stuart England

To the extent that English government utilized the new methods of professional administration developed in the fifteenth and sixteenth centuries, it was potentially as absolute as any divine-right monarchy. But the slow growth of representative government checked this potential, generating a set of rules not to be altered easily by the ordinary processes of government.

---

[*]Quoted in G. R. R. Treasure, *Seventeenth Century France*, 2nd ed. (London: John Murray, 1981), p. 441.

These rules might be written down, but they might also be unwritten, being a consensus about certain traditions. These rules came to be regarded as limiting the authority not only of the king but even of a government elected by a majority of the people—a guarantee to individuals that they had "civil rights" and might carry out certain acts even though those in authority disapproved. Without such rules and habits of constitutionalism, and without the powerful and widespread human determination to back them up, the machinery of English parliamentary government could have been as ruthlessly absolute as any other government.

French kings and ministers could govern without the Estates General. In England, however, King Charles I, who had governed for eleven years without calling Parliament, felt obliged in 1640 to summon it and, although he dismissed it at once when it refused to do his bidding, he had to call another in the same year. This was the Long Parliament, which sat—with changes of personnel and with interruptions—for twenty years and which made the revolution that ended the threat of absolute divine-right monarchy in England.

Charles was ultimately obliged to call Parliament for two basic reasons that go back to medieval history. First, in the English Parliament the House of Commons represented two different social groups not brought together in one house elsewhere: the aristocratic knights of the shire and the burgesses of the towns and cities. The strength of the Commons lay in the practical working together of both groups, which intermarried quite freely and, despite economic and social tensions, tended to form a single ruling class, with membership open to talent and energy from the lower classes. Second, local government continued to be run by magistrates who were not directly dependent on the Crown. True, England had its bureaucrats, its clerks and officials in the royal pay, but where in France and in other Continental countries the new bureaucracy tended to take over almost all governmental business, especially financial and judicial affairs, in England the gentry and the higher nobility continued to do important local work. The Elizabethan Poor Law of 1601 put the care of the needy not under any national ministry but squarely on the smallest local units, the parishes, where decisions lay ultimately with the amateur, unpaid justices of the peace, recruited from the local gentry. In short, the privileged classes were not thrust aside by paid agents of the central government; nor did they, as in Prussia, become agents of the Crown. Instead, they preserved secure bases in local government and in the House of Commons. When Charles I tried to govern without the consent of these privileged classes, when he tried to raise money from them and their dependents to run a bureaucratic government, they had a solid institutional and traditional basis from which to resist his unusual demands.

Because Elizabeth I was childless, she was succeeded by the son of her old rival and cousin, Mary Queen of Scots, in 1603. James Stuart, already king of Scotland as James VI, became James I of England (1603–1625), thus bringing the two countries, still legally separate, under the same personal rule. James was a well-educated pedant, sure of himself, and above all certain that he ruled by divine right. As a Scottish foreigner, he was an object of distrust to his English subjects. He totally lacked the Tudor heartiness and tact, the gift of winning people to him. His son Charles I (1625–1649), under whom the divine-right experiment came to an end, had many more of the social graces of a monarch than his father, but he was still no man to continue the work of the Tudors. Although he was quite as sure as his father had been that God had called him to rule England, he could neither make the compromises the Tudors made nor revive their broad popular appeal. Thus an accident of personality was also important in shaping the outcome of divine-right theories in England.

The business of state was also gradually growing in scope and therefore in cost. The money required by the Stuarts—and indeed by the Bourbons, Habsburgs, and all monarchs—did not go only for high living by royalty and to support hangers-on; it also went to run a government that was beginning to assume many new functions. Foreign relations, for example, were beginning to take on modern forms, with a central foreign office, ambassadors, clerks, travel allowances, and the like, all requiring more money and personnel. James I and Charles I failed to get the money they needed because those from whom they sought it, the ruling classes, had succeeded in placing the raising and spending of it in their own hands through parliamentary supremacy. The Parliament that won that supremacy was a kind of committee of the ruling classes; it was not a democratic legislature, since only a small fraction of the population could vote for members of the Commons.

In this struggle between Crown and Parliament, religion helped weld both sides into cohesive fighting groups. The struggle for power was in part a struggle to impose a uniform worship on England. The royalist cause was identified with High Church Anglicanism, that is, with bishops and a liturgy and theology that made it a sacramental religion relatively free from left-wing Protestant austerities. The parliamentary cause, at first supported by many moderate Low Church Anglicans, also attracted strong Puritan or Calvinist elements; later it came under the control of Presbyterians and then of extreme Puritans, the Independents of Congregationalists. The term *Puritanism* in seventeenth-century England is confusing because it covered a wide range of religious groups, from moderate evangelical Anglicans all the way to radical splinter sects. But the core of Puritanism went back to Zwingli and Calvin, to the repudiation of Catholic sacramental religion and the rejection of most music and the adornment of churches; it emphasized sermons, simplicity in church and out, and "purifying" the tie between the worshiper and God. To understand the context it is necessary to go back to the first Stuart reign.

James I, 1603–1625

In the troubled reign of James I there were three major points of contention—money, foreign policy, and religion. In all three issues the Crown and its opposition each tried to direct constitutional development in its own favor. In raising money James sought to make the most of revenues that did not require a parliamentary grant; Parliament sought to make the most of its own control over the purse strings by insisting on the principle that it had to approve any new revenues. When James levied an import duty without a parliamentary grant, an importer of dried currants refused to pay; the case was decided in favor of the Crown by the Court of Exchequer, and the decision attracted much attention because the judges held the king's powers in general to be absolute. Then a royal appeal for a general "benevolence"—a euphemism for a contribution exacted from an individual—was resisted with the support of the chief justice, Sir Edward Coke (1552–1634). James summarily dismissed Coke from office for asserting the independence of the judiciary and thereby drew attention once again to his broad use of the royal prerogative.

The Tudors had regarded foreign affairs as entirely a matter for the Crown. The delicate problem of a marriage for Elizabeth I, for instance, had concerned her parliaments and the public; but Parliament made no attempt to dictate a marriage, and Elizabeth was careful not to offend her subjects in her own tentative negotiations. On the other hand, when James I openly sought a princess of hated Spain as a wife for his son Charles, the Commons in 1621 petitioned publicly against the Spanish marriage. When James rebuked them for meddling, they drew up the Great Protestation, the first of the major documents of the English Revolution, in which they used what they claimed were the historic privileges of Parliament to assert what was in fact a new claim for parliamentary control of foreign affairs. James responded by dissolving Parliament and imprisoning four of its leaders. The Spanish marriage fell through, but the betrothal of Charles in 1624 to the French princess Henrietta Maria, sister of Louis XIII, who was also Catholic, was hardly more popular with the English people.

Although refusing to permit public services by Catholics and Puritans, Elizabeth had allowed much variety of practice within the Anglican church. James summed up his policy in the phrase "no bishop, no king"—by which he meant that the enforcement of the bishops' authority in religion was essential to the maintenance of royal power. James at once took steps against what he held to be Puritan nonconformity. He called a conference of Anglican bishops and leading Puritans at Hampton Court in 1604, at which he presided in person and used the full force of his scholarship against the Puritans. After the conference dissolved with no real meeting of minds, royal policy continued to favor the High Church, anti-Puritan party.

Despite James's failure to achieve anything like religious agreement among his subjects, his reign is a landmark in the history of Christianity among English-speaking peoples, for in 1611, after seven years' labor, a committee of forty-seven ministers authorized by him completed the English translation of the Bible that is still one of the most widely used. The King James version was a masterpiece of Elizabethan prose, perhaps the most remarkable literary achievement a committee has ever made.

Charles I, 1625–1642

Under his son, Charles I, all James's difficulties came to a head very quickly. England was involved in a minor war against Spain, and although the members of Parliament hated Spain, they were most reluctant to grant Charles funds to support the English forces. Meanwhile, despite his French queen, Charles became involved in a war against France, which he financed in part by a forced loan from his wealthier subjects and by quartering troops in private houses at the householders' expense. His financial position was tenuous; as a French observer remarked, "They wish for war against heaven and earth, but lack the means to make it against anyone." The military preparations were the greatest since 1588, when there had been a visible enemy; in 1626–1628 Charles's subjects were less certain of the need for extraordinary measures. Consequently, in 1628 Parliament passed the Petition of Right—"the Stuart Magna Carta"—which for the first time explicitly stated some of the most basic rules of modern constitutional government: no taxation without the consent of Parliament; no billeting of soldiers in private houses; no martial law in time of peace; no imprisonment except on a specific charge and subject to the protection of regular legal procedures. All of these were limitations on the Crown.

Charles consented to the Petition of Right to secure new grants of money from Parliament. But he also collected duties not sanctioned by Parliament, which thereupon protested not only against his unauthorized taxes but also against his High Church policy. The king now switched from conciliation to firmness. In 1629 he had the mover of the resolutions, arrested, together with eight other members. He then dissolved Parliament, in part for refusing to vote supplies to the king, in part because he felt Parliament was meddling in matters of religion beyond its authority, and in part because those arrested sought to appeal over the king's head to the country.

For the next eleven years, 1629–1640, Charles governed without a Parliament. He squeezed every penny he could get out of royal revenues that did not require parliamentary authorization, never quite breaking with precedent by imposing a wholly new tax but stretching precedent beyond what his opponents thought reasonable. For example, ship money had been levied by the Crown before, but only on coastal towns for naval expenditures in wartime; Charles now imposed ship money on inland areas and in peacetime. John Hampden (1594–1643), a rich member of Parliament from inland Buckinghamshire, refused to pay it. He lost his case in court (1637) but gained wide public support for challenging the king's fiscal expedients.

In religious matters Charles was guided by a very High Church archbishop of Canterbury, William Laud (1573–1645), who systematically enforced Anglican conformity and deprived even moderate Puritan clergymen of their pulpits. Puritans were sometimes brought before the Star Chamber, an administrative court that denied the accused the safeguards of the common law. In civil matters Charles relied on an opportunist conservative, Thomas Wentworth, first earl of Strafford (1593–1641), who had deserted the parliamentary side and went on to become lord lieutenant of Ireland.

England was seething with repressed political and religious passions underneath the outward calm of these years of personal rule. Yet to judge from the imperfect statistics available, the relative weight of the taxation that offended so many Englishmen was less than on the Continent (and far less than taxation in any modern Western state). The members of Parliament who resisted the Crown by taking arms against it were not downtrodden, poverty-stricken people revolting out of despair, but self-assertive people defending their concept of civil rights and their own forms of worship, as well as seeking power and wealth for themselves.

Why, then, was there a revolution? Historians are not agreed, especially about the economic motivations of the English revolutionaries. There is evidence that the more capitalistic gentleman farmers—rural bourgeoisie—supported the Puritans; but other scholars argue that the elements from the gentry who supported the Puritans were those who saw themselves sinking on the economic scale, because of inflation, because of the enclosure of once common lands for sheep farming, and because of competition by the new secular owners of the old monastic lands. This debate about the nature and role of the gentry illustrates two problems faced by the historian: first, that of definitions, since the debate turns in part on how social classes are defined, or defined themselves in the past; second, that of interpretation, since two historians examining the same evidence, or different evidence that overlaps at certain points, may arrive at quite different conclusions about the meaning of that evidence. Was the English Revolution caused by despair—a declining gentry seeking to turn the clock back, so that the revolution was actually conservative in its goals—or was it caused by the perception of the need to modernize, to change the institutions of government to more rational, efficient purposes—that is, the final stage of the long movement away from feudalism? Was "the gentry" even central to the mid-century crisis?

The English Revolution did not, in fact, greatly alter the face of England. The laboring poor played almost no role in the Revolution. Nor did women of any class, except behind the scenes, unlike in the French Revolution over a century later. Nonetheless, a precedent of great significance was established, for a king was brought to trial and executed and his office abolished; an established church was disestablished and its property taken; less emphasis was placed on deference. All this would later be undone, the monarchy and the established church restored. Yet in the process, many would perceive that human beings could alter their world if they chose, and many would see the importance of the political process. And they would see that the Crown was neither rational nor truly responsible in various aspects of finance; in government credit, in the use of improper taxes for purposes considered immoral, and in placing the government's financial interest before its social responsibilities. Thus religion, economics, and politics would prove inseparable, a linked chain of causation.

Charles I could perhaps have weathered his financial difficulties if he had not had to contend with the Scots. Laud's attempt to enforce the English High Church ritual and organization came up against the three-generations-old Scottish Presbyterian *kirk* (church). In 1638 a Solemn League and Convenant bound the members of the kirk to resist Charles by force if need be. Charles marched north against the Scots and worked out a compromise with them in 1639. But even this mild campaign was too much for the treasury, and in 1640

The Written Record

WIFELY SUBMISSION

In 1632 one Thomas Edgar, writing as T.E. on the application of the laws to women's rights, summarized his understanding of the situation. He takes his authority from the Bible (Genesis 3:16) and omits to mention that many upper- or even middle-class married women could secure property rights at the time of marriage through a settlement.

Now Man and Woman are One

See here the reason . . . women have no voice in Parliament, they make no laws, they consent to none, they abrogate none. All of them are understood either married or to be married and their desires [are?] subject to their husbands. I know no remedy, though some women can shift it well enough. The common law here shaketh hands with divinity. . . .

As soon as a man and woman are knit and fast linked together in bands of wedlock, they are in common parlance . . . yoke-fellows, that in an even participation, must take all fortunes equally. Yet law permits not so great an *intervallum* [space] betwixt them as society . . . rather it affirms them to be *una caro* [one flesh], regarded to many intents merely as one undivided substance. . . .

The Woman Marrying Changeth her Name, Dignity, etc

The wife must take the name of her husband, Alice Green becometh Alice Musgrave. She that in the morning was Fairweather, is at night perhaps Rainbow or Goodwife Foul; Sweetheart going to Church, and Hoistbrick coming home. . . .

That which the Husband Hath is his Own

But the prerogative of the husband is best discerned in his dominion over all external things in which the wife by combination divesteth herself of propriety in some sort, and casteth upon her governor, for here practice everywhere agrees with the theoric of law, and forcing necessity submits women to the affection thereof. Whatsoever the husband had before coverture [legal responsibility for the protection of his wife] either in goods or lands, it is absolutely his own; the wife hath therein no seisin [legal possession] at all. If anything when he is married be given him, he taketh it by himself distinctly to himself. . . .

. . . The very goods which a man giveth to his wife are still his own; her chain, her bracelets, her apparel are all the goodman's goods.

. . . A wife how gallant soever she be, glittereth but in the riches of her husband, as the moon hath no light, but it is the sun's. . . .

As quoted in Nitti Keeble, ed., *The Cultural Identity of Seventeenth-Century Woman* (London: Routledge, 1994), p. 146.

Charles had to call Parliament back into session. This Short Parliament denied him any money unless the piled-up grievances against Charles and his father were settled; it was dissolved almost at once. Then the Scots went to war again, and Charles, defeated in a skirmish, bought them off by promising the Scottish army £850 a day until peace was made. Since he could not raise the money, he had to call another Parliament, which became the Long Parliament of the revolution.

Since the Scottish army would not disband until it was paid off, the Long Parliament held it as a club over Charles's head and put through a series of reforms striking at the heart of the royal power. It abolished ship money and other disputed taxes and disbanded the unpopular royal administrative courts, such as the Star Chamber, which had become symbols of Stuart absolutism. Up to now Parliament had been called and dismissed at the pleasure of the Crown; the Triennial Act of 1640 required that Parliament be summoned every three years, even if the Crown did not wish to do so. Parliament also attacked the royal favorites, whom Charles reluctantly abandoned; Archbishop Laud was removed, and Strafford was declared guilty of treason and executed in May 1641.

Meanwhile, Strafford's harsh policy toward the Irish had led to a rebellion that amounted to an abortive war for national independence by Irish Catholics and caused the massacre of thirty thousand Protestants in the northern Irish region of Ulster. Parliament, unwilling to trust Charles with an army to put down this rebellion, drew up in 1641 a Grand Remonstrance summarizing all its complaints. Charles now made a final attempt to repeat the tactics that had worked in 1629. Early in 1642 he ordered the arrest of five of his leading opponents in the House of Commons, including Hampden of the ship money case. The five took refuge in the privileged political sanctuary of the City of London, where the king could not reach them. Charles left for the north and in the summer of 1642 rallied an army at Nottingham. Parliament simply took over the central government, and the Civil War had begun.

During these years of political jockeying, signs were already evident that strong groups in England and in Parliament wanted something more than a return to the Tudor balance between Crown and Parliament, between religious conservatives and religious radicals. In politics the Nineteen Propositions that Parliament submitted to the king in June 1642 would have established parliamentary supremacy over the army, the royal administration, the church, and even the rearing of the royal children. Charles turned down the propositions, and they became the parliamentary positions in the war that followed.

The Civil War, 1642–1649

England was split along lines that were partly ethnic and territorial, partly social and economic, and partly religious. Royalist strength lay largely in the north and west, relatively less urban and less prosperous than other parts, and largely controlled by gentry who were loyal to throne and altar. Parlia-

Sir Anthony Van Dyck (1599–1641) painted King Charles I hunting. Probably completed in 1638 and now in the Louvre, this portrait shows the king informally dressed, having dismounted from his horse. The arrogant pose, with hand on hip and cane, was used from medieval times to represent nobility. Contrast the dress and compare the pose with Rigaud's portrait of Louis XIV (p. 10). (Erich Lessing/Art Resource, NY)

mentary strength lay largely in the south and east, especially in London and in East Anglia, where Puritanism commanded wide support. The Scots were a danger to either side, distrustful of an English Parliament but equally distrustful of a king who had sought to put bishops over their kirk.

In the field, the struggle was at first indecisive. The royalists, or Cavaliers, recruited from a class used to riding, had the initial advantage of superior cavalry. What swung the balance to the side of Parliament was the development of a special force recruited from ardent Puritans in the eastern counties and gradually forged under strict discipline into the Ironsides. Their leader was a Puritan, Oliver Cromwell (1599–1658), who won a crucial battle at Marston Moor in 1644. The parliamentary army, reorganized into the New Model Army and staffed by radicals in religion and politics, stood as Round-heads (from their short-cropped hair) against the Cavaliers. At the battle of Naseby in 1645, the New Model Army was completely victorious, and Charles in desperation took refuge with the Scottish army, who turned him over to the English Parliament in return for their £400,000 back pay.

A situation now arose that was to be repeated, with variations based on time and place, in the French Revolution in 1792 and the Russian Revolution in 1917. The moderates who had begun the revolution and who controlled the Long Parliament were confronted by a much more radical group who controlled the New Model Army. In religion the moderates, seeking to retain some ecclesiastical discipline and formality, were Presbyterians or Low Church Anglicans; in politics they were constitutional monarchists. The rad-icals, who were opposed to churches disciplined from a central organization, were Independents or Congregationalists, and they already so distrusted Charles that they were thinking about a republican England. The situation was further complicated by the Presbyterian Scots, who regarded the Round-heads as religious anarchists.

The years after 1645 were filled with difficult negotiations, during which Charles stalled for time to gain Scottish help. In 1648 Cromwell beat the invad-ing Scots at Preston, and his army seized the king. Parliament, with the mod-erates still in control, now refused to do what the army wanted—to dethrone Charles. The Roundhead leaders then ordered Colonel Thomas Pride (d. 1658) to exclude by force from the Commons ninety-six Presbyterian members. This the colonel did in December 1648, with no pretense of legality. After "Pride's Purge" only some sixty radicals remained of the more than five hundred orig-inal members of the Long Parliament; this remnant was known thereafter as the Rump Parliament. The Rump brought Charles to trial before a special high court of radicals, fifty-nine of whom condemned him to death. On January 30, 1649, Charles I was beheaded. To the end he insisted that a king could not be tried by any superior jurisdiction on earth, that his cause was the cause of the people of England, and that if he could be silenced, so might all others. The monarchs of Europe now had a martyr, and Parliament was, in the eyes of many in England, stained by a clearly illegal act.

Cromwell and the Interregnum, 1649–1660

The next eleven years are known as the Interregnum, the interval between two monarchical reigns. England was now a republic under a government known as the Commonwealth. Since the radicals did not dare to call a free election, which would almost certainly have gone against them, the Rump Parliament continued to sit. Thus, from the start, the Commonwealth was a dictatorship of a radical minority come to power through the tight organization of the New Model Army. From the start, too, Cromwell dominated the new government. In religion an earnest and sincere Independent, a patriotic Englishman,

Oliver Cromwell is invariably depicted as stern and dedicated, staring into the future. This painting by Rober Hutchinson, after one by Samuel Cooper (1609–1672), who specialized in miniature portraits of figures from the Commonwealth and Restoration, emphasizes Cromwell's sense of force by focusing solely on the head, devoid of background or distracting detail. (National Portrait Gallery, London)

strong-minded, stubborn, if now power-mad, still by no means unwilling to compromise, Cromwell was nevertheless a prisoner of his position.

Cromwell faced a divided England, where the majority was royalist at heart and certainly sick of the fighting, the confiscations, the endless confusing changes of the last decade. He faced a hostile Scotland and an even more hostile Ireland, where the disorders in England had encouraged the Catholic Irish to rebel once more in 1649. In 1650 Charles II, eldest son of the martyred Charles I, landed in Scotland, accepted the Covenant (thereby guaranteeing the Presbyterian faith as the established Scottish kirk), and led a Scottish army against the English. Once more the English army proved unbeatable, and young Charles took refuge on the Continent after an escape in disguise. Cromwell then faced a war with Holland (1652–1654) brought on by the Navigation Act of 1651, which forbade the importation of goods into England and the colonies except in English ships or in ships of the country producing the imported goods, thus striking at the Dutch carrying trade.

In time Cromwell mastered nearly all his foes. He himself went to Ireland and suppressed the rebellion with extreme bloodshed. In the so-called Cromwellian Settlement of 1652–1654, he dispossessed rebel Irish landholders in favor of Protestants, achieving order in Ireland but not peace. He brought the naval war with the Dutch to a victorious close in 1654. Later Cromwell also waged an aggressive war against the Spanish (1656–1658), from whom the English acquired the rich Caribbean sugar island of Jamaica. Even in time of troubles, the British Empire kept growing.

Cromwell, however, could not master the Rump Parliament, which brushed aside his suggestions for an increase in its membership and a reform of its procedures. In April 1653 he forced its dissolution by appearing in Parliament with a body of soldiers. In December he took the decisive step of inaugurating the regime called the Protectorate, with himself as lord protector of England, Scotland, and Ireland, and with a written constitution, the only one Britain has ever had: the Instrument of Government. It provided for a Parliament with a single house of 460 members, who were chosen solely by Puritan sympathizers since no royalist dared vote. Even so, the lord protector had constant troubles with his parliaments, and in 1657 he yielded to pressure and modified the Instrument to provide for a second parliamentary house and to put limits on the lord protector's power. Meanwhile, to maintain order, Cromwell had divided the country into twelve military districts, each commanded by a major general.

Oliver Cromwell died in 1658 and was succeeded as lord protector by his son Richard. The army soon seized control, and some of its leaders regarded the restoration of the Stuarts as the best way to end the chronic political turbulence. To ensure the legality of the move, General George Monck (1608–1670), commander of the Protectorate's forces in Scotland, summoned back the Rump and readmitted the surviving members excluded by Pride's Purge. This partially reconstituted Long Parliament enacted the formalities of restoration, and in 1660 Charles Stuart accepted an invitation to return from exile in the Netherlands and reign as Charles II.

The Revolution in Review

At the height of their rule in the early 1650s some Puritans had attempted to enforce on the whole population the austere life of the Puritan ideal. This enforcement took the form of "blue laws": prohibitions on horse racing, gambling, cock fighting, bear baiting, dancing on the greens, fancy dress, the theater, and a host of ordinary pleasures of daily living. Yet this attempt to legislate morality, coming too early for modern techniques of propaganda and regimentation, was not entirely effective. Many an Anglican clergyman, although officially "plundered"—that is, deprived of his living—continued worship in private houses, and many a cock fight went on in secluded spots. Nevertheless, the strict code was there, with earnest persons to try to enforce it and with implacable enemies to oppose it.

The events in Britain of 1640–1660 are of major importance in the history of the West. For the first time a monarch was challenged in a major revolt by politically active private citizens. Although the Stuarts were ultimately

OLIVER CROMWELL

Even today the character of Oliver Cromwell is the subject of much debate. Judgments on the English Civil War are shaped in some measure by opinions about Cromwell's motives, actions, and policies. His supporters and detractors are no less firmly committed today than in Cromwell's time, especially in Britain, where the role of the monarchy continues to be debated even now. Some commentators feel that Cromwell, as Lord Protector, simply replaced the king; others argue that he fundamentally transformed England, despite the eventual restoration of the monarchy. One of the most interesting commentaries is by Cromwell's contemporary, the poet (and official in Cromwell's government) John Milton. In 1654 Milton wrote, in his *Second Defense of the People of England*, one of the most far-reaching defenses of Cromwell, entitled "To You Our Country Owes Its Liberties":

The whole surface of the British empire has been the scene of [Cromwell's] exploits, and the theatre of his triumphs. . . . He collected an army as numerous and as well equipped as any one ever did in so short a time; which was uniformly obedient to his orders, and dear to the affections of the citizens; which was formidable to the enemy in the field, but never cruel to those who laid down their arms; which committed no lawless ravages on the persons or the property of the inhabitants; who, when they compared their conduct with the turbulence, the intemperance, the impiety and the debauchery of the royalists, were wont to salute them as friends and to consider them as guests. They were a stay to the good, a terror to the evil, and the warmest advocates for every exertion of piety and virtue.

But when you saw that the business [of governing the realm] was artfully procrastinated, that every one was more intent on his own selfish interest than on the public good, that the people complained of the disappointments which they had experienced, and the fallacious promises by which they had been gulled, that they were the dupes of a few overbearing individuals, you put an end to their domination.

In this state of desolation which we were reduced to, you, O Cromwell! alone remained to conduct the government and to save the country. We all willingly yield the palm of sovereignty to your unrivalled ability and virtue, except the few among us who, either ambitious of honors which they have not the capacity to sustain, or who envy those which are conferred on one more worthy than themselves, or else who do not know that nothing in the world is more pleasing to God, more agreeable to reason, more politically just, or more generally useful, than that the supreme power should be vested in the best and the wisest of men. Such, O Cromwell, all acknowledge you to be. . . .

But if you, who have hitherto been the patron and tutelary genius of liberty, if you, who are exceeded by no one in justice, in piety and goodness, should hereafter invade that liberty which you have defended, your conduct must be fatally operative, not only against the cause of liberty, but the general interests of piety and virtue. Your integrity and virtue will appear to have evaporated, your faith in religion to have been small; your character with posterity will dwindle into insignificance, by which a most destructive blow will be leveled against the happiness of mankind.*

---

*As reprinted in Perry M. Rogers, ed., *Aspects of Western Civilization: Problems and Sources in History*, 2nd ed. (Englewood Cliffs, N.J.: Prentice Hall, 1992), II, pp. 32–33.

restored, no English king could ever hope to rule again without a Parliament, or revive the court of Star Chamber, or take ship money, benevolences, and other controversial taxes. Parliament thereafter retained that critical weapon of the legislative body in a limited monarchy, control of the public purse by periodic grants of taxes.

Another basic freedom owes much to this English experience. Freedom of speech was a fundamental tenet of the Puritans, even though at the height of their power they did not observe it themselves. It received its classic expression in 1644 by the poet John Milton (1608–1674), in his *Areopagitica*. While Milton defended free speech principally for an intellectual and moral elite, one of his arguments was characteristically pragmatic and English, namely, that attempts to curb free expression just would not work.

The voluminous pamphlet literature of the early years of the great turmoil was a lively manifestation of free speech in action. The extraordinary rise of radical minorities foreshadowed modern political and social thought. One such group, the Levelers, found many sympathizers in the revolutionary army and advanced a program later carried by emigrants to the American colonies. They called for political democracy, universal suffrage, regularly summoned parliaments, progressive taxation, separation of church and state, and the protection of the individual against arbitrary arrest. There were even hints of economic equality, a goal then closely tied to biblical ideas. The Diggers, for example, were a small sect that preached the sharing of earthly goods in a kind of communism. They advocated plowing up common and waste land throughout England, regardless of ownership, in the interests of social reform. The Ranters attacked "respectable" beliefs, arguing that sin hardly existed, that a reformation in behavior would free the oppressed from the nobility and gentry. Fifth Monarchy advocates, Millenarians, and a dozen other radical sects preached the Second Coming of Christ and the achievement of a utopia on earth.

Still more important, there emerged from the English Revolution, even more clearly than from the religious wars on the Continent, the concept of religious toleration. The Independents, while they were in opposition, stood firmly for the right of religious groups to worship God as they wished. Although in their brief tenure of power they showed a readiness to persecute, they were never firmly enough in the saddle to make England into a seventeenth-century version of John Calvin's Geneva. At least one sect, the Quakers, led by George Fox (1624–1691), held to the idea and practice of religious toleration as a positive good. The Quakers denounced all worldly show, finding even buttons ostentatious. They found the names of the days and months indecently pagan, the polite form "you" in the singular a piece of social hypocrisy, and the taking of legal oaths impious. Hence they met for worship on what they called the First Day rather than the day of the sun god; they addressed each other as "thee" or "thou"; and they took so seriously the Protestant doctrine of the priesthood of the believer that they eliminated any formal ministry. In the Religious Society of Friends, as they were properly known, any worshiper who felt the spirit move might testify—give what other sects would call a sermon. The Friends felt too deeply the impossibility of coercing anyone to see the "inner light" for them to force people to accept their faith. They would abstain entirely from force, particularly from war, and would go their own way in Christian peace.

Among the Quakers the religious rights of women reached new heights. Any Friend could speak and prophesy; Fox declared that the subjection of women, which had been decreed at the fall of man in the garden of Eden, was ended through the sacrifice made by the Redeemer. Women were priests, and Christ was both male and female. Thus women played a major role in Quakerism and, from 1671, held women's meetings, which gave them a share in church government. The Civil War sects also gave women important, if not equal, roles to play, challenging orthodox arguments for the exclusion of women from church office. The sects focused often on the family and its ethical and moral role; combined with the spread of religious toleration, this led to some weakening of the idea of paternal authority, with spheres being defined in which maternal authority was to govern.

The Restoration, 1660–1688

The Restoration of 1660 left Parliament essentially supreme but attempted to undo some of the work of the Revolution. Anglicanism was restored in England and Ireland, although not as a state church in Scotland. Protestants who would not accept the restored Church of England were termed dissenters. Although they suffered many legal disabilities, dissenters remained numerous, especially among artisans and middle-class merchants. As time went on they grew powerful, so that the nonconformist conscience became a major factor in English public life. Indeed, the three-century progression of names by which these non-Anglican Protestants were called shows their rise in status: the hostile term "dissenter" became "nonconformist" in the nineteenth century, and "free churchman" in the twentieth.

The Restoration was also a revulsion against Puritan ways. The reign of Charles II (r. 1660–1685) was a period of moral looseness, of lively court life, of Restoration drama with its ribald wit, and of the public pursuit of pleasure, at least among the upper classes.

But the new Stuarts were not as adept at public relations as the Tudors had been. Charles II dissipated some of the fund of goodwill with which he started by following a foreign policy that seemed to patriotic Englishmen too subservient to Louis XIV. Yet Charles's alliance with Louis in 1670 did result in the extinction of any Dutch threat to English sea power, and it confirmed an important English acquisition, that of New Amsterdam, now New York, first taken in the Anglo-Dutch War of 1664–1667.

What really undid the later Stuarts and revealed their political ineptitude was the Catholic problem. Charles II had come under Catholic influence through his French mother and probably became a Catholic before he died in 1685. Since he left no legitimate children, the crown passed to his brother, James II (1685–1688), who was already an open Catholic. To enlist the support

The Written Record

BLACKSTONE ON THE LAW

By the eighteenth century the English recognized that a unique constitution had evolved from the period of their Civil War. Basically unwritten, rooted in the common law, this constitution would contribute to a remarkable period of political stability. In 1765 an English jurist, William Blackstone (1723–1780), would prepare a lengthy set of commentaries on the laws of England in which the process dramatically accelerated by the English Revolution was described in terms of the theory of checks and balances:

And herein indeed consists the true excellence of the English government, that all the parts of it form a mutual check upon each other. In the legislature, the people are a check upon the nobility, and the nobility a check upon the people; by the mutual privilege of rejecting what the other has resolved; while the king is a check upon both, which preserves the executive power from encroachments. And this very executive power is again checked and kept within due bounds by the two houses, through the privilege they have of inquiring into, impeaching and punishing the conduct (not indeed of the king which would destroy his constitutional independence; but, which is more beneficial to the public,) of his evil and pernicious counsellors. Thus every branch of our civil polity supports and is supported, regulates and is regulated, by the rest. . . . Like three distinct powers in mechanics, they jointly impel the machine of government in a direction different from what either, acting by itself, would have done . . . a direction which constitutes the true line of the liberty and happiness of the community.

William Blackstone, *Commentaries on the Laws of England*, 15th ed. (London: A. Stralan, 1809), I, 153.

of the dissenters for the toleration of Catholics, James II issued in 1687 a Declaration of Indulgence, granting freedom of worship to all denominations in England and Scotland. While this was, in the abstract, an admirable step toward full religious liberty, to the majority in England Catholicism still seemed a great menace, and it was always possible to stir them to an irrational pitch by an appeal to their fear of "popery" and of Spain and France, Catholic countries. Actually, by the end of the seventeenth century most of the few remaining Catholics in England were glad to accept the status of the dissenters and were no real danger to an overwhelmingly Protestant country. In Ireland, however, the Catholics remained an unappeasable majority, and Ireland posed a genuine threat.

The political situation was much like that under Charles I: the Crown had one goal, Parliament another. Although James II made no attempt to dissolve Parliament or to arrest its members, he went over Parliament's head by issuing decrees based on what he called the "power of dispensation." Early in his

By 1651 the House of Commons was depicted on the Great Seal of England as used by the Commonwealth—testimony to the symbolic significance that Cromwell attached to the House. This scene is a Dutch rendition of Cromwell's dissolution of Parliament in 1653. The owl and small lion made to look like a dog are intended as a satirical commentary on the debate and dissolution. (New York Public Library Picture Collection)

reign he had used a minor rebellion by the duke of Monmouth, a bastard son of Charles II, as the excuse for two ominous policies. First, his judges punished suspected rebel sympathizers with a severity that seemed out of all proportion to the extent of the rebellion. Second, he created a standing army of thirty thousand men, part of which he stationed near London in what appeared as an attempt to intimidate the capital. To contemporaries it looked as though James were plotting to force both Catholicism and divine-right monarchy on an unwilling England.

The Glorious Revolution and Its Aftermath, 1688–1714

The result was the Glorious Revolution, a coup d'état engineered at first by a group of James's parliamentary opponents who were called Whigs, in contrast to the Tories who tended to support at least some of the policies of the later Stuarts. The Whigs were the heirs of the moderates of the Long Parliament, and they represented an alliance of the great lords and the prosperous London merchants.

James II married twice. By his first marriage he had two daughters, both Protestant—Mary, who had married William of Orange, the Dutch opponent of Louis XIV, and Anne. Then in 1688 a son was born to James and his Catholic second wife, thus apparently making the passage of the crown to a Catholic heir inevitable. The Whig leaders responded with propaganda, including rumors that the queen had never been pregnant, that a baby had been smuggled into her chamber in a warming pan so that there might be a Catholic heir. Then the Whigs and some Tories negotiated with William of Orange (that is, William III, Stadtholder of Holland and Leeland), who could hardly turn down a proposition that would give him the solid assets of English power in his struggle with Louis XIV. He accepted the invitation to take the English crown, which he was to share with his wife, the couple reigning as William III (r. 1689–1702) and Mary II (r. 1689–1694). On November 5, 1688, William landed at Torbay on the Devon coast with some fourteen thousand soldiers. When James heard the news he tried to rally support in the West Country, but everywhere the great lords and even the normally conservative gentry were on the side of a Protestant succession. James fled from London to France in December 1688, giving William an almost bloodless victory.

Early in 1689 Parliament (technically a convention, since there was no monarch to summon it) formally offered the crown to William. Enactment of a Bill of Rights followed. This document, summing up the constitutional practices that Parliament had been seeking since the Petition of Right in 1628, was, in fact, almost a short written constitution. It laid down the essential principles of parliamentary supremacy: control of the purse, prohibition of the royal power of dispensation, and frequent meetings of Parliament.

Three major steps were necessary after 1689 to convert Britain into a parliamentary democracy with the Crown as the purely symbolic focus of patriotic loyalty. These, were, first, the concentration of executive direction in a committee of the majority party in the Parliament, that is, a cabinet headed by a prime minister, achieved in the eighteenth and early nineteenth centuries; second, the establishment of universal suffrage and payment to members of the Commons, achieved in the nineteenth and twentieth centuries; and third, the abolition of the power of the House of Lords to veto or significantly retard legislation passed by the Commons, achieved in the early twentieth century. Thus democracy was still a long way off in 1689, and William and Mary were real rulers with power over policy.

Childless, they were succeeded by Mary's younger sister Anne (r. 1702–1714), all of whose many children were stillborn or died in childhood. The exiled Catholic Stuarts, however, did better; the little boy born to James II in 1688 and brought up near Paris grew up to be known as the "Old Pretender." Then in 1701 Parliament passed an Act of Settlement that settled the crown— in default of heirs to Anne, then heir presumptive to the sick William III—not on the Catholic pretender, but on the Protestant Sophia of Hanover or her issue. Sophia was a granddaughter of James I and the daughter of Frederick of the Palatinate, the "Winter King" of Bohemia in the Thirty Years' War. On Anne's death in 1714, the crown passed to Sophia's son George, first king of the house of Hanover. This settlement made it clear that Parliament, and not the divinely ordained succession of the eldest male in direct descent, made the kings of England.

To ensure the Hanoverian succession in both Stuart kingdoms, Scotland as well as England, the formal union of the two was completed in 1707 as the United Kingdom of Great Britain. Scotland gave up its own parliament and sent representatives to the parliament of the United Kingdom at Westminster. Although the union met with some opposition from both English and Scots, on the whole it went through with ease, so great was Protestant fear of a possible return of the Catholic Stuarts.

The Glorious Revolution did not, however, settle the other chronic problem—Ireland. The Catholic Irish rose in support of the exiled James II and were put down at the battle of the Boyne in 1690, a battle still commemorated by Protestant Irish to this day. William then attempted to apply moderation in his dealings with Ireland, but the Protestants there soon forced him to return to the Cromwellian policy. Although Catholic worship was not actually forbidden, many galling restrictions were imposed on the Catholic Irish, including the prohibition of Catholic schools. Moreover, economic persecution was added to religious, as Irish trade came under stringent mercantilist regulation. This was the Ireland whose deep misery inspired the writer Jonathan Swift (1667–1745) in 1729 to make a satirical "modest proposal," that the impoverished Irish sell their babies as articles of food. Swift's ferocious suggestion highlights the destitution of the Catholic Irish at this time. It is difficult today to know just how destructive the sectarian wars were: certainly six thousand Unionists and Ulster Protestants were massacred by Catholics in 1641 (although Protestants at the time insisted and most likely believed there were upward of 200,000 victims). Cromwell's own physician-general estimated that 616,000 died on both sides between 1641 and 1652. By the 1690s the Protestant population had grown from 5 percent to 20 percent of the population, and in time would hold 85 percent of the land. By the eighteenth century Ireland had become a complex and at times paradoxical English colony.

The English experience provided the most dramatic check to absolutism in all the major European states. Although English monarchs continued to exercise considerable political influence, they could not be effective without the support of Parliament. As a result, the English aristocracy was able to recover some of the power it had lost under the Tudors. Indeed, the establishment of Parliamentary supremacy institutionalized aristocratic power until the coming of democracy at the end of the nineteenth century. The result was not a smaller national state, but a larger one. The two wars England fought with France under William and Mary and Queen Anne provided an ideal opportunity for the English aristocracy to expand the trough of patronage. Over the eighteenth century, methods of distributing this welfare for the wealthy would become more regularized through the development of a two-party system. Taxes in England would become heavier per person than they would be in France, and the establishment of the Bank of England, which organized the borrowing efforts of the state, provided a relatively cheap and efficient method for expanding government expenditures still further. A growing economy and a recently found political stability would enable England to exert influence over European affairs as it never had before.

Century of Genius/Century of Everyman

In the seventeenth century the cultural, as well as the political, hegemony of Europe passed from Italy and Spain to Holland, France, and England. Especially in literature, the France of *le grand siècle* set the imprint of its classical style on the West through the writings of Corneille, Racine, Molière, Bossuet, and a host of others. Yet those philosophers and scientists who exerted the greatest influence on modern culture were not exclusively French. Their arguments were expressed in political and economic constructs that justified or attacked the conventional wisdom of the age. In all fields of intellectual endeavor the seventeenth century saw such a remarkable flowering that historians have called it "the century of genius."

Progress and Pessimism

Scientists and rationalists helped greatly to establish in the minds of the educated throughout the West two complementary concepts that were to serve as the foundations of the Enlightenment of the eighteenth century: first, the concept of a "natural" order underlying the disorder and confusion of the universe as it appears to unreflecting people in their daily life; and, second, the concept of a human faculty, best called reason, which is obscured in most of humanity but can be brought into effective play by good—that is, rational—perception. Both of these concepts can be found in some form in the Western tradition at least as far back as the ancient Greeks. What gave them novelty and force at the end of the seventeenth century was their being welded into the doctrine of progress—the belief that all human beings can attain here on earth a state of happiness, of perfection, hitherto in the West generally thought to be possible only in a state of grace, and then only in a heaven after death.

Not all the great minds of the seventeenth century shared this optimistic belief in progress and in the infallibility of reason. The many-sided legacy of this century of genius is evident, for example, in the contrast between two of the most important political writings issuing from the English Revolution: Thomas Hobbes's *Leviathan* and John Locke's *Second Treatise of Government*. Published in 1651 and much influenced by the disorders of the English Civil War, *Leviathan* was steeped in Machiavellian pessimism about the inherent sinfulness of human beings. The state of nature, when people live without government, is a state of war, Hobbes argued, where people prey upon each other and human life is "solitary, poor, nasty, brutish, short." The only recourse is for people to agree among themselves to submit absolutely to the Leviathan—an all-powerful state that will force peace upon humankind.

This is the illustration from the title page of Hobbe's Leviathan. *While it shows the ruler in absolute control over the land, his body symbolically consists of all those individuals whose self-interest is served by their consent to accept the collective rule of the state for the general welfare. All look to him, and each loses individuality, but the mass is, nonetheless, composed of individual figures. This title page is considered to be a masterpiece, summarizing a philosopher's view in a single illustration. The Latin quotation from the book of Job translates, "Upon the earth there is not his like."* (Beinecke Rare Book and Manuscript Library, Yale University)

Hobbes (1588–1679) turned the contract theory of government upside down by having people consent to give up all their liberties; Locke (1632–1704) put the contract right side up again. Locke was a close associate of the Whig leaders who engineered the Glorious Revolution. In his *Second Treatise of Government*, published in 1690 as a defense of their actions, Locke painted a generally hopeful picture of the state of nature, which suffers only from the "inconvenience" of lacking an impartial judicial authority. To secure such an authority, people contract among themselves to accept a government—not an omnipotent Leviathan—that respects a person's life, liberty, and property; should a king seize property by imposing unauthorized taxes, then his subjects are justified in overthrowing their monarch. Locke's relative optimism and his enthusiasm for constitutional government nourished the major current of political thought in the next century, and his ideas were incorporated into the principles of some of the North American colonies. They culminated in the American and French revolutions. But events after 1789 brought Hobbesian despair and authoritarianism to the surface once more.

Meantime, exponents of the older Christian tradition continued to flourish on the Continent. One example is Blaise Pascal (1623–1662), a one-man personification of the complexities of the century of genius. He won an important place in the history of mathematics and physics by his work with air pressure and vacuums and, at the practical level, by his invention of the calculating machine and his establishment of the first horse-drawn bus line in Paris. Yet he was also profoundly otherworldly and became a spokesman for the high-minded, puritanical Jansenists, whose doctrines he defended with skill and fervor. He dismissed as unworthy the concepts of God as mere master geometer or engineer and sought instead for the Lord of Abraham and the Old Testament prophets. He advocated acts of charity, especially by those with wealth and status, for God's incomprehensible love had placed on them the obligation to look after the weak and poor. One night in November 1654, he underwent a great mystical experience in which he felt with absolute certainty the presence of God and of Christ. He spent his final years in religious meditation. In his *Pensées*, or *Thoughts*, published posthumously in 1670, he wrote of the presumed conflict between faith and science, posing that life was a gamble that favored faith: if God exists, believers win everlasting life; if God does not exist, believers were no worse off than nonbelievers.

Another example is Baruch Spinoza (1632–1677), the century's most controversial thinker, who was the son of a Jewish merchant in Amsterdam. Spinoza tried to reconcile the God of Science and the God of Scripture. He constructed a system of ethical axioms as rigorously Cartesian and logical as a series of mathematical propositions. He also tried to reunite the Cartesian opposites—matter with mind, body with soul—by asserting that God was present everywhere and in everything. His pantheism led to his ostracism in Holland by his fellow Jews and also by the Christians, who considered him an atheist; his rejection of rationalism and materialism offended intellectuals. Spinoza found few admirers until the romantic revolt against the abstractions and oversimplifications of the Enlightenment over a century later.

Literature

Just as Henry IV, Richelieu, and Louis XIV brought greater order to French politics after the civil and religious upheavals of the sixteenth century, so the writers of the seventeenth century brought greater discipline to French writing after the Renaissance extravagance of a genius like Rabelais. It was the age of classicism, which insisted on the observance of elaborate rules, on the authority of models from classical antiquity, and on the employment of a more polite, stylized vocabulary. In the early 1600s the example of greater refinement in manners and speech was set by the circle who met in the Paris *salon* (reception room) of an aristocratic hostess, the marquise de Rambouillet (1588–1665). Later, proper behavior was standardized by the court ceremonial at Versailles,

The Written Record

A LETTER CONCERNING TOLERATION

In his *Letters Concerning Toleration*, written between 1689 and 1693, John Locke took up the question of the separation of church and state.

The toleration of those that differ from others in matters of religion, is so agreeable to the Gospel of Jesus Christ, and to the genuine reason of mankind, that it seems monstrous for men to be so blind as not to perceive the necessity and advantage of it in so clear a light. I will not here tax the pride and ambition of some, the passion and uncharitable zeal of others. These are faults from which human affairs can perhaps scarce ever be perfectly freed; but yet such as nobody will bear the plain imputation of, without covering them with some specious color; and so pretend to commendation, whilst they are carried away by their own irregular passions. But, however, that some may not color their spirit of persecution and unchristian cruelty with a pretense of care of the public weal and observation of the laws; and that others, under pretense of religion, may not seek impunity for their libertinism and licentiousness; in a word, that none may impose either upon himself or others, by the pretenses of loyalty and obedience to the prince, or of tenderness and sincerity in the worship of God I esteem it above all things necessary to distinguish exactly the business of civil government from that of religion, and to settle the just bound that lie between the one and the other. If this be not done, there can be no end put to the controversies that will be always arising between those that have, or at least pretend to have, on the one side, a concernment for the interest of men's souls, and, on the other side, a care of the commonwealth.

The commonwealth seems to me to be a society of men constituted only for the procuring, preserving, and advancing their own civil interests.

Civil interests I call life, liberty, health, and indolency of body; and the possession of outward things, such as money, lands, houses, furniture, and the like.

It is the duty of the civil magistrate, by the impartial execution of equal laws, to secure unto all the people in general, and to every one of his subjects in particular, the just possession of these things belonging to this life. If any one presume to violate the laws of public justice and equity, established for the preservation of those things, his presumption is to be checked by the fear of punishment, consisting of the deprivation or diminution of those civil interests, or goods, which otherwise he might and ought to enjoy. But seeing no man does willingly suffer himself to be punished by the deprivation of any part of his goods, and much less of his liberty or life, therefore is the magistrate armed with the force and strength of all his subjects, in order to the punishment of those that violate any other man's rights.

Now that the whole jurisdiction of the magistrate reaches only to these civil concernments, and that all civil power, right, and dominion, is bounded and confined to the only care of promoting these things; and that it neither can nor ought in any manner to be extended to the salvation of souls, these following considerations seem unto me abundantly to demonstrate.

First, because the care of souls is not committed to the civil magistrate, any more than to other men. It is not committed unto him, I say, by God; because it appears not that God has ever given any such authority to one man over another, as to compel anyone to his religion. Nor can any such power be vested in the magistrate by the consent of the people, because no man can so far abandon the care of his own salvation as blindly to leave to the choice of any other, whether prince or subject, to prescribe to him what faith or worship he shall embrace. For no man can, if he would, conform his faith to the dictates of another. All the life and power of true religion consist in the inward and full persuasion of the mind; and faith is not faith without believing. Whatever profession we make, to whatever outward worship we conform, if we are not fully satisfied in our own mind that the one is true, and the other well pleasing unto God, such profession and such practice, far from being any furtherance, are indeed great obstacles to our salvation. For in this manner, instead of expiating other sins by the exercise of religion, I say, in offering thus unto God Almighty such a worship as we esteem to be displeasing unto him, we add unto the number of our other sins those also of hypocrisy, and contempt of his Divine Majesty.

In the second place, the care of souls cannot belong to the civil magistrate, because his power consists only in outward force; but true and saving religion consists in the inward persuasion of the mind, without which nothing can be acceptable to God. And such is the nature of the understanding, that it cannot be compelled to the belief of anything by outward force. Confiscation of estate, imprisonment, torments, nothing of that nature can have any such efficacy as to make men change the inward judgment that they have framed of thing. . . .

In the third place, the care of the salvation of men's souls cannot belong to the magistrate; because, though the rigor of laws and the force of penalties were capable to convince and change men's minds, yet would not that help at all to the salvation of their souls. For there being but one truth, one-way-to-heaven, what hope is there that more men would be led into it if they had no rule but the religion of the court, and were put under the necessity to quit the light of their own reason, and oppose the dictates of their own consciences, and blindly to resign themselves up to the will of their governors, and to the religion which either ignorance, ambition, or superstition had chanced to establish in the countries where they were born? In the variety and contradiction of opinions in religion, wherein the princes of the world are as much divided as in their secular interests, the narrow way would be much straitened; one country alone would be in the right, and all the rest of the world put under an obligation of following their princes in the ways that lead to destruction; and that which heightens the absurdity, and very ill suits the notion of a Deity, men would owe their eternal happiness or misery to the places of their nativity.

These considerations, to omit many others that might have been urged to the same purpose, seem unto me sufficient to conclude that all the power of civil government relates only to men's civil interests, is confined to the care of the things of this world, and hath nothing to do with the world to come.

and proper vocabulary by a great dictionary of the French language that the experts of the academy founded by Richelieu finished compiling in the 1690s, after more than half a century of labor. Nicholas Boileau (1636–1711), the chief literary critic of the day, set the rules for writing poetry with his Cartesian pronouncement, "Think well, if you wish to write well." Exaggerated notions of propriety outlawed from polite usage the French counterparts of such terms as *spit* and *vomit* and obliged writers to seek euphemisms for dozens of commonplace activities. Indeed, many of our notions of which words are vulgar or obscene derive from this time, although they were later reinforced by Victorian prudery and class concern for "nicety" in the nineteenth century. Already there were indications of the social divisions that would produce the Revolution of 1789 in the enormous gap between the classical French speech of the court and the plainer, coarser language of the average French person.

On the other hand, the linguistic standards of the seventeenth-century court also brought substantial benefits to literature. Without its discipline, French would not have won its unique reputation for clarity and elegance. The leading tragic dramatists of *le grand siècle* made observance of all the classical dos and don'ts not an end in itself but a means to probe deeply into the endless variety of human personalities. Pierre Corneille (1606–1684) and Jean Racine (1639–1699) created moving portraits of people upholding exalted ideals of honor or crushed by overwhelming emotion. The French tragedies of the seventeenth century were worthy successors to the Greek dramas of the fifth century b.c., not merely because of their classical form but also because of their powerful rhetoric, complex structure, psychological insight, and clarity of expression.

As a writer of comedies, Jean Baptiste Poquelin, known as Molière (1622–1673), the other great French dramatist of the age, was less constrained to employ a dignified vocabulary and to heed the rules of classicism. The main characters of his satirical comedies were not only sharply etched personalities but social types as well—overrefined pedantic ladies of the salons, the hypocrite in *Tartuffe* (1664), the ignorant and self-important newly rich in *Le Bourgeois Gentilhomme* (1670). In Molière, as in all good satire, there is more than a touch of moralizing. Didactic overtones are also present in two other characteristic works of the Great Century: the *Fables* of Jean de La Fontaine (1621–1695) reworked in lively fashion tales borrowed from antiquity; the *Maxims* of the duc de la Rochefoucauld (1613–1680) were even more disenchanted in their estimates of human nature. "Judged by most of its reactions, love is closer to hatred than to friendship." "Men would not get on for long in society if they did not fool one another." "In general, we give praise only that we may get it." But la Rochefoucauld could also write, "Perfect courage means doing unwitnessed what we would be capable of with the world looking on," and "The fame of great men should always be judged by the methods they employed to achieve it."*

The Maxims of La Rochefoucauld, trans. Louis Kronenberger (New York: Random House, 1959), maxims 72, 87, 146, 216, 157.

Seventeenth-century English literature also had its cynics, notably William Wycherley (c. 1640–1716), William Congreve (1670–1729), and other playwrights who wrote witty, bawdy, and disillusioned Restoration comedies. Under Charles II and his successors the pendulum of public taste and morality made a particularly violent swing as a reaction to the midcentury Puritans, who had closed down the theaters as dens of sinfulness. One of those Puritans, John Milton (1608–1674), secretary of the council of state, produced his major work of literature, *Paradise Lost* (1667), the only English epic in the grand manner that still attracts many readers, after going blind. Although Milton was a classical scholar of great learning, his often complex style and his profound belief in Christian humanism really made him a belated representative of an earlier literary age, the last great writer of the English Renaissance.

What was needed to prepare for the classical age of English letters was the modernization of the English language by pruning the elaborate flourishes, standardizing the chaotic spelling, and eliminating the long flights of rhetoric characteristic of Elizabethan and early seventeenth-century prose. Under the influence of John Dryden (1631–1700), English began to model itself on French, adopting a straightforward word order, comparatively brief sentences, and the polish, neatness, and clarity of the French school. English letters were entering the Augustan Age, which lasted through the first half of the eighteenth century.

The Baroque Era

Baroque, the label usually applied to the arts of the seventeenth century, probably comes from the Portuguese *barroco*, "an irregular or misshapen pearl." Some critics have seized upon the suggestion of deformity to criticize the impurity of seventeenth-century art in contrast with the purity of the Renaissance. Especially among Protestants, the reputation of baroque suffered because it was identified with the Counter-Reformation and many of its leading artists appeared to be propagandists for Rome. Many viewers were also repelled by the flamboyance of baroque works.

Baroque art was closely associated with the Jesuits, with the successors of Philip II in Spain, and above all with Rome during the century following the Council of Trent. Catholic reformers enlisted the arts in propagating the faith and endowing it with greater emotional intensity. But not all the baroque masters were Catholic—Rembrandt, for instance, was a Mennonite, and Sir Christopher Wren an Anglican—nor were all their patrons Catholic prelates or grandees. Portraits of the Protestant Charles I of England brought Van Dyck fame and wealth; and in the Dutch republic, where the Calvinist churches frowned on all ornamentation, painters won support from the business community and sometimes became prosperous businessmen themselves.

The unprecedented financial success of some artists is one of the distinguishing characteristics of the baroque period. Rubens, Van Dyck, and Wren lived like lords, in contrast to the relatively austere existence of such Renaissance masters as Leonardo and Michelangelo. A second characteristic is the baroque stress on sheer size, as exemplified by the vast canvases of Rubens, the immense palace of Versailles, and Bernini's decorative canopy over the high altar in St. Peter's in Rome. A third characteristic is theatricality, as painters intensified the illusion of brilliant lighting and placed figures in the immediate foreground of a canvas to draw the spectator into the scene. A final characteristic is the realistic depiction of a wide range of humanity— clowns, beggars, gypsies, cardsharps, cripples, and dwarfs, as well as ordinary people, praying, laughing, or eating. In France, for example, Georges de La Tour (1593–1652) took everyday subjects and people—a woman retrieving a flea as she undresses, a hurdy-gurdy player, and, at the height of the seventeenth-century devotional cult of Mary Magdalen, a painting of her pensively contemplating a candle—and executed them in a nighttime setting that permitted dramatic contrasts of light and shadow.

Painting.   The most restrained baroque painter was probably Diego Velásquez (1599–1660), who spent thirty-four years at the court of Philip IV of Spain. Velásquez needed all his skill to soften the receding chins and large mouths of the Habsburgs and still make his portraits of Philip IV and the royal family instantly recognizable. His greatest feat of technical wizardry is *The Maids of Honor.* A little princess, having her portrait painted, is surrounded by a pet dog, dwarfs, and other attendants; it is the moment when the royal parents are looking in on the scene, but only their reflections are seen in a mirror at the rear of the room. As Velásquez turns to greet them and looks at the viewer, the latter realizes he is standing where the royal couple must have stood. With its adroit use of mirrors, *The Maids of Honor* is a splendid example of baroque attempts to make the spectator an active participant.

Unlike the aristocratic Velásquez, the Flemish Peter Paul Rubens (1577– 1640) was the baroque counterpart of the Renaissance universal man. A diplomat, a linguist, and a student of antiquity and archaeology, he amassed a fortune from his painting and collected such impressive honors as being knighted by Charles I of England and elevated to the nobility by the king of Spain. Rubens made his studio, with its two hundred students, a factory of art. He himself is estimated to have contributed to over two thousand pictures, whose subjects ranged from simple portraits to ambitious political themes. He was commissioned by Marie de' Medici, widow of Henry IV of France, to execute a series of canvases glorifying Henry and herself. As monarchs by divine right, Henry and Marie were portrayed more as mythological figures than as mere mortals.

One of Ruben's pupils was a fellow Fleming, Anthony Van Dyck (1599– 1641), whose portraits of Charles I captured the casual elegance and confident authority of the Stuart monarch. Although courtly style was not highly valued by the Flemings' northern neighbors in the Netherlands, the officers of Dutch civic guards, the governing boards of guilds, and other important organizations of Dutch merchants liked to be portrayed for posterity. Dutch middle-class families favored small, cheerful pictures, preferably showing the leisure activities cherished by these hard-working people. The consequence was a

Diego Velásquez painted many portraits of Spain's King Philip IV, but perhaps his most famous royal painting is The Maids of Honour. *Here is Princess Margarita, only four years old, dressed as the times and her station required. With her are two young noblewomen, the court jester, a female dwarf, and others. The child is receiving cold, perfumed water to drink.   (Erich Lessing/Art Resource, NY)*

veritable explosion of artistic output that coincided with the heyday of Dutch prosperity during the first two-thirds of the century. With the French invasion of the 1670s, both the economic and artistic hegemony of the Dutch began to fade.

Seventeenth-century Dutch painters were admired both for their subtle depiction of light and color in landscapes and for their realistic representations of the interiors of Dutch houses, with their highly polished or well-scrubbed floors and their strong contrasts of light and shade. The best-known baroque painters in the Netherlands were Frans Hals (c. 1580–1666) and Rembrandt Van Rijn (1606–1669). Hals used bold strokes to paint cheerful contingents of civic guards, laughing musicians, and tavern drunks. As he aged, he himself became a chronic drinker; yet in his eighties, a penniless inmate in a poorhouse, he painted the most remarkable group portrait in baroque art—*The Women Regents of the Haarlem Hospital*, dour, formidable, and aging matrons in all their Calvinist severity.

Rembrandt, too, attained fame early, then slipped into obscurity and poverty; he documented his troubles in a series of moving self-portraits. He also executed famous group portraits—*The Night Watch* and *The Syndics of the Drapers' Guild*. Rembrandt painted an exceptional scientific subject, *The Anatomy Lesson of Dr. Tulp*, in which a physician is explaining the structure of blood vessels and tendons in the arm of an executed criminal, the only kind of cadaver available to anatomists. By the twentieth century Rembrandt would be one of the most renowned artists of all time.

Architecture and the Art of Living.   Baroque architecture and urban planning were at their most flamboyant in Rome, where Urban VIII (1623–1644) and other popes sponsored churches, palaces, gardens, fountains, avenues, and piazzas in their determination to make their capital once again the most spectacular city in Europe. St. Peter's Church, apart from Michelangelo's dome, is a legacy of the baroque rather than the Renaissance.

In the last third of the century the France of Louis XIV set the trends in architecture, landscape gardening, town planning, and furniture—especially at Versailles and in Paris. Vienna, Munich, Madrid, Warsaw, and Prague also became major baroque cities, although their styles tended to be imitative of the Italian or French. Great architectural feats sometimes took two generations or more, and the post-1630 period (known as high baroque) was marked by constant building, even in lesser cities like Würzburg or Dresden.

In England baroque building was much diluted by classicism. Under Charles II the chief architect was Sir Christopher Wren (1632–1723), a talented engineer and professor of astronomy who was deluged with commissions after a great fire destroyed much of the city of London in 1666. St. Paul's Cathedral, in particular, for which Wren had drawn up new plans only a week before the fire, drew upon Wren's capacity to fuse varying styles into a harmonious whole. Of the eighty-eight churches destroyed by the great fire, Wren supervised the rebuilding of fifty-three, placing his stamp firmly on the city.

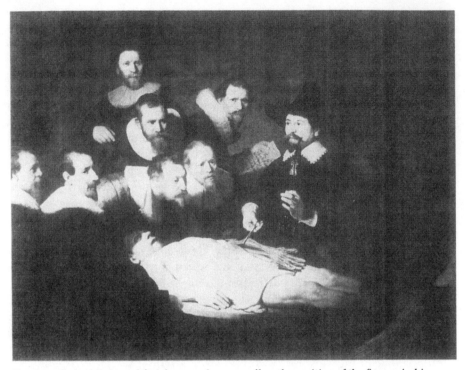

Rembrandt used light and facial expressions as well as the position of the figures in his paintings to capture a sense of psychological truth. Here, in The Anatomy Lesson of Dr. Nicolaeus Tulp, *the first commission he completed after moving from Leiden to Amsterdam in 1632, he showed a demonstration given by the leading professor of anatomy at the time. Those around him are members of the surgeon's guild. Each figure is individually realized, as Rembrandt draws attention to the developing science of pathology.   (Erich Lessing/Art Resource, NY)*

The arts of good living made substantial progress in the seventeenth century, despite the ravages of disease and famine that reduced the European population in some areas between 1600 and 1700. The expansion of Europe overseas made available the new beverages of coffee, tea, and cocoa, the new cotton fabrics, and luxuries like Chinese porcelain and lacquer ware. Exotic tropical woods were used to inlay and veneer furniture. On the whole, furniture was becoming more specialized: dining chairs replaced dining benches; chairs were made both with arms and, to accommodate hoop skirts, without. Table napkins came into use; individual plates and glasses replaced communal bowls and goblets. Families of moderate means could afford these innovations, as well as a teapot, a pitcher, and a few items of plain cutlery, and thus shared in what amounted to a revolution in domestic arrangements.

Music.   Baroque composers, especially in Italy, moved further along the paths laid out by their Renaissance predecessors. In Venice, Claudio Monteverdi (1567–1643) wrote the first important operas. The opera, a characteristically baroque mix of music and drama, proved so popular that Venice soon had sixteen opera houses, which focused on the fame of their chief singers rather than on the overall quality of the supporting cast and the orchestra. The star system reached its height at Naples, where conservatories (originally institutions for "conserving" talented orphans) specialized in voice training. Many Neapolitan operas were loose collections of songs designed to show off the talents of the individual stars. The effect of unreality was heightened by the custom of having male roles sung by women and some female roles sung by *castrati*, male sopranos who had been castrated as young boys to prevent the onset of puberty and the deepening of their voices.

In England, Henry Purcell (c. 1659–1695), the organist of Westminster Abbey, produced a masterpiece for the graduation exercises of a girls' school, the beautiful and moving *Dido and Aeneas*. Louis XIV, appreciating the obvious value of dance and opera in enhancing the resplendence of his court, imported from Italy the talented Jean-Baptiste Lully (1632–1687). In his operas Lully united French and Italian musical, dance, and literary traditions and took over the artificiality, gaiety, and weight of court ballet. No artist of the time was more representative, and none was more distant from the concerns of the people who, although they might admire the majesty of the court from a distance, could know no part in it—the common people, who saw little if any of the art and architecture, read none of the literature and heard none of the music of baroque high society.

Social Trends

Recession and the Family.   Most people during the seventeenth century were caught in a seemingly endless cycle of poverty, disease, violence, and death. Living in rural villages and dependent on agriculture for their livelihood, the vast majority of the population did not own enough land to support a family and therefore had to rent land, sharecrop, or work part-time for others. Peasants were vulnerable to pestilence and weather changes that could easily destroy the crop of an entire region, thereby inflating bread prices, causing widespread misery, and raising the prospect of starvation. To pay for food under such circumstances, peasants frequently had to sell their land, their only substantial asset. This meant trading away not only the material foundation of the family, but also its social status in the village. Once a family sold its land, it would likely be reduced to begging and break apart.

The gradual commercialization of agriculture—the process whereby crops were produced and sold for the market—created new dangers, since it meant relying upon an ever-shifting demand, which could collapse. Soil erosion, war, and epidemics added to the hardships of the peasantry, as did a tax burden that increased many times over in most countries during the seventeenth century. Despite the growth of royal power, lords still had the ability to tyrannize their peasants. Indeed, empowerment of the king in eastern Europe gave nobles a freer hand with their peasants, since in return for serving the king, the nobility was invited to brutally enserf the peasant population. The processes that would ultimately improve the lot of the peasantry—growth of the economy and law-and-order states—for the time being probably made it little better, and in some areas worse.

Demographically, the seventeenth century represented a slowdown. Whereas the aggregate European population had grown by 20 million in the sixteenth century, it grew a mere 7 million over the next, and in some countries—notably Spain and Germany—the population declined precipitously. As indicated by the fact that bread prices fell over the century, this relative stagnation probably did not result from a "Malthusian crisis"—a critical situation caused by an inability to grow enough food to supply the population. Rather, it stemmed from various combinations of disease, colder weather, war, economic dislocations, and—most interestingly—deliberate choice. Whereas demographers for a long time thought that premodern families exercised little control over family size since mechanical contraception was unknown or unavailable until later, we now know that in the seventeenth century European families did deliberately seek to limit births in the face of a contracting economy. One method—*coitus interruptus*, withdrawal before ejaculation—was certainly practiced, but with unknown frequency. More important, undoubtedly, was nonmarriage for as much as 10 to 15 percent of the population, and late marriage for the rest, which may have reduced fertility rates by one or two children per married female. The average age of marriage in western Europe climbed from the early twenties in 1600 for both sexes to the late twenties for males and mid-twenties for females by 1700— very high for a population in which only a minority lived to age fifty.

Delayed marriage had a number of wider implications. For one thing, it meant that people postponed sexual intercourse until relatively late in life, as indicated by the fact that delayed marriage did not cause illegitimacy rates to rise appreciably. How people coped with sexual frustration is not clear. Commercial sex was sometimes available. Yet prostitution did not account for most illegitimate births, which usually resulted from sex before marriage, not outside it. Another implication was that the two-generational nuclear family became the norm, not the exception. Given the later average age of marriage and the early average age at death, most people did not live to see their grandchildren, which meant that immediate parents exercised full control over family fortunes. Finally, the effort to restrict births involved a modified attitude toward the care of children. Responding to growing infant and child mortality rates—perhaps as much as 40 percent of all offspring died by adolescence during this period—parents tried to increase the chances their family line would not disappear by concentrating their scarce resources on fewer children.

Gender and Witchcraft.   It is difficult to know what impact worsening conditions had on gender roles, which probably did not change dramatically during the seventeenth century. If anything, the economic and other disorders of the time tended to reinforce male dominance as part of a movement to strengthen traditional authority in general. One French historian has noted the evolution of a "family-state compact"—a tacit agreement between kings and fathers to mutually reinforce their respective spheres of authority. Together they worked to enact and enforce laws that defined sovereignty in strongly masculine terms and increased paternal control over family property and the marriage choices of their children.

Evidence of this development can be found elsewhere, as, for example, in a work appropriately entitled *Patriarcha* (posthumous, 1680) by the prominent English royalist Robert Filmer (c. 1589–1653). Building upon a commonly invoked analogy between the kingdom and the family, Filmer justified the absolute power of kings by arguing that as literal or figurative descendants of the first father, Adam, kings were no more accountable to their subjects than were ordinary fathers accountable to their households. The implications of such arguments for women were clear. Despite the rule of an occasionally strong woman sovereign, female power was stigmatized in most countries on the notion that women were naturally weak and incapable. Those women who exercised power behind the scene—most notably, royal mistresses—were much feared, resented, and vilified because they transgressed conventional gender roles. Thus, Madame de Maintenon—Louis XIV's last mistress—was slandered in the street as a witch, a demon, and a whore.

This vision of women did not go unchallenged. Among the literate, the old debate over the relative capabilities of men and women continued, and there were some who spoke up in favor of women and their talents. Moreover, although women generally were ever more limited to poorer paid, low-status jobs and were denied the same education received by men, some did manage to evade the constriction of economic opportunities to the extent and in the manner that their social position and resources allowed. Women developed a sense of vocation through a variety of activities they could engage in—from midwifery to writing. One study of the French church has shown that it became progressively more feminized, as it recruited ever greater numbers of women to work in its schools and charities. In short, overt repression was met with generally quiet, but often determined, resistance.

Although it surely had other roots as well, economic pressures and the contested social role of women contributed to the rise in witchcraft accusations, which has been one of the most intensively studied and hotly debated developments of the sixteenth and seventeenth centuries. Belief in the magical powers of healers and sorcerers had been part of European popular culture for centuries. At the end of the Middle Ages, such popular beliefs were fused with more elitist notions of an elaborate Devil cult in many areas of Europe. During the Reformation, witchcraft also became closely associated with heresy, a growing concern in both Catholic and Protestant camps, which were defining their versions of Christian orthodoxy ever more rigidly. The role of economic stress and the growth of misogyny is perhaps most evident in the selection of the accused. Approximately 80 percent of those charged with witchcraft were women (often accused by women), and most often these women came from the poorer classes of society.

Witchcraft accusation was a complex phenomenon open to multiple interpretations. Was it principally a means of repressing socially deviant women, among them, those who resisted new restrictions? A mechanism of the

---

The Written Record

ADVICE TO A DAUGHTER

By the time of the Glorious Revolution there had been many subtle shifts in concepts of wifely responsibilities, especially among the rich. The idea of "compan-
ionative marriage" had grown, weakening the notion of the firmly subjugated
wife, and Puritan speeches had increasingly spoken of wives as helpmeets, not servants. In 1688 George Savile, the Viscount Halifax (1633–1695), one of those who
requested William and Mary to accept the crown, wrote *Advice to a Daughter* (collected for publication, 1700).

That which challengeth the next place in your thoughts is how to live with a
husband. . . .
   It is one of the disadvantages belonging to your sex that young women are
seldom permitted to make their own choice; their friends' care and experience
are thought safer guides to them than their own fancies, and their modesty
often forbiddeth them to refuse when their parents recommend, though their
inward consent may not entirely go along with it. In this case there remaineth
nothing for them to do but to endeavour to make that easy which falleth to their
lot. . . .
   You must first lay it down for a foundation in general, that there is inequality in the sexes, and that for the better economy of the world the men, who were
to be the lawgivers, had the larger share of reason bestowed upon them; by
which means your sex is the better prepared for the compliance that is necessary for the better performance of those duties which seem to be most properly
assigned to it. This looks a little uncourtly at the first appearance, but upon
examination it will be found that Nature is so far from being unjust to you that
she is partial on your side. She hath made you such large amends by other
advantages for the seeming injustice of the first distribution that the right of
complaining is come over to our [the male] sex. You have it in your power not
only to free yourselves but to subdue your masters, and without violence throw
both their natural and legal authority at your feet. We are made of differing
tempers, that our defects may the better be mutually supplied: your sex wanteth our reason for your conduct, and our strength for your protection; ours
wanteth your gentleness to soften and entertain us. The first part of our life is a
good deal subjected to you in the nursery, where you reign without competition, and by that means have the advantage of giving the first impressions.
Afterwards you have stronger influences, which, well managed, have more
force in your behalf than all our privileges and jurisdictions can pretend to have
against you. You have more strength in your looks than we have in our laws,
and more power by your tears than we have by our arguments.
   It is true that the laws of marriage run in a harsher style towards your sex.
Obey is an ungenteel word, and less easy to be digested by making such an
unkind distinction in the words of the contract, and so very unsuitable to the
excess of good manners which generally goes before it. Besides, the universal-

ity of the rule seemeth to be a grievance, and it appeareth reasonable that there might be an exemption for extraordinary women from ordinary rules, to take away the just exception that lieth against the false measure of general equality. . . .

But the answer to it in short is, that the institution of marriage is too sacred to admit a liberty of objecting to it; that the supposition of yours being the weaker sex having without all doubt a good foundation maketh it reasonable to subject it to the masculine dominion; that no rule can be so perfect as not to admit some exceptions, but the law presumeth there would be so few found in this case who would have a sufficient right to such a privilege that it is safer some injustice should be connived at in a very few instances than to break into an establishment upon which the order of human society doth so much depend.

You are therefore to make your best of what is settled by law and custom, and not vainly imagine that it will be changed for your sake.

As quoted in Nitti Keeble, ed., *Seveteenth-Century Woman* (London: Routledge, 1994), pp. 167–168.

---

wealthier classes to regulate the poor? A desperate effort to account for and reverse economic hardship? A protection of the powerful against charges of heresy? Most likely, combinations of forces were at work, and just as the incidence of these accusations varied over time and place, so did the reasons for the phenomenon. What is certain is its vast scale: from 1580 to 1650 about 100,000 cases of witchcraft were prosecuted in Europe as a whole. Even in England, where the common law prohibited torture to extract confessions, there were more than a thousand witchcraft trials.

If the reasons for the rise of witchcraft accusation remain muddy, equally so are the reasons for its decline, which began in the early eighteenth century, as did the decline in attention given to the Devil. Legal difficulties in establishing "proof" may have played a role; so, too, might lessening interest in prosecuting heresy and the easing of economic hardship. In addition, European elites, who at this time were cultivating a more refined lifestyle that distinguished them from the common people, adopted a scientific outlook discouraging belief in witches and other supernatural phenomena. Almost certainly, this was less because belief in such phenomena was intellectually inconsistent with the findings and methods of the new science than because such belief smacked too much of popular culture. For the line between the natural and the supernatural remained extremely fuzzy, even among elites. The eighteenth-century upper classes may have honored the physics of Newton, but they also indulged in pseudoscientific fads such as Mesmerism—a *salon* craze offering medical cures in bizarre settings through infusions of "universal fluid" (in reality, mild electrical shocks).

The Problems of the Rich.   Although economic recession certainly devastated the poor far more than other classes, the rich, too, had to manage their family fortunes carefully in the seventeenth century by investing well and marrying well. Marrying well normally meant choosing a mate of at least equal status and wealth, although asymmetric alliances could also be desirable, as, for example, when poor nobles married their sons bearing titles to the daughters of merchants with fat dowries. Such considerations did not, of course, enter into unions among the poorest classes, since without titles and property to bestow, parents had little control over the selection of their children's spouses. In this one area, at least, poverty offered more freedom than did affluence.

Since the main goal of most families was self-perpetuation and the accumulation of prestige and wealth over generations, producing a strategically desirable number of heirs was critical. Too few heirs meant that a family could die out, which frequently happened in an age of staggeringly high infant and child mortality rates. A most prominent example was that of Queen Anne of England, who gave birth to seventeen children and was survived by none of them. But too many heirs meant that wealth might be divided into so many small portions that the prospects of each heir and his or her family branch would be compromised. To prevent this eventuality, some countries, most notably England, practiced primogeniture, that is, the deeding of noble titles and landed estate to the eldest son alone. But, of course, this institution raised the question of how to provide for younger siblings.

Especially in such countries, but also in those where primogeniture was not practiced, the state became increasingly useful as a provider of welfare for the rich. Commissions in the army and navy, appointments to remunerative clerical posts, commercial contracts, and outright pensions grew in number with the expansion of the state, thereby providing additional opportunities and sources of revenue for hard-pressed aristocratic families. The state also offered opportunities to lend money at interest. If such loans did not always pay high dividends, they usually offered considerable security for family fortunes. In addition, the state provided for the policing the poor. Soaring bread prices often provoked popular riots in town and country, thereby disrupting the profitable grain trade and threatening other proprietary interests. Although most states enacted policies aimed at keeping grain at affordable prices, they could and did put down grain riots with terrific military force when unrest occurred. Laws were passed to ensure that the poor did not poach on landed estates, with the threat of harsh punishments if offenders were caught.

When looked at from this perspective, the differences between absolutist regimes such as that in France and nonabsolutist regimes such as that in England appear much less striking than they do from a purely constitutional viewpoint. After 1689, the English Parliament became the main conduit of

St. Paul's Cathedral in London, built between 1673 and 1710, became the architectural model for much public architecture well into the nineteenth century. The cathedral is seen here in a painting done by Giovanni Antonio Canaletto (1697–1768). (Giraudon/Art Resource, NY)

state patronage for the wealthy, whereas in France the court was its main dispenser. But in both cases state building and elite family-building went hand in hand.

"The past is a foreign country: they do things differently there."* The past summarized so scantily in this volume is indeed, to the present age, a vast foreign land—more different by virtue of the distance of time than modern countries may be from one another despite the distances imposed by language and technology. In 1513 Niccolò Machiavelli had written in *The Prince*, "There is nothing more difficult to take in hand, more perilous to conduct, or more uncertain in its success, than to take the lead in the introduction of a new order of things." Soon the introduction of new orders of things would become frequent, even seem commonplace, as the pace of known history—of recorded events that bear directly upon our understanding of the present—speeded up dramatically. To tread on the dust of the past, as the early nineteenth-century English poet Lord Byron wrote, is to feel the earthquake waiting below.

---

*From the twentieth-century English novelist L. P. Hartley, *The Go-Between* (London: Harnish Hamilton, 1953), p. 9.

SUMMARY

The seventeenth century was dominated by France. During the reign of Louis XIII, Cardinal Richelieu created an efficient centralized state. He eliminated the Huguenots as a political force, made nobles subordinate to the king, and made the monarchy absolute. Louis XIV built on these achievements during his long reign. Louis XIV moved his capital from the turbulence of Paris to Versailles, where he built a vast palace and established elaborate court rituals that further limited the power of the nobles.

From Versailles, the Sun King demanded unquestioning obedience from his subjects, seeing himself as the representative of God on earth and ruling by divine right. In religion, Louis XIV encouraged the evolution of the Gallican church. In 1685, he revoked the Edict of Nantes, ending toleration of Huguenots. Mercantilism, practiced by Colbert, was central to French economic policy. Colbert's policies promoted foreign trade and the expansion of industry.

Hoping to expand France to its "natural frontiers," Louis XIV pursued an aggressive foreign policy that embroiled the nation in numerous wars. In the War of the Spanish Succession (1701–1714), England, Holland, the Holy Roman Empire, and German states joined forces to prevent a union of Spain and France. The treaties of Utrecht (1713) preserved the balance of power in Europe but left many unresolved issues.

In England, the Stuart monarchs James I and Charles I violated traditions limiting royal authority and protecting individual rights. Their attempts to rule without Parliament brought matters to violent conflict between the Crown and the members of Parliament. During the Civil War (1640–1649), England was split between royalists and parliamentarians. Under Puritan leader Oliver Cromwell, the New Model Army decisively defeated the king. Radicals in the Rump Parliament tried and condemned the king to death in 1649.

During the Interregnum, England was a republic dominated by Oliver Cromwell and the Puritans. They faced opposition at home and abroad. In 1660, the monarchy was restored. But the Interregnum marked the first successful challenge to a monarch by a politically active citizenry. Moreover, the events of the Civil War affirmed the existence of an unwritten constitution rooted in English common law. Belief in freedom of speech and religious toleration also emerged in this period.

During the Restoration, Parliament was supreme. The Catholic sympathies of James II so alienated his subjects that he was toppled by the Glorious Revolution of 1688, which put William of Orange and Mary on the throne. Parliament then enacted the Bill of Rights of 1689, which embodied the principles of parliamentary supremacy. In the next two hundred years, England would become a parliamentary democracy.

The seventeenth century was an age of intellectual ferment dominated by France, Holland, and England. Two concepts underlay thought: the idea of a natural order and the importance of reason. In England, Thomas Hobbes in

Leviathan (1651) and John Locke in his *Second Treatise of Government* (1690) set out ideas on government and human nature that would greatly influence political thought. On the Continent, Pascal and Spinoza made equally significant contributions to Western thought.

During the Age of Classicism, French dramatists such as Corneille, Molière, and Racine dominated literature just as the court of Louis XIV influenced all of Europe. In *Paradise Lost*, John Milton combined classical scholarship and profound Christian faith.

Baroque masters produced flamboyant works of art that emphasized size and theatrically. Flemish and Dutch painters including Rubens, Rembrandt, and Van Dyck won widespread acclaim.

Families tried to cope with their difficulties by limiting births, strengthening paternal authority, and, when possible, seeking help from the state.

TWO

The Old Regimes

The term *Old Regime* is used to describe the institutions prevailing in Europe, and especially in France, before 1789. This was the "Old Regime" of the eighteenth century, in contrast to the "New Regime" that was to issue from the French Revolution. On the surface, the Old Regime followed the pattern of the Middle Ages, although the forces that were to transform the economy, society, and politics of modern Europe were already at work. To be sure, the economy was still largely agrarian, for most Europeans lived in farming villages and retained the localized outlook of the peasant.

The social foundations of the Old Regime rested on the medieval division of society into the first estate of the clergy, the second estate of the nobility, and the third estate of the commoners, which included the urban bourgeoisie and working people as well as the peasantry. Within the third estate, only those at the top exerted much political influence—well-to-do business leaders in England and Holland, French lawyers or merchants wealthy enough to purchase government office, women who had married well or who had the ear of the influential people who attended their salons. Every government in Europe tended to represent the interests of the few rather than the many. In this respect, it made little difference whether it was an absolute monarchy like France or Prussia, a developing constitutional monarchy like Britain, or a republic like the Dutch United Provinces.

As the eighteenth century advanced, the political and social status quo came under increasing attack from the leaders of the intellectual movement known as the Enlightenment (see Chapter 3). The economic foundations of the Old Regime were eroding under the pressure of revolutionary change, and the balance of power achieved by the Utrecht settlement was undermined. The defeat and death of Louis XIV did not end the worldwide rivalry of England and France. Meanwhile, further shifts in the international balance resulted from the appearance of two important newcomers: Russia and the German state of Brandenburg-Prussia.

A Closer Look

THE COFFEEHOUSE

The thriving maritime trade changed public taste, as it brought a variety of new produce into the British and Continental markets. Dramatic examples are the rise of the coffeehouse and the drinking of tea at home. In the seventeenth and early eighteenth centuries the coffeehouse was referred to as the "penny university," for the price of entry, which was a penny (and two pennies extra for the coffee itself), admitted one to a room where the daily newspaper could be found and where animated political discussion was taking place. The Turks had called coffeehouses "schools of the wise," and the tendency for them to become centers for subversion led the Russians to attempt to suppress them.

In 1675 England's Charles II tried to close coffeehouses, acting upon the pretext that coffee was injurious to health, as a pamphlet, *The Women's Petition against Coffee, representing to public consideration the grand inconveniences accruing to their sex from the excessive use of the drying and enfeebling liquor,* had argued. In truth, as his proclamation showed, Charles was more concerned that "in such Houses . . . divers False, Malitious and Scandalous Reports are devised and spread abroad, to the Defamation of his Majestie's Government, and to the Disturbance of the Peace and Quiet of the Realm." Eleven days later the king withdrew the edict of prohibition on the grounds of "royal compassion." Until the end of the reigns of the early Georges, the coffeehouse, at least in London, remained a male social center; in Queen Anne's time there were five hundred such houses.

In 1706 Ned Ward somewhat satirically described a Whiggish day in *Wealthy Shopkeeper:*

Rise at 5; counting-house till 8; then breakfast on toast and Cheshire cheese; in his shop for two hours then a neighbouring coffee house for news; shop again, till dinner at home (over the shop) at 12 on a "thundering joint"; 1 o'clock on Change; 3, Lloyd's Coffee House for business; shop again for an hour; then another coffee house (not Lloyd's) for recreation, followed by "sack shop" to drink with acquaintants, till home for a "light supper" and so to bed, "before Bow Bell rings nine."

Quoted in G. M. Trevelyan, *Illustrated English Social History,* Vol. III. *Eighteenth Century* (London: Longmans, Green, 1951), p. 30.

The Economic "Revolutions"

The changes that undermined the Old Regime were most evident in western Europe. They were in some respects economic revolutions. In the eighteenth century the pace of economic change was slower than it would be in the nineteenth or twentieth, and it provided less drama than such political upheavals as the American and French revolutions. Yet in the long run the consequences of the economic "revolutions" were fully as revolutionary as were the political and social ones of 1776 and 1789.

Commerce and Finance, 1713–1745

Many of the basic institutions of European business life had developed before 1715—banks and insurance firms in the Renaissance, for example, and chartered trading companies in the sixteenth century. Mercantilism had matured in the Spain of Philip II, in the France of Louis XIV and Colbert, and in Britain between 1651 and the early eighteenth century. The steady growth of seaborne trade, stimulated by an increasing population and a rising demand for food and goods, was a main force in quickening the pace of commerce.

The growing maritime trade increased the demand for insurance of ships and cargoes. In London early in the century marine insurance brokers gathered at Edward Lloyd's coffeehouse in Lombard Street to discuss business, news, and politics. Thus was born Lloyd's of London, a firm that developed the standard form of policy for marine insurance and published the first detailed and accurate shipping newspaper. Another great London institution to emerge from the informal atmosphere of the coffeehouse was the stock exchange.

Marine insurance prospered in part because improved charts and the installation of lighthouses and buoys made navigation safer. Captains could determine their geographical position at sea by using two new instruments, the sextant and the chronometer. The sextant, an elaboration of the telescope, showed the altitude of the sun at noon and thus indicated the ship's latitude. The chronometer, a clock unaffected by the motion of the ship, was kept on Greenwich mean time (the time at the meridian running through Greenwich, near London). The two new instruments also made it possible to calculate the ship's longitude.

On land, improvements in communication and transport came much more slowly. Except for the relatively good highways of France, European roads were scarcely more than wide paths. The shipments of goods overland remained slow, unsafe, and expensive until after 1750, when the construction of turnpikes and canals gradually improved the situation.

Business people faced the handicaps imposed by restrictive guild regulations, by the many different coins, weights, and measures, and by the numerous local tolls. Sweden, for example, minted only copper money, including a coin weighing 43 pounds. Baden, one of the smaller German states, had 112 separate measures for length, 65 for dry goods, 123 for liquids, and 163 for cereals, not to mention 80 different pound weights. Even in France, a relative model for uniformity and centralization, all sorts of local taxes and other obstacles to internal trade persisted.

The survival of local vested interests showed the limitations of the power of the mercantilist state. Although mercantilism required the regulation of trade on a national basis, no eighteenth-century government had the staff

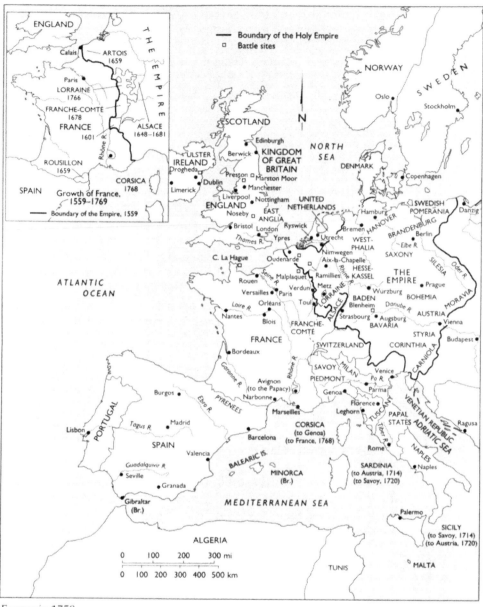

Europe in 1750

needed to make national regulation effective. Austria, Prussia, and some other German states endeavored to assimilate mercantilism into a more systematized policy called *cameralism* (from *camera*, the council or chamber dealing with expenditures and income). Their main effort was directed toward planning state budgets, especially the increase of revenues. Other states often relied heavily on private companies and individuals to execute economic policies.

Thus the English and Dutch East India companies exercised not only a trading monopoly in their colonial preserves but also virtual sovereign powers, including the right to maintain soldiers and conduct diplomacy. Inventors worked on their own, not in government facilities. On the whole, private initiative accomplished more than governments did, although it could also get out of control, as demonstrated by two speculative booms early in the century—the Mississippi Bubble in France and the South Sea Bubble in England.

In 1715 hardly a state in Europe could manage the large debts that had piled up during the recent wars. Yet all of them had to find some way of meeting at least part of the large annual interest on bonds and other obligations or else go bankrupt. The governments of France and England transferred the management of state debts to joint-stock companies, which they rewarded for their risk taking with trading concessions. The commerce of the companies, it was hoped, would prove so lucrative that their profits would cover the interest charges on government bonds.

John Law (1671–1729), a Scottish mathematical wizard and financier, presided over the experiment in France. Law asserted that the limited supply of silver and gold made it difficult to increase the amount of *specie* (coined money) circulating in any country, and therefore made it difficult to promote business. Paper money, Law concluded, was the solution—paper money backed by a nation's wealth in land and trade.

The death of Louis XIV gave Law his opportunity. The regent for Louis XV, the duke of Orléans, permitted Law to set up a central bank in Paris. Law's bank issued paper notes of stable value. Business activity at once increased. Next, Law set up the Compagnie des Indies, commonly called the Mississippi Company, which received a monopoly of commerce to and from the Louisiana colony.

Law's system reached to almost every corner of the French economy. Merging with the royal bank, his company took over the government debt and agreed to accept government bonds in partial payment for shares of Mississippi stock. Many bondholders responded enthusiastically to Law's offer. Law, however, had to sell additional shares of Mississippi stock to obtain sufficient working capital for his company and to absorb his paper money. To attract cash purchasers, he promoted a boom in Mississippi stock. Investors caught the fever of speculation, and by the close of 1719 Mississippi stock was selling at forty times its par value.

The Mississippi Bubble soon burst. As the price of Mississippi shares rose higher and higher, cautious investors decided to cash in. They sold their shares, received payment in banknotes, then took the notes to Law's bank and demanded their redemption in specie. The bank exhausted its reserves of gold and silver and suspended specie payments in February 1720. Law was forced to resign in May 1720; he fled France shortly thereafter. The consequences of the failure of Law's system were long-ranging. Although other reformers proposed banking schemes to solve the government's fiscal problems in later years, Law's failure made it impossible to establish a true national bank until the French Revolution. Most observers were now convinced that an absolute monarch would always wind up destroying the credit of such a bank by using his power to drain its assets. As a result, the French government had to pay a much higher rate of interest than did the English government, which meant the French could afford to borrow less. This was one contributing factor to the government bankruptcy of the 1780s, a major precipitant of the French Revolution.

Within a few weeks of Law's resignation the South Sea Bubble burst in London. Management of the English government's debt had been assigned to the Bank of England. Founded in 1694 as a private institution, the bank issued notes and performed other services for the government during the last wars against Louis XIV; but in negotiations for the privilege of managing the debt, the bank was outbid by the new South Sea Company, which paid the government an exorbitant sum. The resources of the company were slim, consisting largely of the right to exploit the trading concessions that Britain obtained at the end of the War of the Spanish Succession. These privileges were limited to furnishing Spain's American colonies with forty-eight hundred slaves annually and sending one ship a year to Panama for general trade.

The South Sea Company invited government creditors to transfer their bonds into company stock. The directors of the company bought and sold shares in secret to create a more lively market, encouraged purchases of stock with a down payment of only 10 percent in cash, and spread reports of forthcoming sailings by the company's ships on voyages that did not take place. The gullibility of the investing public, although remarkable, was not inexhaustible. South Sea shares fell; Parliament ordered an investigation and, to protect the company's creditors, seized the estates of its directors, who had in the meantime destroyed the company's books and fled the country.

The bubbles were an extreme instance of the economic growing pains suffered as Europe groped for solutions to new and baffling financial problems. Law's system released French business from the depression induced by the defeats of Louis XIV. It also stimulated settlement in Louisiana. The Mississippi Company, reorganized after 1720, consistently made a large profit. In England the strongest institutions rode out the bursting of the South Sea Bubble; the East India Company continued to pay an annual dividend of 5 to 10 percent, and the Bank of England again became the financial mainstay of the realm.

In the political shakeup following the collapse of the Bubble, the Whig statesman Robert Walpole (1676–1745) came to power with a program of honoring the debt as a *national* debt. This was a novel concept in an age when most states treated their debts as the monarch's personal obligation. No subsequent stock crisis assumed the proportions of that of 1720, and thereafter British banking grew rapidly and on a stable foundation.

Over the next century, the British government went deeply into debt in order to finance its empire, but because interest rates were low, it was able to do so at relatively modest cost. This was one of its major sources of strength.

Agricultural Improvements

The agricultural revolution—the second force transforming the modern economy—centered on improvements that enabled fewer farmers to produce more crops. The Netherlands were the leaders, producing the highest yields per acre while also pioneering in the culture of new crops like the potato, the turnip, and clover. Turnips furnished feed for livestock until the spring pasturing season began, thus eliminating the necessity for massive slaughtering of stock at the onset of winter. Clover, by fixing nitrogen in the soil, increased the fertility of the land and ended the need to have fields lie fallow every third year. Livestock breeding was also improved.

In England the new crops were taken up by Lord ("Turnip") Townshend (1674–1738), whose plan for a four-year rotation—planting a field in turnips, barley, clover, and wheat in successive years—became standard on many English estates. Jethro Tull (1674–1741) adapted French methods to the grain fields of England. In place of the inefficient custom of scattering seed broadcast, he planted it deep in regular rows with a horse-drawn hoe. The improvements of Tull and Townshend won enthusiastic praise from Arthur Young (1741–1820), who published lengthy reports on his frequent trips through the farming districts of Britain and the Continent. Young won an international following that included George III, George Washington, the marquis de Lafayette, and Catherine the Great.

The agricultural revolution of the eighteenth century came close to ending wholesale famines in Europe, even if it did not prevent recurring food shortages. It also marked an important stage in the gradual shift from the largely self-sufficient manor of the Middle Ages to the capitalist farm producing specialized crops. The "improving landlords" needed large amounts of capital and large plots of land that were not subdivided or otherwise used in common by many farmers. There was a mounting demand that common fields be fenced off as the private lands of single landlords. Enclosures, which in Tudor England were introduced to extend sheep pastures, were now sought to increase cropland.

Enclosure created large farms well suited to drill-planting, horse-hoeing, and crop rotation, but it also caused social dislocations. The development of large estates ruined many small farmers, or yeomen, who could not survive without the right to use common lands, and who could not afford to buy tools and install fences. Many of them became hired hands on big farms or sought work in the expanding towns. Some became poachers, illegally taking game from the great estates. In 1723 Parliament passed the Waltham Black Act, which was aimed at controlling new crimes that were, in effect, socially defined, such as being armed with weapons and appearing in forests or enclosed lands with faces blackened, which was taken as evidence of the intention to steal or kill animals, to take crops or wood, or to set fire to the property of the owners.

Colonies and Slavery

It is one of the bitterest ironies of the eighteenth century that a period best known for the Enlightenment and revolutions on behalf of liberty experienced the massive enslavement of Africans to work in the European trans-Atlantic colonies. Slavery had long existed in Africa under a variety of conditions, but the coming of the Europeans turned it into a routinized big business. The roots of the trans-Atlantic slave trade lay in the chronic shortage of labor in the American colonies. After plundering the gold and silver of the New World in the sixteenth century, Europeans increasingly sought to exploit their American colonies for such products as tobacco, sugar, and coffee, which were finding a growing market at home. But the reluctance of most Europeans to go abroad and the demise of millions of Native Americans following their exposure to European diseases meant that to exploit these markets Europeans had to look elsewhere for laborers. Beginning in the seventeenth century, enterprising European merchants began to enter into mutually advantageous pacts with African chieftains to supply them with slaves. Thus indirectly Africa also increasingly came to "discover" Europe.

Before 1700 most African slaves were sent to Brazil and the Caribbean; after that date, there was a marked increase in the number of slaves sent to the North American mainland. Although the vast majority worked on plantations in relatively warm climates, slaves performed many other services; as far north as New York approximately 15 percent of the population were slaves at the time of the American Revolution. What is most striking are the total numbers. By 1850, roughly 11 million slaves had been imported into the Americas, a figure that does not include those who died in transit. At the height of the slave trade—the late eighteenth century—nearly 100,000 Africans were imported into the Americas every year. By this time, in the French colony of Saint Domingue (later Haiti) alone, nearly a half-million slaves worked the sugar plantations, overseen by about twenty thousand Europeans.

The conditions under which Europeans uprooted Africans and sent them to live in the New World were appalling, even in comparison to those of the vast majority of the European population, who worked long hours at near subsistence levels. Branded, shaved, shackled, and scourged, the slaves were packed tightly into ships for the three-month voyage across the Atlantic, during which many died. Once they landed, those slaves who had survived the harrowing crossing were parceled out to plantation owners with life-and-death powers over their newly acquired laborers. Proprietary interest dictated good treatment of slaves, but in a system that involved frequent beatings, rape, inadequate food rations, and the breakup of families, the will to

degrade victims and to commit violence against them often overrode economic considerations. Cruelty was an endemic part of the system, and just as
slaves sought to subvert it as best they could, masters lived in constant fear
of revolts.

To answer the occasional critics of this institution, masters and their apol-
ogists invoked various justifications. Slavery, it was noted, had been practiced in biblical times. John Locke, the great defender of "natural liberty," justified slavery in the Carolinas as an extension of the rights of victors over
their captives. By the eighteenth century, racism was increasingly deployed
to portray Africans as animals who merited enslavement. As voices opposing
slavery grew louder, opponents of abolition contended that slaves were
property and should be freed only if their owners were compensated.

The Beginnings of the Industrial Revolution, to 1789

By increasing productivity and promoting population growth, the revolution
in agriculture contributed to that in industry. Industry also required raw materials, markets, and capital to finance the building and equipping of factories.
Thus the prosperity of commerce also nourished the growth of industry.

The first major changes were in textile manufacture, where the making of
yarn and cloth had long been organized under the putting-out system, in
which spinners and weavers worked at home with wheels and looms. Often
they did not buy their own raw materials or market their finished products,
but worked as wage-laborers for someone who furnished the raw materials
and sold the finished products. In other industries, however, production was
sometimes organized in simple factories, which brought together many
laborers in a large workshop. These factories were particularly common in
enterprises requiring close supervision for reasons of state, like cannon
foundries, or because they used expensive materials, like gold or silver
threads for luxury cloth.

The industrial revolution made the putting-out system obsolete and transformed the early factory system. Machines superseded the spinning wheel,
hand loom, and other hand tools, and water or steam replaced human mus-
cle and animal energy as the chief source of power. Because power-driven
machines were often cumbersome and complicated, larger factories were
needed to house them.

Coal mining was becoming a big business, largely because of increased
demand for coke by iron smelters, which had previously used charcoal to
make ore into iron. Ordinary coal could not replace charcoal as smelter fuel
because the chemicals in coal made the iron too brittle. The Darby family of
Shropshire discovered how to remove the chemical impurities from coal by
an oven process that converted it into coke. The Darbys and other private
firms were the pioneers in metallurgy.

The revolution in textiles focused on the cheaper production of cotton
cloth. The flying shuttle, a technical device first applied to the hand loom in
England (1733), enabled a single weaver to do the work that had previously

| A Closer Look |

SLAVE LAWS OF THE FRENCH WEST INDIES

A code of laws tells historians of public fears and possible occurrences, since a law is seldom established against activities that have not taken place. The French Black Code reveals much about the realities of slavery in the French West Indian colonies. The code drew together and added to all relevant previous laws from those first promulgated in 1685 to 1785.

Art. 1. We wish and intend that the Edict of the late King, of glorious memory, our most honored lord and father, dated 23 April 1615, be carried out in the Islands; for the which, we enjoin all our officials to expel all the Jews who have there established their abode. We order them, as declared enemies of the Christian faith, to depart within three months, counting from the day of publication of the present Edict, on pain of confiscation of their bodies and goods.

Art. 2. All the slaves in our Islands are to be baptized and instructed in the Roman Catholic and Apostolic Religion. We order those inhabitants who purchase newly arrived Negroes, to notify the Governor and Intendant of the said Islands, within eight days at the latest, on pain of an arbitrary fine, that those officials may give the necessary orders to have them baptized and instructed in a reasonable time.

Art. 3. We forbid the public practice of any religion, other than the Roman Catholic and Apostolic; we desire that those who contravene this be punished as rebels, and disobedient to our orders. We forbid any assemblies for the purpose of practicing other religions, and declare them to be illicit and seditious, and subject to the same penalties, which are to apply even to any masters who permit their slaves to take part in such assemblies.

Art. 4. No person is to be placed in charge of Negroes, who does not profess the Roman Catholic and Apostolic Religion; on pain of the confiscation of the said Negroes from any master who places such persons over them, and arbitrary punishment of those persons placed in charge.

Art. 5. We forbid our subjects, who profess the Protestant Religion, to cause any trouble or hindrance to our other subjects and their slaves, in their free practice of the Roman Catholic and Apostolic Religion, on pain of exemplary punishment.

Art. 6. We enjoin all our subjects, of whatever quality and condition, to observe the Sundays and Feast Days kept by our subjects of the Roman Catholic and Apostolic Religion. We forbid them to work, or to cause their slaves to work, on those days, from midnight on the one day to midnight on the next, whether at cultivating the land, manufacturing sugar, or any other form of labor, on pain of a fine and arbitrary punishment for the masters, and confiscation of all the sugar and slaves who are surprised during such work by our officials.

Art. 7. We similarly forbid the holding of slave markets and any other markets on those days, on pain of similar punishment, with confiscation of any goods found at the markets, and an arbitrary fine for the merchants.

Art. 8. We declare those of our subjects who are not of the Roman Catholic and Apostolic Religion incapable of contracting a legal marriage from this time on. We declare the children who shall be born of such unions to be bastards, and we wish such unions to be held and reputed as true concubinage.

Art. 9. Free men who have one or more children by concubinage with their slaves, together with the masters who permit this, shall each be condemned to a fine of two thousand pounds of sugar. And if they are the masters of the slave, by whom they have had such children, we order that in addition to the fine, they be deprived of the said slave and children, that these be confiscated for the profit of the Hospital, and never be emancipated. . . .

Art. 12. The children born of marriages between slaves, shall be slaves, and shall belong to the master of the female slave, and not to the master of her husband, if the slaves belong to different masters.

Art. 13. We wish that if a slave marry a free woman, the children shall be free, following the condition of the mother, notwithstanding the servile condition of the father; and that if the father be free and the mother a slave, the children shall likewise be slaves.

Art. 14. Masters are to bury their slaves, who have been baptized, in holy ground, in the cemeteries destined for this purpose; as to those who die without benefit of baptism, they are to be buried by night in a field close to the place where they die.

Art. 15. We forbid slaves to carry any offensive weapons, or large sticks, on pain of whipping, and of the confiscation of the weapons for the benefit of whoever discovers them in their possession; with the sole exception of those slaves sent hunting by their masters, and who are provided by them with notes or accustomed marks of recognition.

Art. 16. We likewise forbid slaves belonging to different masters to gather together by day or night on pretext of a wedding or anything else either at their masters' residences or elsewhere, and still less on the high roads or in remote places, on pain of corporal punishment not less than whipping or branding; and in case of repeated offenses or more serious circumstances, they may be punished by death, as shall be decided by the judges. We enjoin all our subjects to pursue the offenders, arrest them and take them to prison, even if they are not officials, and there is no decree ordering this. . . .

Art. 18. We forbid slaves to sell sugar cane, on any occasion, even with the permission of their masters. . . .

Art. 19. We also forbid slaves to offer for sale in the market or to carry to private houses for sale any form of provisions—including fruits, vegetables, firewood, edible plants, food for the animals of the sugar manufactures—without express permission of their masters in the form of a note or recognized mark. . . .

Art. 21. We permit all our subjects who inhabit the Islands to seize everything that they find in the possession of slaves, who are not provided with notes or recognized marks from their masters. . . .

Art. 22. The masters shall be responsible for providing weekly for their slaves aged ten years and above, for their subsistence, two and one half pots (of the local measure) of manioc flour, or three cassavas each weighing at least two and a half pounds, or the equivalent, with three pounds of salt beef, or three pounds of fish, or other food in proportion; and for the children, from the time they are weaned until they are ten, half the victuals specified above.

Art. 23. We forbid the masters to give the slaves distilled spirits of cane, instead of the subsistence specified in the preceding article. . . .

Art. 25. The masters shall be required to provide each slave annually with two linen garments, or four ells of linen cloth, as the master wishes. . . .

Art. 27. Slaves who are infirm through illness, age, or other cause, whether the illness be incurable or not, are to be fed and kept by their masters; and if they are abandoned, the said slaves shall be committed to the Hospital, to which the masters shall be condemned to pay six sous per day for the food and keeping of each slave. . . .

Art. 33. A slave who strikes his master, or his master's wife, his mistress, or her children in the face or causing a contusion is to be put to death.

Art. 34. Crimes and violence committed by slaves against free persons are to be severely punished, even with the sentence of death, if the case require it.

Art. 35. Grand thefts and thefts of horses, mares, mules, cows, and bulls, which are committed by slaves or emancipated slaves, are to be punished by corporal penalties and even by death should the case require it.

Art. 36. Thefts by slaves of sheep, goats, pigs, poultry, sugar cane, peas, manioc, or other vegetables, are to be punished according to the gravity of the theft; if the case merit it, the judges may condemn them to be flogged with rods by the Executioner of High Justice and branded on the shoulder with the *fleur-de-lys*. . . .

Art. 38. A runaway slave who is absent for more than one month, to be reckoned from the day his master informs the authorities, is to have his ears cut off, and to be branded on one shoulder with the *fleur-de-lys*; if the offense is repeated, for another month, similarly reckoned from the date of notification, he is to be hamstrung, and branded on the other shoulder with the *fleur-de-lys*; the third time, the slave is to be punished by death.

Art. 39. Freed slaves who harbor runaways in their houses are to be fined three hundred pounds of sugar for every day that they harbor them, to be paid to the masters of the runaways.

Art. 40. Any slave who suffers the death penalty because of the report or denunciation of his master (who is not implicated in the crime) is to be valued by two of the principal inhabitants of the Island to be chosen by the judge, and the value of the slave paid to the master; to meet the cost of this, a tax is to be levied by the Intendant on every Negro on whom duty is payable. . . .

Art. 42. Masters who believe their slaves deserving of punishment may chain them up and flog them with rods or cords; they are forbidden to torture their slaves, or mutilate their limbs, on pain of confiscation of the slaves, and extraordinary proceedings against the masters.

Art. 43. We order our officials to prosecute any masters or overseers who kill a slave in their charge or under their command, the master to be punished according to the seriousness of the crime; and if there should be cause for pardon, we permit our officials to grant it to the said masters or overseers without there being any need for Letters of Grace from us.

Art. 44. We declare slaves to be movable property, and as such to be part of the family property, not liable to proceedings for mortgage, and divisible equally among the co-heirs without preference or right of primogeniture; not to be subject to customary dowry settlements, to feudal or familial recovery or resumption, to feudal or seigneurial dues, to formal decrees, or to reductions of four-fifths, in the event of disposal through death or testament.

Art. 45. Nevertheless we do not intend by this to deprive our subjects of the right to declare slaves to be their personal property, or their family's, on their side, as is practiced with regard to money and other movable goods. . . .

Art. 55. Masters over the age of twenty years may emancipate their slaves by legal action or testament without having to give any reason for the emancipation and without the advice and concurrence of relatives, even if they are less than twenty-five years old. . . .

Art. 57. We declare that emancipations made in our Islands shall be equivalent to birth in those Islands, and that emancipated slaves do not require Letters of Naturalization from us in order to enjoy the privileges of subjects born in our kingdom, and the lands and countries owing obedience to us, even if they were born in foreign lands.

Art. 58. We command emancipated slaves to maintain a special respect toward their former masters, their widows, and children, so that any wrong they may do them is to be punished more severely than if it were done to another person. . . .

Art. 59. We grant to emancipated slaves the same privileges, rights, and immunities as are enjoyed by persons born free; we desire that they should be worthy of the freedom they have gained, that it may produce in them with respect both to their persons and their goods the same effects that the blessing of natural liberty offers to all our other subjects. . . .

As quoted and translated in Geoffrey Symcox, ed., War, Diplomacy, and Imperialism 1618–1763 (New York: Harper & Row, 1973), pp. 309–318.

required the services of two. Looms equipped with the flying shuttle used up the supply of hand-spun thread so rapidly that a private organization, the London Society for the Encouragement of Arts, Manufacturers and Commerce, offered a prize for improving the spinning process. James Hargreaves (d. 1778) won the prize in 1764 with his spinning jenny, a series of wheels geared together to make eight threads simultaneously. Soon the jenny was adapted to water power, and its output was increased to more than a hundred threads at once. The eventual emancipation of industry from dependence on unreliable water power was foreshadowed in the 1760s when the Scotsman James Watt (1736–1819) introduced the steam engine.

Although Britain had nearly 150 cotton mills in 1789, woolens and dozens of other basic commodities were still made by hand. Full industrial development would not occur until the canals and railroads permitted cheap transport of heavy freight and until shortages of capital and skilled labor were overcome. The difficulty of making precisely machined parts for Watt's engine delayed its production in large quantities. Although the eighteenth century had taken many of the initial steps in the industrial revolution, it remained for the next century to apply them on a truly revolutionary scale.

James Hargreave's spinning jenny revolutionized the textile industry. Put into use about 1764, it rapidly increased the production of thread. It also assured women a place in the work force, taking them out of the home, their wages a boon at first to hard-pressed families. (Culver Pictures, Inc.)

The Established Powers

Spain had been the dominant European power in the late sixteenth century, and France in the late seventeenth century. The Dutch had experienced a Golden Age of trade and wealth in the seventeenth century as well. In the eighteenth century, the European nations were more evenly balanced. Some countries that had lost ground in the seventeenth century—such as Spain and Austria—rebounded, while France, although it remained the strongest nation on land, slowly declined. The centers of power moved from the interior of Europe to the eastern and western peripheries. In the East, Russia began to play a significant role in European affairs for the first time, and Prussia emerged as major player by the middle of the century, despite its small size and slender economic base. In the north, Protestant Sweden lost ground to Russia. In the West, Britain rivaled and on the sea surpassed France, thereby exercising an influence on the Continent that it had never enjoyed before.

Britain, 1714–1760

In the eighteenth century British merchants outdistanced their old trading rivals, the Dutch, and gradually took the lead over their new competitors, the French. Judged by the touchstones of mercantilism—commerce, colonies, and sea power—Britain was the strongest state in Europe. The British colonial empire, however, was not a mercantilist undertaking in the fullest sense. Supervision of the colonies rested with the Board of Trade, which followed a policy of "salutary neglect." In the long run, salutary neglect did not satisfy the colonists, who found British policy neither salutary nor neglectful, but in the short run it promoted the colonists' prosperity and self-reliance.

The Royal Navy enjoyed the assets of a disciplined officer corps and more ships than any other power possessed. Future captains went to sea at the age of sixteen or even younger and passed through long practical training before receiving commissions. Britain had a two-to-one advantage over France in number of warships, a six-to-one lead in merchant ships, and a ten-to-one lead in total number of experienced seamen, merchant and naval. In wartime the fleet could draw on the merchant marine for additional sailors and auxiliary vessels.

The British army, by contrast, was neither large nor impressive. Its officers were reputed to be the worst in Europe, and many of its soldiers were mercenaries from the German state of Hesse-Cassel, or Hessians. Neglect of the army was a deliberate decision. The British Isles were relatively safe from invasion; moreover, the English people feared a standing army as an instrument of potential absolutism.

The Glorious Revolution, which had done much to confirm distrust of the army, had also confirmed the supremacy of Parliament. Parliament had approved the accession of William and Mary in place of James II. When Anne, Mary's sister and the last Stuart monarch, died in 1714, Parliament had already arranged for the succession of the house of Hanover.

Under the first kings of the new house—George I (r. 1714–1727) and George II (r. 1727–1760)—the cabinet was only starting to gain authority. George I and George II by no means abdicated all the old royal prerogatives. They often intervened in the conduct of war and diplomacy. They chose their cabinet ministers from the Whig party, then in control of the Commons. They did so, however, not because they were required to, but because it suited their convenience and because they distrusted the Tories, some of whom were involved in Jacobite plots to restore to the throne the descendants of James II (Jacobite from *Jacobus*, Latin for "James").

From 1721 to 1742 Robert Walpole, who led the Whigs in the Commons, headed the cabinet; he was in fact prime (or first) minister, although the title was still unofficial. Walpole was a master politician who maintained his majority in the Commons by skillful manipulation. The task was not easy, for party discipline did not yet exist. The terms *Whig* and *Tory* referred to shifting interest groups, not to parties in a formal sense.

Under the first two Georges the Whigs were a coalition of landed and "funded" gentry—that is, of nobles and squires from the country and of business and professional men from London and provincial towns. The Whigs thus renewed a political alliance that had first appeared in the later Middle Ages when the knights of the shire had joined the burgesses to form the Commons. Family ties, common political aims, and common respect for property bound together the rural and urban Whigs.

What did terms like *gentry* and *squire* connote about social class in the eighteenth century? Historians generally agree that they referred to a class just below the titled nobility. The ranks of the gentry included the younger sons of nobles, technically not nobles themselves since a seat in the House of Lords passed only to the eldest son. They also included other owners of landed estates, all of whom were addressed verbally as "sir" and in writing as "Esquire." Historically, the gentry lived off the revenues of landed property, but by the eighteenth century many of them also had a stake in commerce. Successful businessmen sometimes bought country estates and set themselves up as gentlemen. But recent research has shown that in England movement by successful businessmen into the aristocracy was limited, less than it was in France, where venality provided a mechanism for transforming wealth into noble status.

In its social and political structure the Britain of Walpole was not democratic. Only gentlemen could hope to rise in the professions, to become army and navy officers, lawyers, clergymen, and physicians. In local affairs the landed gentry alone supplied the justices of the peace, who presided over courts, fixed wage scales, superintended the relief of the poor, maintained bridges and highways, and defended the propertied classes. Until the 1740s only gentlemen had the right to vote for members of Parliament. The small number of voters in many constituencies encouraged corruption, particularly in the "rotten" or "pocket" boroughs, which had such a tiny electorate that control of their vote reposed in the "pocket" of some wealthy lord who readily used bribery to achieve his ends.

Thus the ruling classes governed the generally voteless masses. London was already big enough to have slums, crimes of violence, and traffic jams— accompanied by an almost complete lack of police and fire protection. Children generally began to work when they were eight years old. Yet the British ruling classes, selfish and narrow though they often were, had at their best a sense of public spirit and civic-mindedness toward the less fortunate. Furthermore, the memory of Cromwell's rebellion and the recurrent food riots because of the effects of the enclosure movement also provided sharp incentives for the nobility to maintain political control.

France, 1715–1774

Although relatively few merchants and not many professionals rose into the landed aristocracy in England during the eighteenth century, the size and influence of the middle class grew considerably. In France, by contrast, it was comparatively easy to gain a noble title through purchase of a high government office, yet the middle class was proportionately smaller. In part the French middle class was smaller because most of the profits from expanded commerce went to the coastal cities, while in England the equivalent profits were more widely shared. Although French colonial policies discouraged French migration to the New World, port cities grew considerably in size and wealth as a result of the booming trade with the French sugar-producing Caribbean colonies.

The French navy needed greater resources and better leadership. Since Dutch and British vessels carried much of French commerce, the merchant marine was small. French naval officers, rigorously trained in the classroom, lacked the practical experience gained by captains with a lifetime at sea.

French rulers neglected the navy in favor of the army, since France was, above all, a land power, and its vulnerable northeastern frontier invited invasion. However, the troops were poorly trained, and the organization was top-heavy; there was one officer to fifteen men, compared with one to thirty-five in the more efficient Prussian army. Many aristocratic officers regarded a commission as simply a convenient way of increasing their personal wealth.

Both the navy and the army were reformed after the defeats suffered by France in the Seven Years' War (1756–1763). The number of warships was increased, the army officer corps was cleared of much deadwood, and more aggressive military tactics were introduced. These improvements accounted in part for the excellent showing made by France in the American Revolutionary War and in the military campaigns resulting from its own revolution. They came too late, however, to save the vanishing prestige of the Old Regime.

One of the French government's chief weaknesses was Louis XIV's creation of so grandiose a role for the French king that neither of his successors could adequately perform it. Louis XV was only five years old when he acceded to the throne in 1715, and until 1743 he ruled through a succession of regents and prime ministers. Although he was an intelligent and diligent king, his remote personality and long period of indirect rule created the impression that he cared more about his private pleasures than about public affairs and the welfare of his subjects. In the 1740s he took up with a long series of mistresses, most notably Madame de Pompadour (1721–1764). Her strong personality, intelligence, and influence at court helped confirm widespread impressions that she was the true power behind the throne. Louis XV was a secretive ruler, so much so that in his later reign he personally conducted a foreign policy through agents whose true mission was unknown to his own foreign minister. His many sudden shifts of policy and changes of high government appointees strongly suggested he lacked the strong consistent will of Louis XIV—a fatal flaw in a system of government that relied so heavily on the king himself.

Problems that would become unmanageable later already surfaced under the Regency government established in 1715 under the Duke d'Orléans. First, there was the increasing opposition to the Crown from within the government, especially from the Parlement of Paris. The Parlement was a high royal court staffed by members of the service nobility that exercised the right to "register" (that is, formally inscribe) royal edicts before they went into effect. Because his authority as Regent was disputed, the Duke of Orléans cut a deal

William Hogarth was especially known for his satirical view of the political and social cus-
toms of the English. He intended to be a silversmith but became an engraver of satirical
prints for publishers instead; he then extended his work to moral commentaries on everyday
life. His Election series shows both fine draftsmanship and skill as a caricaturist. Here he
shows a campaign in progress, in Canvassing for Votes. *(Memorial Art Gallery of the Uni-*
versity of Rochester, gift of Mr. and Mrs. Herman Cohn)

with the Parlement: in exchange for their supporting his claims to the
Regency, Orléans, upon assuming power, reestablished the court's right to
protest edicts before it registered them, a right the Parlement had lost under
Louis XIV.

Although this right was limited later, the Parlement had effectively
regained the authority to challenge royal initiatives, and it did so almost
immediately. Two issues dominated these noisy disputes. First, there was the
fiscal crisis left over from the previous reign, which the Regent ultimately
tried to resolve through the risky system of John Law (as described in Chapter 1). Suspicious of Law's intentions, the Parlement opposed the system
even before its collapse—a prelude to the opposition royal fiscal policies
received from the Parlement later on. A second major issue was the papal bull
Unigenitus published in 1713 that condemned ideas allegedly contained in a
Jansenist treatise. The Parlement was particularly sensitive about its enforcement, in part because there was a vocal minority of Jansenist magistrates
within the Parlement and in part because the Parlement claimed to have

jurisdiction over the French church and was resentful of papal interference (Jansenist nuns also ran influential schools). Despite Orléans's efforts to moderate the conflict, the Parlement objected to his compromises. Increasingly frustrated, Orléans ordered the exile of the Parlement from Paris in 1720, a weapon the Crown would use later in similar conflicts. A temporary settlement was soon reached, but the matter was hardly settled once and for all. Jansenism would remain a major bone of contention in French politics for the next half-century. Equally important, the Jansenist lobby made effective use of appeals to public opinion through the publication of hundreds of pamphlets and, starting in 1728, an underground newspaper that condemned the government for its "despotic" policies.

Under the ministry of Cardinal Fleury, which began in 1726, a major controversy over Jansenism erupted in 1730–1732, but otherwise the nation was calmer than in the stormy period of the Orléans Regency. Fleury was personally sympathetic to *Unigenitus* and imprisoned many peddlers of Jansenist literature, but his goal in this area was to lessen controversy. Another important goal was to restore health to the French economy and to royal finances, largely by avoiding expensive military conflicts abroad. Under his administration, the government nearly balanced the budget for the first time in living memory, which permitted the government to escape potential bitter disputes over taxes for a time. However, by Fleury's death in 1743 the nation was again entering a period of protracted warfare, which sparked a new round of ultimately fatal threats to the solvency and authority of the government.

Other States of Western Europe

Spain was the only other state in western Europe with a claim to great power status. Sweden and the Dutch republic could no longer sustain the major international roles they had undertaken during the seventeenth century. The Great Northern War had withered Sweden's Baltic empire. The Dutch, exhausted by their wars against Louis XIV, could not afford a large navy or an energetic foreign policy. Still, Dutch seaborne trade remained substantial, and the republic settled down to a life of relative prosperity and decreased international significance.

Spain suffered comparatively little damage from the War of the Spanish Succession of the early 1700s. The loss of Belgium and parts of Italy in the Utrecht settlement of 1713 reduced the unwieldy Spanish domains to more manageable size, and Philip V (r. 1700–1746), the first Bourbon monarch, infused fresh life into the country's traditional institutions. Philip and his advisers cut down the excessive formalities and long delays of Spanish administration, reasserted the authority of the monarchy over the nobility and clergy, improved the tax system, encouraged industry, built up the navy, and fortified strategic points of the Spanish Empire in America.

This new administration, however, did not strike at the root causes of Spanish decline. The greed of governors and the restrictions of mercantilism still checked the growth of the colonies. The mother country remained

Beautiful, intelligent, and ambitious, Madame de Pompadour was Louis XV's most powerful mistress. This portrait, by Francois Boucher (1703–1770), a master of the rococo style, provides the historian with valuable details concerning clothing, hairstyles, decorations, and furniture. (*Reproduced by permission of the Trustees of The Wallace Collection, London, England*)

impoverished, burdened with noble and clerical castes, and hampered by inadequate resources. Philip V himself was neurotic and was dominated by his strong-willed second wife, Elizabeth Farnese. Since Philip's son by his first marriage would inherit Spain, Elizabeth was determined to find thrones for her own two sons, and her persistent attempts to secure Italian states for them repeatedly threatened the peace of Europe.

During this time Spain was also preoccupied with events in Italy. By 1715 the Italian states had lost much of the political and economic power they had enjoyed during the Renaissance. The opening of new lands overseas and the rise of the Atlantic powers had diminished the importance of the Mediterranean. In the Mediterranean itself, the Ottoman Turks and their satellites in

North Africa had long menaced Italian shipping and trade. Moreover, from the time of the French invasion of 1494 the Italian states had lived in fear of conquest by one or another of the new national monarchies.

It was the Spanish Habsburgs who had made that conquest. For almost two centuries they ruled Milan, Naples, and Sicily directly and dominated the rest of the peninsula. By 1720 Austria was firmly established in Lombardy, flanked by the decaying commercial republics of Venice and Genoa. In the mountainous northwest was the small but rising state of Piedmont-Savoy (technically the kingdom of Sardinia after its acquisition of that island in 1720). Farther down the peninsula were the grand duchy of Tuscany (formerly the republic of Florence), the Papal States, and the kingdom of Naples and Sicily. None of these states was more than a minor power.

Yet Italy could not be written off as a negligible quantity in the eighteenth century. Rome remained the capital of Catholicism, Venice still produced fine painters, and Naples remained the school for European musicians. Lombardy, Tuscany, and Naples all contributed to the economic and intellectual advances of the century.

In the 1730s a series of exchanges gave Naples and Sicily to Elizabeth's older son, while the Austrians gained the right to succeed the last Medici grand duke of Tuscany. In 1768 Genoa sold the island of Corsica to France. Italy was, in an old phrase, merely "a geographical expression"—not a single political entity but a series of parts manipulated by ambitious dynasts and empire builders from outside the peninsula.

In some respects Germany deserved even more to be called a geographical expression, for it was divided into three hundred states. The Peace of Westphalia in 1648 had enhanced the sovereign rights of the particular German states and virtually extinguished the authority of their nominal overlord, the Holy Roman emperor. Unlike Italy, however, Germany did include two considerable powers—one long established (Austria) and one recently arrived (Prussia).

The Habsburg rulers of Austria won a series of military and diplomatic victories in the two decades before 1715. In 1699, by the Peace of Carlovitz, they had recovered much of Hungary from the Ottoman Turks. In 1713, although they failed to keep the old Habsburg crown of Spain from going to the Bourbon Philip V, they were compensated with Spain's Belgian and Italian territories, and in 1718 they acquired the rest of Hungary.

Charles VI (r. 1711–1740) spent much of his reign persuading his own noble subjects to ratify the Pragmatic Sanction, the constitutional agreement that established the principle of linking together the scattered family territories, whereby, in the absence of sons, Charles's daughter Maria Theresa (1717–1780) would succeed him in all his lands, and in 1724 he succeeded. Much, however, remained to be done to consolidate Habsburg rule over an assemblage of lands that represented many different nations and would never be forged into a single national monarchy. In three key national areas—German Austria, Czech Bohemia, and Magyar Hungary—the nobles still kept most of their medieval prerogatives and, by dominating local estates and diets, controlled grants of taxes and the appointment of officials. Still, the financial

---

The Written Record

AN AGE OF MANNERS

In 1729 a French guide to behavior for the "civilized Christian" covered such subjects as speech, table manners, bodily functions, nose blowing, and behavior in the bedroom. This guide to good manners was reissued with increasingly complex advice through 1774, although with significantly changing emphases, as certain behavior (blowing one's nose into a kerchief no longer worn about the neck but now carried in the hand, hence *handkerchief*) became acceptable, and other behavior more closely observed. These guides emphasized class differences, pointing out that behavior found acceptable in the presence of one's social inferiors was to be avoided in the presence of one's equals or social superiors.

It is a part of decency and modesty to cover all parts of the body except the head and hands. You should take care ... not to touch with your bare hand any part of the body that is normally uncovered. ... You should get used to suffering small discomforts without twisting, rubbing, or scratching. ... It is far more contrary to decency and propriety to touch or see in another person, particularly of the other sex, that which Heaven forbids you to look at yourself. When you need to pass water, you should always withdraw to some unfrequented place. And it is proper (even for children) to perform other natural functions where you cannot be seen. It is very impolite to emit wind from your body when in company, either from above or from below, even if it is done without noise. ... It is never proper to speak of the parts of the body that should be hidden, nor of certain bodily necessities to which Nature has subjected us, nor even to mention them. ... You should avoid making a noise when blowing your nose. ... Before blowing it, it is impolite to spend a long time taking out your handkerchief. It shows a lack of respect toward the people you are with to unfold it in different places to see where you are to use it.

Sieur La Salle, *Les Règles de la bienséance et de la civilité Chrétienne* (Rouen, 1729), quoted in Norbert Elias, *The History of Manners*, vol. I: *The Civilizing Process*, trans. Edmund Jephcott (New York: Pantheon, 1982), pp. 132, 156.

---

and military weakness of the Habsburg regime was underlined by the fact that when Charles VI died in 1740, the treasury was nearly empty and the pay of both army and civil service was more than two years overdue. The Elector of Bavaria thereupon made a claim for succession on behalf of his wife, challenging Maria Theresa.

The Newcomers

Prussia and the Hohenzollerns, 1715–1740

Prussia's territories were scattered across north Germany from the Rhine on the west to Poland on the east. Consisting in good part of sand and swamp, these lands had meager natural resources and supported relatively little trade. With fewer than 3 million inhabitants in 1715, Prussia ranked twelfth among the European states in population. Its capital city, Berlin, had few of the obvious geographical advantages enjoyed by Constantinople, Paris, London, and other great capitals. The Hohenzollerns had been established since the fifteenth century as electors of Brandenburg, which lay between the Elbe and Oder rivers. In 1618, when East Prussia fell to the Hohenzollerns, it was separated from Brandenburg by Polish West Prussia and was still nominally a fief held from the Polish king. In western Germany in the meantime the Hohenzollerns had acquired (1614) Cleves, Mark, and some other parcels in the lower Rhine valley and Westphalia. Thus, when Frederick William, the Great Elector (r. 1640–1688), succeeded to the Hohenzollern inheritance, his lands consisted of a nucleus in Brandenburg with separate outlying regions to the east and west. With extraordinary persistence, the rulers of Brandenburg-Prussia for the next two hundred years devoted themselves to the task of making a solid block of territory out of these bits and pieces.

The Great Elector won recognition from Poland as the full sovereign of Prussia. He also tried, with less success, to dislodge the Swedes from the Pomeranian territories between Brandenburg and the Baltic that they had acquired in 1648. In domestic policy his accomplishments were more substantial. He had found his domains largely ruined by war, the farms wasted, the population cut in half, the army reduced to a disorderly rabble of a few thousand men. The Great Elector repaired the damage thoroughly. To augment the population, he encouraged the immigration of Polish Jews and other refugees from religious persecution. He built a small, efficient standing army. In peacetime he assigned the soldiers to the construction of public works, including a canal between the Elbe and the Oder.

The Great Elector initiated the Hohenzollern pattern of militarized absolutism. On his accession he found that in all three territories—Prussia, Brandenburg, and Cleves-Mark—the authority of the ruler was limited by the estates, medieval assemblies representing the landed nobles and the townspeople. He battled the estates for supremacy and won, thereby delaying for two centuries the introduction of representative government into the Hohenzollern realm. He gradually gathered into his own hands the crucial power of levying taxes.

Like Louis XIV, the Great Elector reduced the independence of the aristocracy; unlike Louis, however, he relied not on bourgeois officials but on a working alliance with the landed gentry, particularly the Junkers of East Prussia. He confirmed the Junkers' absolute authority over the serfs on their estates and their ascendancy over the towns, and he encouraged them to serve the state, especially as army officers. Even more than in other monarchies, the absolutism of the Hohenzollerns rested on the cooperation of the sovereign and the aristocracy, not on their mutual antagonism.

The Great Elector's son, Frederick I (r. 1688–1713), assumed the title "King of Prussia" and insisted on international recognition of his new status as the price for his entry into the War of the Spanish Succession. The next king, Frederick William I (r. 1713–1740), devoted himself entirely to economy, absolutism, and the army. His frugality enabled him to undertake occasional projects that he thought worthwhile, such as financing the immigration of twelve thousand south German Protestants to open up new farmlands in eastern Prussia.

To strengthen royal control over the apparatus of state, Frederick William I instituted a small board of experts charged both to administer departments of the central government and to supervise provinces. The arrangement detached provincial administration from local interest and brought it under closer royal control.

Frederick William I doubled the size of the standing army and established state factories to provide guns and uniforms. To conserve the strength of the laboring force in his underpopulated state, he furloughed troops to work on the farms nine months a year. He was too cautious to undertake an adventurous foreign policy; his only significant military campaign was against Sweden in the last phase of the Great Northern War, whereby Prussia obtained in 1720 part of Swedish Pomerania and also the important Baltic port of Stettin at the mouth of the Oder River.

Eighteenth-century observers rightly called the Prussia of Frederick William an armed camp. The king neglected the education of his subjects, showed little concern for the arts, and carried miserliness to the extreme of refusing pensions to soldiers' widows. Yet in terms of power, his regime worked extremely well. The Junkers were intensely loyal to the Hohenzollerns and made excellent officers. The army, although smaller than those of France, Russia, or Austria, was the best drilled and disciplined in Europe.

Russia and Peter the Great, 1682–1725

Even more spectacular than the rise of Prussia was the emergence of Russia as a major power during the era of Peter the Great (r. 1682–1725). In 1682, at the death of Czar Fëdor Romanov, Russia was still a backward country, with few diplomatic links with the West and very little knowledge of the outside world. Contemporaries, Russians as well as foreigners, noted the brutality, drunkenness, illiteracy, and filth prevalent among all classes of society. Even most of the clergy could not read.

Czar Fëdor died childless in 1682, leaving a retarded brother, Ivan, and a capable sister, Sophia, both children of Czar Alexis (r. 1645–1676) by his first wife. The ten-year-old Peter was the half-brother of Ivan and Sophia, the son of Alexis by his second wife. A major court feud developed between the partisans of the family of Alexis's first wife and those of the family of the second. At first the old Russian representative assembly, the Zemski Sobor, elected Peter czar. But Sophia, as leader of the opposing faction, won the support of the *streltsi,* or "musketeers," a special branch of the military. Undisciplined and angry with their officers, the streltsi were a menace to orderly government. Sophia encouraged the streltsi to attack the Kremlin, and the youthful Peter saw the infuriated troops murder some of his mother's family. For good measure, they killed many nobles living in Moscow and pillaged the archives where the records of serfdom were kept. Sophia now served as regent for both Ivan and Peter, who were hailed as joint czars. In the end, however, the streltsi deserted Sophia, who was shut up in a convent in 1689; from then until Ivan's death in 1696 Peter and his half-brother technically ruled together.

The young Peter was almost seven feet tall and extremely energetic. Fascinated by war and military games, he had set up a play regiment as a child, staffed it with full-grown men, enlisted as a common soldier in its ranks (promoting himself from time to time), ordered equipment for it from the Moscow arsenals, and drilled it with unflagging vigor. When he discovered a derelict boat in a barn, he unraveled the mysteries of rigging and sail with the help of Dutch sailors living in Moscow. Maneuvers, sailing, and relaxing with his cronies kept him from spending time with his wife, whom Peter had married at sixteen and eventually sent to a convent. He smoked, drank, caroused, and seemed almost without focus; at various times he took up carpentry, shoemaking, cooking, clock making, ivory carving, etching, and dentistry. Peter was a shock to Muscovites, and not in keeping with their idea of a proper czar. Society was further scandalized when Peter took as his mistress a girl who had already been mistress to many others; after she gave birth to two of his children, he finally married her in 1712. This was the empress Catherine (c. 1684–1727), a hearty and affectionate woman who was able to control her difficult husband as no one else could.

Meanwhile, Peter led a campaign against the Turks around the Black Sea. With the help of Dutch experts, he sailed a fleet of river boats down the Don and defeated the Turks at Azov in 1696. The project of forming an anti-Turkish league with the states of western Europe now gave Peter a pretext for the first trip outside Russia taken by a Russian sovereign since the Kievan period. What fascinated him was Western technology, especially in naval matters, and he planned to go to Holland, England, and Venice. He hired several hundred technicians to work in Russia, raised money by selling the monopoly of tobacco sales in Russia to an English peer, and on his journey visited every sort of factory, museum, or printing press he could find.

Before Peter reached Venice, his trip was interrupted by news that the streltsi had revolted again; Peter rushed home and personally participated in their hideous punishment. Although many innocent men suffered torture and death, Peter broke the streltsi as a power in Russian life. He was more determined than ever to modernize his country, and on the day of his return summoned the court jester to assist him as they went about clipping off courtiers' beards. This was an act full of symbolism, for the tradition of the Orthodox church held that God was bearded; if man was made in the image of God, man must also have a beard; and if he was deprived of it, he became a candidate for damnation. Peter now decreed that Russian nobles must shave or else pay a substantial tax for the privilege of wearing their beards. Peter also commanded that all *boyars* (members of the gentry class) and the city population in general must abandon long robes with flowing sleeves and tall bonnets, and adopt Western-style costume. The manufacture of traditional clothes was made illegal, and Peter took up his shears again and cut off the sleeves of people wearing them.

Peter's policies at home can be understood only in light of his ever-mounting need to support virtually incessant warfare, together with his intense desire to modernize Russia. His plan for an international crusade against the Turks collapsed when the Austrians and the Ottoman Empire agreed to the Peace of Carlovitz in 1699. Feeling that Austria had betrayed Russia, Peter made a separate peace with the Turks in 1700. By then he was already planning to attack Sweden. Peter's allies in the enterprise were Denmark and Poland.

Led by Charles XII (r. 1697–1718), Sweden won the opening campaigns of the Great Northern War (1700–1721). Charles knocked once-powerful Denmark out of the fighting, frustrated Poland's attempt to take the Baltic port of Riga, and completely defeated a larger but ill-prepared Russian force at Narva (1700). Instead of marching into Russia, however, Charles detoured into Poland, where he spent seven years pursuing the king, who finally had to abandon both the Russian alliance and the Polish crown. Charles thereupon secured the election of one of his protégés as king of Poland.

In the interim, Peter rebuilt his armies and took from the Swedes the Baltic provinces nearest to Russia—Ingria and Livonia. In the marshes of the former, he founded in 1703 the city of St. Petersburg, to which he eventually moved the court from Moscow. In 1708 Charles swept far to the south and east into the Ukraine in an effort to join forces with the Cossacks. Exhausted by the severe winter, the Swedish forces were defeated by the Russians in the decisive battle of Poltava (1709). Peter now reinstated his king of Poland, but he was not able to force the Turks to surrender Charles, who had taken refuge with them.

To avenge his defeat Charles engineered a war between Turkey and Russia (1710–1711), during which the Russians made their first appeal to the Balkan Christian subjects of the Turks on the basis of their common faith. Bearing banners modeled on those of Constantine, first emperor of Byzantium, Russian forces crossed into the Ottoman province of Moldavia. Here the Ottoman armies trapped Peter in 1711 and forced him to surrender; the Turks proved unexpectedly lenient, requiring only the surrender of the port of Azov and the creation of an unfortified no man's land between Russian and Ottoman territory.

On the diplomatic front Russia made a series of alliances with petty German courts. The death of Charles XII in 1718 cleared the way for peace negotiations, although it took a Russian landing in Sweden proper to force a decision. At Nystadt (1721) Russia handed back Finland and agreed to pay a substantial sum for the former Swedish possessions along the eastern shore of the Baltic. The opening of this "window on the West" meant that seaborne traffic no longer had to sail around the northern edge of Europe to reach Russia.

Constant warfare requires constant supplies of men and money. Peter's government developed a form of conscription according to which a given number of households had to supply a given number of recruits. Although

Russian Expansion in Europe, 1689–1796

more of these men died of disease, hunger, and cold than at the hands of the
enemy, the very length of the Great Northern War meant that survivors
served as a tough nucleus for a regular army. Peter also built a Baltic fleet at
the first opportunity, but a Russian naval tradition never took hold. From
eight hundred ships (mostly very small) in 1725, the fleet declined to fewer
than twenty a decade later; there was no merchant marine at all.

To staff the military forces and the administration, Peter rigorously
enforced the rule by which all landowners owed service to the state. For those
who failed to register he eventually decreed "civil death," which removed

them from the protection of the law and made them subject to attack with impunity. State service became compulsory for life; at the age of fifteen every male child of the service nobility was assigned to his future post in the army, in the civil service, or at court. When a member of this class died, he was required to leave his estate intact to one of his sons, not necessarily the eldest, so that it would not be divided anew in every generation. Thus the service nobility was brought into complete dependence upon the czar. The system opened the possibility of a splendid career to men with talent, for a person without property or rank who reached a certain level in any branch of the service was automatically ennobled and received lands.

To raise cash, Peter debased the currency, taxed virtually everything—sales, rents, real estate, tanneries, baths, and beehives—and appointed special revenue finders to think of new levies. The government held a monopoly over a variety of products, including salt, oil, coffins, and caviar. However, the basic tax on each household was not producing enough revenue, partly because the number of households had declined as a result of war and misery, and partly because households were combining to evade payment. Peter's government therefore substituted a head tax on every male. This innovation required a new census, which produced a most important, and unintended, social result. The census-takers classified as serfs many who were between freedom and serfdom; these people thus found themselves and their children labeled as unfree, to be transferred from owner to owner.

In administration, new ministries (*prikazy*) were first set up to centralize the handling of funds received from various sources. A system of army districts adopted for reasons of military efficiency led to the creation of provinces. Each province had its own governor, and many of the functions previously carried on inefficiently by the central government were thus decentralized.

Ultimately, Peter copied the Swedish system of central ministries to supersede the old prikazy and created nine "colleges"—for foreign affairs, the army, justice, expenditure, and the like—each administered by an eleven-man collegium. This arrangement discouraged corruption by making any member of a collegium subject to checking by his colleagues; but it caused delays in final decisions, which could only be reached after lengthy deliberations.

To educate future officers and also many civil servants, Peter established naval, military, and artillery academies. Because of the inadequacy of Russian primary education, which was still controlled by the church, foreigners had to be summoned to provide Russia with scholars. At a lower level, Peter continued the practice of importing technicians and artisans to teach their skills to Russians. The czar offered the inducements of protective tariffs and freedom from taxation to encourage manufacturing. Although sometimes employing many laborers, industrial enterprises remained inefficient. Factory owners could buy and sell serfs if the serfs were bought or sold as a body together with the factory itself. This "possessional" industrial serfdom did not provide much incentive for good work.

Peter also brought the church under the collegiate system. Knowing how the clergy loathed his new regime, he began by failing to appoint a successor when the patriarch of Moscow died in 1700. In 1721 he placed the church under an agency called at first the spiritual college and then the Holy Directing Synod, headed by a layman. Churchmen of the conservative school were more and more convinced that Peter was the Antichrist himself.

The records of Peter's secret police are full of the complaints his agents heard as they moved about listening for subversive remarks. Peasant husbands and fathers were snatched away to fight on distant battlefields or to labor in the swamps building a city that only Peter appeared to want. The number of serfs increased. Service men found themselves condemned to work for the czar during the whole of their lives and were seldom able to visit their estates.

Among the lower orders of society resistance took the form of peasant uprisings, which were punished with extreme brutality. The usual allies of the peasant rebels, the Cossacks, suffered mass executions, and sharp curtailment of their traditional independence. The leaders of the noble and clerical opposition focused their hopes on Peter's son Alexis. Alexis fanned their hopes by indicating that he shared their views. Eventually, he fled abroad and sought asylum with his brother-in-law, the Austrian emperor Charles VI. Promising him forgiveness, Peter lured Alexis back to Russia and had him tortured to death in his presence.

In many respects Peter simply fortified already existing Russian institutions and characteristics. He made a strong autocracy even stronger, a universal service law even more stringent, a serf more of a serf. His trips abroad, his fondness for foreign ways, his regard for advanced technology, his mercantilism, his wars, all had their precedents in Russian history before his reign. Before he attacked it, the church had already been weakened by the schism of the Old Believers. Perhaps Peter's true radicalism was in the field of everyday manners and behaviors. His attacks on beards, dress, the calendar (he adopted the Western method of dating from the birth of Christ), his hatred of ceremony and fondness for manual labor—these were indeed new; so, too, were the exceptional vigor and passion with which he acted. They were decisive in winning Peter his reputation as a revolutionary—Peter the Great.

In foreign affairs Russia found itself persistently blocked, even by its allies; whenever Russia tried to move into central or western Europe, Prussia or Austria would desert any alliance with the Russians. As a result, Russian rulers distrusted European diplomacy and followed an essentially defensive policy. The Russians had become a formidable military power capable of doubling their artillery in a single year, with perhaps the best infantry and most able gunnery in Europe by the mid-eighteenth century. A lack of heavy horses held back the cavalry, as did the undisciplined nature of Cossack warfare. But by the time the Russians occupied East Prussia (from 1758–1761), the Cossacks, too, were noted for their discipline, and European monarchs, fearful of Russian influence, increasingly used propaganda against the czars, even when allied to them.

The Polish and Ottoman Victims

By the early eighteenth century, Poland and the Ottoman Empire still bulked large on the map, but both states suffered from incompetent government, a backward economy, and the presence of large national and religious minorities. The Orthodox Christians in Catholic Poland and Muslim Turkey were beginning to look to Russia for protection. Moreover, the evident decay of both states stimulated the aggressive appetites of their stronger neighbors. Poland would disappear as an independent power before the end of the century, partitioned by Russia, Austria, and Prussia. Turkey would hold on, but was already beginning to acquire its reputation as "the Sick Man of Europe."

The Polish government was a political curiosity. The monarchy was elective: Each time the throne fell vacant, the Diet chose a successor, usually the candidate who had offered the largest bribes, and sometimes even a foreigner. Once elected, the king was nearly powerless. The Diet was dominated by the nobility and since the 1650s had practiced the *liberum veto*, whereby any one of its members could block any proposal by shouting "I do not wish it!" The Diet was not a parliament but as assembly of aristocrats, each of whom acted as a power unto himself; unanimity was therefore almost impossible. This loosely knit state had no regular army, no diplomatic corps, no central bureaucracy.

The Ottoman Empire was still a functioning state, yet it was falling further and further behind the major European powers, particularly in fiscal stability and technology. Not until the nineteenth century did it produce a sultan who would attempt the kind of massive assault on tradition that Peter the Great had mounted. In the eighteenth century, with rare exceptions, the sultans were captives of harem intrigue and could do little to discipline such powerful groups as the *janissaries*—members of the elite military caste—who exploited their privileges and neglected their soldierly duties. This cumbersome government did at least govern, however, and it showed considerable staying power in war. The so-called Polish and Turkish questions would dominate international politics for the next half-century.

War and Diplomacy, 1713–1763

In the early eighteenth century the international balance was precarious. Should the strong states decide to prey upon the weak, the balance was certain to be upset. One such upset resulted from the Great Northern War, which enabled Russia to replace Sweden as the dominant power in the Baltic. The expansion of Russia continued to threaten the balance during most of the eighteenth century, and the chief victims were Poland and Turkey. A second major threat to the balance came from the expansion of Prussia at the expense

of Austria, Poland, and Sweden. A third arose out of the colonial and commercial rivalry between Britain and the French and Spanish Bourbons.

These were not the only international issues of the day. The old competition between Austria and France remained lively. It was complicated by the
ambitions of Elizabeth Farnese, second wife of Philip V of Spain, who won
the support of France and threatened Austrian power in Italy. The Austrian
Habsburgs were vigorous expansionists, aiming to drive the Turks from the
Danube and extend their own domains southeast to the Black Sea.

Although the interplay of all these rivalries led to frequent shifts in power,
an international balance was generally maintained. The limited financial
resources of the governments of the Old Regime generally permitted only
limited warfare. On the battlefield, generals were reluctant to risk losing soldiers who represented a costly investment in training; they favored sieges
executed according to conventions well understood by all belligerents. At the
peace table, diplomats were reluctant to destroy an opponent; they generally
sought to award a bit of territory or a minor throne as compensation for a
greater loss. The handling of the Polish and the Turkish questions afforded
clear examples of conventional international politics in operation.

The Turkish and Polish Questions, 1716–1739

In 1716 the Ottoman Empire became embroiled in a war with Austria that
resulted in the Treaty of Passarowitz (1718), by which Charles VI recovered
the portion of Hungary still under Turkish rule, plus some other Ottoman
lands in the Danube valley. Another Austro-Turkish war (1735–1739) modified the Passarowitz settlement. In this war Austria was allied with Russia,
but they fell to quarreling over division of the prospective spoils. In the end
there was little to divide, and Charles VI had to hand back to Turkey the
Danubian lands annexed in 1718. During the negotiations leading to the Austro-Turkish settlement of 1739, France gave the Ottoman Empire powerful
support. In the early 1730s Bourbons and Habsburgs also chose opposing
sides in a crisis over the kingship of Poland. The stage was set for the War of
the Polish Succession (1733–1735), pitting a Polish contender, Stanislas Leszcynski, protégé of Charles XII, plus France and Spain, against Augustus III, a
protégé of Peter the Great, who also had Austrian support.

The diplomats quickly worked out a compromise settlement. Much to the
satisfaction of Austria and Russia, Augustus III secured the Polish throne. Yet
from the French standpoint, Stanislas Leszcynski was well compensated for
his loss. He acquired the duchy of Lorraine on the northeastern border of
France, with the provision that when he died Lorraine would go to his
daughter Marie, wife of Louis XV of France, and thence to the French Crown.
The incumbent duke of Lorraine, Francis, future husband of the Habsburg
heiress Maria Theresa, was awarded the grand duchy of Tuscany. Finally, as
a by-product of the settlement, Elizabeth Farnese of Spain capped twenty
years of perseverance by procuring the kingdom of Naples for her elder son.

The War of the Polish Succession may seem like much ado about a kingship possessing no real power; and the postwar settlement, which affected chiefly Italy and Lorraine, may appear to be a striking case of diplomatic irrelevance. Yet the whole Polish crisis neatly illustrates the workings of dynastic politics and the balance of power. Statesmen regarded thrones as diplomatic prizes, to be assigned without reference to the wishes of the populations involved. The complicated arrangements of the 1730s preserved the balance of power by giving something to almost everyone. Although the diplomats had not prevented a little war over Poland, they did keep it from becoming a big one.

The Austrian Succession, 1739–1748

Britain and France collaborated in the 1720s and 1730s because both Walpole and Fleury sought stability abroad to promote economic recovery at home. The partnership, however, collapsed over the competition between the two Atlantic powers for commerce and empire. Neither Walpole nor Fleury could prevent the worldwide war between Britain and the Bourbon monarchies that broke out in 1739 and that lasted, with intervals of peace, until the final defeat of Napoleon in 1815. This "Second Hundred Years' War" had, in fact, already begun half a century earlier, in the days of Louis XIV. The Utrecht settlement of 1713 had not fully settled the rivalry between Britain and France (and France's Bourbon partner, Spain). Thus the war of 1739 was as much the renewal of an old struggle as the onset of a new one.

The specific issue behind the crisis of 1739 was the comparatively minor question of British disappointment over the results of the Asiento privilege. As the South Sea Company discovered, the Asiento gave Britain only a token share in the trade of the Spanish American colonies. What British captains could not get legitimately they got by smuggling, and Spain retaliated with a coast guard patrol in American waters to ward off smugglers. British merchants complained of the rough treatment handed out by the Spanish guards, and in 1736 they exhibited to Parliament a Captain Robert Jenkins (fl. 1731–1738), who claimed that Spanish brutality had cost him an ear, which he duly produced, preserved in salt and cotton batting. Asked to state his reaction on losing the ear, he replied, "I commended my soul to God and my cause to my country." In October, to the joyful pealing of church bells, Britain began the War of Jenkins's Ear against Spain. The British fleet lost the opening campaign in the Caribbean, and France showed every sign of coming to Spain's assistance.

In 1740 a chain of events linked the colonial war to the great European conflict over the Austrian succession. On the death of Charles VI in 1740, the Habsburg dominions passed to his twenty-three-year-old daughter, Maria Theresa (r. 1740–1780). The German princes ignored the Pragmatic Sanction guaranteeing her succession and looked forward to partitioning the Habsburg inheritance. The elector of Bavaria, a cousin of the Habsburgs, also hoped to be elected Holy Roman emperor. The first of the German princes to strike, however, was Frederick the Great (r. 1740–1786), who had just inherited the Prussian throne. In December 1740 Frederick suddenly invaded the Habsburg province of Silesia.

In the ensuing War of the Austrian Succession, England and Austria were ranged against France, Spain, Prussia, and Bavaria. The Prussian army astounded Europe by its long night marches, sudden flank attacks, and other surprise tactics quite different from the usual deliberate warfare of sieges. Frederick, however, antagonized his allies by repeatedly deserting them to make secret peace arrangements with Austria. And he did little to support the imperial aspirations of the Bavarian elector, who enjoyed only a brief tenure as Emperor Charles VII.

The Anglo-Austrian alliance worked no better than the Franco-Prussian one. Many of the English felt that the Hanoverian George II was betraying their interests by entangling them in the Austrian succession and other German problems. Nevertheless, British preference for the Hanoverians over the Stuarts, Protestants over Catholics, was evident when Bonnie Prince Charles, grandson of the deposed James II, secured French backing and landed in Britain in 1745. He won significant recruits only among the Highlanders of Scotland, where he was defeated at Culloden in 1746.

In central Europe, the war was a decisive step in the rise of Prussia to the first rank of powers. The new province of Silesia brought not only a large increase in the Prussian population but also an important textile industry and large deposits of coal and iron. Maria Theresa got scant compensation for the loss of Silesia; although her husband, Francis, won recognition as Holy Roman emperor, she had to surrender Parma and some other territorial crumbs in northern Italy to Philip, the second son of Elizabeth Farnese.

The peace made in 1748 at Aix-la-Chapelle lasted only eight years. Then the Seven Years' War of 1756–1763 broke out, caused partly by old issues left unsettled at Aix-la-Chapelle and partly by new grievances arising from the War of the Austrian Succession. In southern India the English and French East India companies fought each other by taking sides in the rivalries of native princes. By 1751 the energetic French administrator Joseph Dupleix (1697–1763) had won the initial round in the battle for supremacy in the Indian subcontinent. Then the English, led by the equally energetic Robert Clive (1725–1774), seized the initiative. In 1754 Dupleix was called home by the directors of the French company, who were unwilling to commit costly resources to his aggressive policy.

In North America English colonists from the Atlantic seaboard had already staked out claims to the rich wilderness between the Appalachians and the Mississippi. But the French, equally intent on mastering the area, moved first and established a string of forts in western Pennsylvania from Presque Isle (later Erie) south to Fort Duquesne (later Pittsburgh). In 1754 a force of Virginians under a youthful George Washington (1732–1799) tried unsuccessfully to dislodge the French from Fort Duquesne, initiating a war that would end in a British victory.

The Diplomatic Revolution and the
Seven Years' War, 1756–1763

In Europe a dramatic shift of alliances called the Diplomatic Revolution immediately preceded the formal outbreak of the Seven Years' War, which had already begun in the colonies. Britain, which had joined Austria against Prussia in the 1740s, now paired off with Frederick the Great. And in the most dramatic move of the Diplomatic Revolution, France joined with its hereditary enemy, Habsburg Austria.

In 1755, the British touched off this Diplomatic Revolution. To enlist a second power in the task of defending Hanover, they concluded a treaty with Russia, which had taken a minor part in the War of the Austrian Succession as an ally of England. The Anglo-Russian treaty alarmed Frederick the Great. In January 1756 the Prussian king concluded an alliance with Britain that detached it from Russia. The alliance between England and Prussia isolated France and gave the Austrian chancellor the opportunity he had been waiting for. What Austria needed to avenge itself on Frederick and regain Silesia was an ally with a large army; this required an alliance with France, not Britain. The last act of the Diplomatic Revolution occurred when Russia joined the Franco-Austrian alliance.

The new war, like its predecessor, was really two separate wars—one Continental, the other naval and colonial. In the European campaigns of the Seven Years' War, Frederick the Great confronted the forces of Austria, France, and Russia, whose combined population was more than fifteen times larger than Prussia's. Frederick had almost no allies except Britain, which supplied financial subsidies but little actual military assistance. To fill up the depleted ranks of his army, he violated international law by impressing soldiers from Prussia's smaller neighbors, Mecklenburg and Saxony. Since British subsidies covered only a fraction of his war expenses, he seized Saxon, Polish, and Russian coins and melted them down for Prussian use.

A final factor in saving Prussia was the shakiness of the coalition arrayed against it. Russia's generals were unexpectedly timid, and those of France and Austria proved incompetent. Moreover, the French, the strongest of the allies, had to fight a two-front war, in Europe and overseas, without the financial resources to do both.

The grand alliance created by the Austrian chancellor, Prince von Kaunitz (1711–1794), suffered to an unusual extent from the frictions, mistrust, and cross-purposes typical of wartime coalitions. In fact, the coalition did not last out the war. When Elizabeth of Russia (r. 1741–1762) died in January 1762, she was succeeded by Czar Peter III, a passionate admirer of Frederick the Great, who at once placed Russia's forces at Frederick's disposal. Although he occupied the Russian throne only until July, Peter's reign marked a decisive turning in the Seven Years' War. In 1763 Prussia won its war.

Meanwhile, Frederick's British partner was losing abroad. During the first year and a half of the fighting the British suffered setbacks on almost every front. At sea they lost the important Mediterranean base of Minorca in the Balearic Islands. In North America the British lost time and again, but the

| *A Closer Look* |

FREDERICK THE GREAT'S INSTRUCTIONS FOR HIS GENERALS, 1753

Why was Frederick the Great's army so effective? In part because he inherited a well-trained army from his father, in part because he was analytical and able to judge a tactical problem accurately and quickly, and in part because he thought and wrote about the qualities of a good officer. For more on Frederick, see Chapter 3.

The strictest care and the most unremitting attention are required of commanding officers in the formation of my troops. The most exact discipline is ever to be maintained, and the greatest regard paid to their welfare; they ought also to be better fed than almost any troops in Europe.

Our regiments are composed of half our own people and half foreigners who enlist for money. The latter only wait for a favorable opportunity to quit a service to which they have no particular attachment. The prevention of desertion therefore becomes an object of importance.

Many of our generals regard one man as good in effect as another, and imagine that if the vacancy be filled up, this man has no influence on the whole; but one does not know how on this subject to make a proper application of other armies to our own.

If a deserter be replaced by a man as well trained and disciplined as himself, it is a matter of no consequence; but if a soldier who for two years has been accustomed to arms and military exercise should desert and be replaced by a bad subject or perhaps none at all, the consequence must prove eventually very material.

It has happened from the negligence of officers in this particular, that regiments have not only been lessened in number, but that they have also lost their reputation.

By accidents of this kind, the army becomes weakened at the very period when its completion is most essentially necessary, and unless the greatest attention be paid to this circumstance, you will lose the best of your forces, and never be able to recover yourself.

Though my country be well peopled, it is doubtful if many men are to be met with of the height of my soldiers: and supposing even that there was no want of them, could they be disciplined in an instant? It therefore becomes one of the most essential duties of generals who command armies or detachments, to prevent desertion. This is to be effected.

First, by not encamping too near a wood or forest, unless sufficient reason require it.

Secondly, by calling the roll frequently every day.

Thirdly, by often sending out patrols of hussars to scour the country round about the camp.

Fourthly, by placing chasseurs in the corn by night and doubling the cavalry posts at dusk to strengthen the chain.

Fifthly, by not allowing the soldiers to wander about and taking care that each troop be led regularly to water and to forage by an officer.

Sixthly, by punishing all marauding with severity, as it gives rise to every species of disorder and irregularity.

Seventhly, by not drawing in the guards, who are placed in the villages on marching days, until the troops are under arms.

Eighthly, by forbidding, under strictest injunctions, that any soldier on a march quit his rank or his division.

Ninthly, by avoiding night marches, unless obliged by necessity.

Tenthly, by pushing forward patrols of hussars to the right and left, while the infantry are passing through a wood.

Eleventhly, by placing officers at each end of a defile, to oblige the soldiers to fall into their proper places.

Twelfthly, by concealing from the soldier any retrograde movement which you may be obliged to make, or giving some specious, flattering pretext for so doing.

Thirteenthly, by paying great attention to the regular issue of necessary subsistence, and taking care that the troops be furnished with bread, meat, beer, brandy, etc.

Fourteenthly, by searching for the cause of the evil, when desertion shall have crept into a regiment or company, inquiring if the soldier has received his bounty and other customary indulgencies, and if there has been no misconduct on the part of the captain. No relaxation of discipline is however on any account to be permitted. It may be said that the colonel will take care of this business, but his efforts alone cannot be sufficient, for in an army, every individual part of it should aim at perfection, to make it appear to be the work of only one man.

An army is composed for the most part of idle and inactive men, and unless the general has a constant eye upon them and obliges them to do their duty, this artificial machine, which with greatest care cannot be made perfect, will very soon fall to pieces, and nothing but the bare idea of a disciplined army will remain.

Constant employment for the troops is therefore indispensably necessary. The experience of officers who adopt such a plan will convince them of its good effects, and they will also perceive that there are daily abuses to be corrected, which pass unobserved by those who are too indolent to endeavor to discover them. . . .

War may be carried on in three different kinds of country: either in our own territories, those belonging to neutral powers, or in the country of an enemy.

If glory were my only object, I would never make war but in mine own country, by reason of its manifold advantages, as every man there acts as a spy, nor can the enemy stir a foot without being betrayed. . . .

When war is carried on in a neutral country, the advantage seems to be equal, and the object of attention then is to rival the enemy in the confidence and friendship of the inhabitants. To attain this end, the most exact discipline must be observed, marauding and every kind of plunder strictly forbidden, and its commission punished with exemplary severity. It may not be amiss also to accuse the enemy of harboring some pernicious designs against the country.

If we are in a Protestant country, we wear the mark of protector of the Lutheran religion and endeavor to make fanatics of the lower order of people, whose simplicity is not proof against our artifice.

In a Catholic country, we preach up toleration and moderation, constantly abusing the priests as the cause of all the animosity that exists between the different sectaries, although, in spite of their disputes, they all agree upon material points of faith. . . .

In a country that is entirely hostile, as Bohemia and Moravia, you are to hazard nothing, and never send out parties, for the reasons already mentioned, as the people there are not to be trusted any farther than you can see them. The greater part of the light troops are to be employed in guarding the convoys, for you are never to expect to gain the affection of the inhabitants of this country. . . .

All that now remains for our management is fanaticism, to know how to inspire a nation with zeal for the liberty of religion and hint to them in a guarded manner how much they are oppressed by their great men and priests. This may be said, to be moving heaven and hell for one's interest. . . .

As quoted in Geoffrey Symcox, ed., War, Diplomacy, and Imperialism, 1618–1763 (New York: Harper & Row, 1973), pp. 190–192, 200–201.

most dramatic of Britain's misfortunes occurred in India. In June 1756, the nawab of Bengal, an ally of the French, crowded 146 British prisoners at Calcutta into a small room with only two windows. The resulting incident, as described by an officer of the English East India Company, came to be known as the Black Hole, an incident in which the British capitalized in shoring up public opinion:

It was the hottest season of the year, and the night uncommonly sultry. . . . The excessive pressure of their bodies against one another, and the intolerable heat which prevailed as soon as the door was shut, convinced the prisoners that it was impossible to live through the night in this horrible confinement; and violent attempts were immediately made to force the door, but without effect for it opened inward. At two o'clock not more than fifty remained alive. But even this number were too many to partake of the saving air, the contest for which and for life continued until the morn. . . .

An officer . . . came with an order to open the prison. The dead were so thronged, and the survivors had so little strength remaining, that they were employed near half an hour in removing the bodies which lay against the door before they could clear a passage to go out one at a time; when of one hundred and forty-six who went in no more than twenty-three came out alive.[*]

William Pitt (1708–1778) turned the tide in favor of Britain. He strengthened the Anglo-Prussian alliance by sending Frederick substantial subsidies and placing English forces in Hanover under an able Prussian commander.

---

[*]Robert Orme, A History of the Transactions of the British Nation in Indostan (London: J. Nourse, 1778), pp. 74, 76.

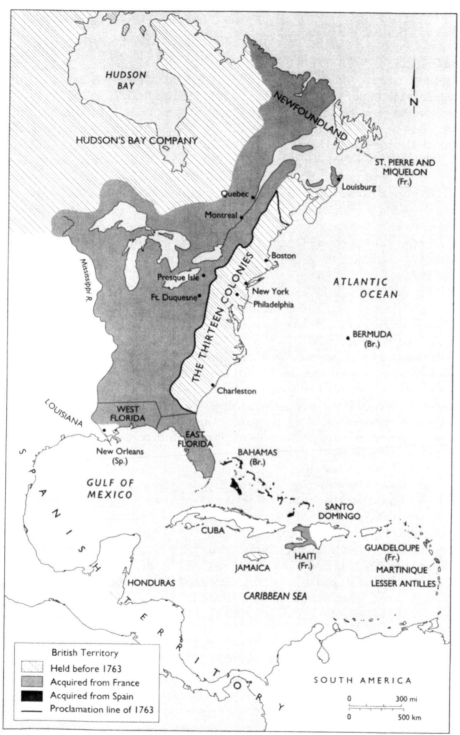

North America and the Caribbean, 1763

He replaced blundering generals and admirals and took energetic measures that transformed the naval and colonial campaigns.

After the Royal Navy at last defeated both the French Atlantic and Mediterranean squadrons (1759), Britain commanded the seas. Britain could thus continue trading abroad at a prosperous pace, while French overseas trade rapidly sank to one sixth of the prewar rate. Cut off from supplies and reinforcements from home and faced by generally superior British forces, the French colonies fell in quick succession. In Africa, Britain's capture of the chief French slaving stations ruined the slavers of Nantes; in India Clive and others avenged the Black Hole by punishing the nawab of Bengal and capturing the key French posts near Calcutta and Madras; in the West Indies the French lost all their sugar islands except for Santo Domingo. In North America the sixty-five thousand French, poorly supplied and poorly led, were helpless against the million British colonists, fully supported by their mother country. Fort Duquesne was taken and renamed after Pitt, and the British went on to other triumphs in the war that the English colonists called the French and Indian War because of the alliance between the French and Native American chiefs. In Canada the English general James Wolfe (1727–1759) took Louisburg (1758); in the next year he lost his life but won immortal fame in a great victory on the Plains of Abraham above Quebec. The remaining French stronghold, Montreal, fell in 1760.

Although Pitt had won the war, he did not make the peace; George III (r. 1760–1820) dismissed him in 1761. In the Peace of Paris (1763) the French recovered their islands in the West Indies, highly valued as a major source of sugar. While British planters in the Caribbean were much relieved, since their markets had been flooded by sugar from captured French islands during the war, it seemed to outraged patriots as though Britain had let a grand prize slip through its fingers.

France, however, lost all its possessions on the mainland of North America. Britain secured both Canada and the disputed territories between the Appalachians and the Mississippi. Moreover, Spain, which had joined France in 1762 when the war was already hopeless, ceded to Britain the peninsula called East Florida and the coast of the Gulf of Mexico as far as the Mississippi called West Florida. In compensation, France gave Spain the city of New Orleans and the vast Louisiana territories west of the Mississippi. In India, France recovered its possessions on condition that it would not fortify them. For Britain the Seven Years' War marked the beginning of virtually complete ascendancy in India; for France it marked the virtual end of its "old Empire."

The International Balance in Review

The peace settlements of Hubertusburg and Paris ended the greatest international crisis that was to occur between the death of Louis XIV and the outbreak of the French Revolution. New crises were to arise, but they did not fundamentally alter the international balance; they accentuated the shifts that had long been underway. And although American independence cost Britain thirteen of its colonies, the maritime and imperial supremacy it had gained in 1763 was not otherwise seriously affected.

Thus the international balance established in 1763 remained largely unchanged until 1789. In the incessant struggle for power during the eighteenth century, the victorious states were Britain, Prussia, and Russia. France, Spain, Austria, Sweden, and Turkey survived, although they suffered loss. As a Spanish diplomat observed early in the century, the weakest units, Poland and Italy, were being "pared and sliced up like so many Dutch cheeses."

The world struggle between Britain and the Bourbon empire did much to justify the mercantilist view that conceived of international relations in terms of incessant competition and strife. According to the mercantilist doctrine of the fixed amount of trade, a state could enlarge its share of the existing supply only if it reduced the shares held by rival states, either through war or through smuggling and retaliatory legislation. All this was borne out by British success (and French failure) in maintaining overseas trade during the Seven Years' War.

Economics did not wholly explain the changes in the international balance during the century. For example, increasingly efficient utilization of Prussian resources played its part in the victories of Frederick the Great. But his success depended still more on his own leadership and the discipline of the army and the society that he headed. Britain seemingly offers evidence for the supreme power of commerce, as Pitt turned the country's formidable financial and commercial assets to practical advantage. Yet Pitt himself cannot be explained solely in economic terms, for his accession as prime minister was made possible by a political system, social concepts, and a pragmatic approach to leadership that enabled the right man to come forward at the right time.

The eighteenth century, despite its wars, was an interlude of comparative social calm between the period of religious strife that had preceded it and the storms of liberalism and nationalism that would be loosed by the French Revolution. The Seven Years' War, for example, did not begin to equal in destructive force the Thirty Years' War, in more ways than just the relative shortness of the war: Few of the combatants had the feeling of fighting for a great cause, like Catholicism or Protestantism or national independence; the fighting itself was conducted in a more orderly fashion than it had been a hundred years before; soldiers were better disciplined and armies were better supplied; troops lived off the land less often and no longer constituted such a menace to the lives and property of civilians. Even warfare tended to reflect the order and reason characteristic of the Age of Enlightenment.

And yet below the reality of this relative sense of order—of reason and compromise, of enlightened despots and rational, even cynical, diplomacy—the great mass of the population continued to live with debt, disease, deprivation, and destitution. The competitive state system, increasingly efficient at the top, seemed increasingly makeshift at the bottom.

Summary

The Old Regime, the institutions that existed in France and Europe before 1789, exhibited features of both the medieval and early modern worlds. The economy was largely agrarian, but in western Europe serfdom had disappeared. The social foundations of the Old Regime were based on three estates. Increasingly, the economic, social, and political order of the Old Regime came under attack in the eighteenth century.

The economic foundations of the Old Regime were challenged in part by the quickening pace of commerce. European states were hard pressed to service debts accumulated in the wars of the seventeenth century. In France, John Law attempted to restore monetary stability by issuing paper money backed by the nation's wealth. Both in France and England, attempts to manage the national debt caused chaos when these experiments resulted in huge speculative bubbles that burst. The failure of the South Sea Company rocked England, but forced the government to establish a more secure banking system.

Another economic revolution occurred in agriculture. Improvements in farming techniques and the use of new crops such as turnips enabled farmers to produce more food. Increased production ended widespread famines in Europe. In England, enclosures caused widespread social dislocations but created a new labor pool.

A third economic revolution was the beginning of the Industrial Revolution, notably in the textile industry. New machines enabled rapid production and led to the organization of simple factories. New techniques in metallurgy helped make coal mining into a big business.

Britain took the lead in these economic revolutions, becoming the wealthiest nation in the world. Under the first two Hanoverian kings, Parliament was supreme, and the cabinet system took shape under Walpole. Yet Britain was not democratic because only "gentlemen" had the right to vote. For the masses, especially in the growing urban slums of London, life was extremely harsh, but the ruling class was responsive to the need for change.

In the eighteenth century France suffered from mediocre leadership. Cardinal Fleury was the exception. He pursued economic policies designed to stabilize coinage and encourage industry. Despite the failure of Louis XV to institute needed reform, France remained a great power, and French culture dominated Europe.

By the eighteenth century Spain was no longer dominant in the European balance of power. Spanish rulers were preoccupied with Italy, where their claims clashed with those of the Austrian Habsburgs.

Since the mid-seventeenth century, the Hohenzollern rulers of Prussia had worked hard to increase their territories and gain international recognition. Their efforts centered on the economy, absolutism, and the army. The miserly Frederick William I built the Prussian army into the finest force in Europe.

Under Peter the Great, Russia emerged as a great power. Fascinated by Western technology, Peter brought foreign experts to teach Russians modern skills. In foreign policy, Peter expanded Russia by engaging in constant warfare. As a result of the Great Northern War against Sweden (1700–1721), Peter gained his "window on the West." His economic and social policies fortified the autocracy.

The expansion of Russia and Prussia, rivalry between Britain and France, and competition between Austria and France frequently threatened the balance of power in the eighteenth century. In the early 1700s Britain and France cooperated diplomatically to maintain the balance. By 1740, however, colonial and commercial rivalry set the two powers at odds. Thus, in the War of the Austrian Succession (1739–1748), Britain and Austria were allied against France, Prussia, Spain, and Bavaria.

A diplomatic revolution occurred on the eve of the Seven Years' War (1756–1763), when Britain and Prussia paired off against France and Austria, traditional enemies. In the power struggles of the eighteenth century, Britain, Prussia, and Russia were the winners. France, Spain, Austria, and Turkey suffered losses.

THREE

The Enlightenment

❦

The Enlightenment was the most influential and distinctive cultural movement of the eighteenth century. Its main goals were to free humankind from error and "superstition" through a critical review of all human knowledge and to free people from unnecessary restraints on their freedom through social and political reform. These two goals were linked in the mind of Enlightenment reformers; to be truly free, people had to have "reason" and sound knowledge of the world. Thus, in issuing the challenge "Dare to know!" the German philosopher Immanuel Kant (1724–1804) also challenged his contemporaries to liberate themselves from the traditional forms of political and social servitude they had imposed on themselves. If the present time was not yet an enlightened age, he observed, at least it was an age of Enlightenment—a time to experiment with new possibilities.

The Enlightenment arose from a combination of factors. One was the growing awareness that changing conditions required new solutions to the problems of European society. The Old Regime had reduced disorder by expanding royal armies and bureaucracies, stiffening social hierarchies, and reinforcing religious orthodoxies. But with order largely restored, it became evident, especially after 1750, that government machinery and social policies required another look, for in many ways the costs of these policies appeared to be outweighing their benefits. So strong did the case for reform appear that by mid-century "progress"—not to be confused with revolution—became a goal almost unto itself. The most prominent French Enlightenment figure, Voltaire (1694–1778), quipped of his associate, Turgot (1727–1781), that he did not know exactly what Turgot wanted, but it was sure to be something new and different.

A second factor was the growing belief among elites that the Scientific Revolution and the new sensationalist epistemology, developed most notably by John Locke in his *Essay Concerning Human Understanding* (1690), had placed many of Europe's traditional notions of the universe and humankind in doubt. The new science had challenged and discarded many traditional concepts of nature, while in his work Locke had broadened the effort "to remove some of the rubbish that lies in the way of knowledge." Taking its cue from

Newton and Locke, the Enlightenment now sought to extend the critical reexamination of received ideas to the most sensitive notions of the state, society, and religion. Because of their wide-ranging intellectual hunt, Enlightenment leaders took the name *philosophes*, the French word for "philosophers."

A third factor was the changing setting of and audience for high culture. Since the Middle Ages, most great works of European philosophy, theology, history, science, and the arts had been produced by intellectuals supported materially and politically by the church, the state, or wealthy aristocrats. In the seventeenth century, the courts of great princes and kings had attracted the efforts of the best and the brightest, with the result that intellectuals had usually shaped their work to please their royal patrons and the courtiers. By the eighteenth century, this situation had changed. To be sure, the state, royal court, and royal academies continued to be important sources of patronage for the philosophes and other intellectuals and artists, and aristocrats remained important consumers of work they produced. Yet the growth and increasing wealth of the middle class in western Europe significantly expanded the paying audience for art, music, literature, history, science, and philosophy. In response, the book trade flourished, while public theaters, public concerts, and public art exhibitions multiplied throughout the eighteenth century. The expansion of the "public" encouraged producers of high culture to criticize established authority more freely, even if state patronage and censorship continued to limit this freedom in practice. Matters of public concern were increasingly discussed and debated not only in the press, but also in the coffeehouses, printing shops, and *salons*, all of which mushroomed across western and central Europe. (*Salons* were periodic informal gatherings of intellectuals and socially prominent people usually held in the homes of hostesses, who regulated and moderated the flow of witty conversation and the sometimes vigorous exchanges of opinions.)

With the growth of the cultural "public" came a greater concern and respect for its judgment. Hardly a new term, "public opinion" acquired greater authority during the eighteenth century both in cultural and political matters. The philosophes certainly sought to advise and influence established authorities, including kings, and they sometimes flattered rulers in craven ways to remain in favor. But they also composed their work to shape the discussion of the new broader, educated "public." "Opinion governs mankind, and the philosophes will little by little change the opinion of all," wrote Voltaire. Given the many opinions they wanted to change, the philosophes were in for a long battle.

The Settings

The philosophes have been portrayed by some historians as impractical dreamers who had little contact with the realities of politics. But, in fact, Enlightenment writers knew a great deal about the political and social institutions they both worked for and criticized. This helps to explain why rulers—even hard-headed, authoritarian ones like Catherine the Great of

Russia and Frederick the Great of Prussia—were willing to sponsor the philosophes and occasionally follow their advice. The philosophes wrote on a broad range of issues: education, health, economics, finance (especially taxation), justice, religion, and science. In a few instances, the philosophes were employed directly by the state to run its operations. Thus, Voltaire was employed as a historian, propagandist, and diplomat by the French government. The economist Turgot spent more than two decades laboring in the French state administration, including two years as the monarchy's chief financial minister.

The writings of the philosophes reflected this practical side. Although they did publish some systematic treatises of philosophy, most of their work took the form of essays, satires, critiques, dialogues, public letters, and novelettes, which were intended less as intellectual monuments to last the ages than as polemical pieces written for specific occasions. The philosophes frequently used sarcasm and ironic humor to make their readers see the absurdity and uselessness of many contemporary practices and institutions, and Voltaire's sneer became a feared force in some circles. Needless to say, their ideas and their methods were not appreciated by those people and institutions they ridiculed. Before the end of the eighteenth century, anti-Enlightenment works flooded the market, especially in southern and eastern Europe, where older ideas had more support.

If the philosophes recognized their obligations to serve their own country, they also felt a responsibility to Western civilization as a whole. Thus, they cultivated friendships and maintained correspondence with like-minded colleagues abroad, whom they frequently visited in person. Some gained the patronage of foreign princes. Voltaire enjoyed the support of both Frederick II of Prussia and Catherine of Russia and became a member of many foreign academies. The French encyclopedist and author Denis Diderot (1713–1784) was also patronized by Catherine, who bought his library and had it transported to Russia when he died. Such webs of associations allowed the philosophes to think of themselves as citizens of an international "republic of letters"—an imagined community of scholars of many nationalities and faiths, in which each member enjoyed the freedom to critique the work of others as well as Western social institutions.

The philosophes' internationalist perspective found its way into their writings. In one of the first and most celebrated Enlightenment works of fiction, *The Persian Letters* (1721), the baron de Montesquieu (1689–1755) held up a critical mirror to French society by imagining how two Persian visitors might perceive the social customs, religious practices, and politics they encountered in Paris. At about the same time, the abbé de Saint-Pierre (1658–1743)—an early philosophe brimming with original ideas for improving society—proposed a league for maintaining international peace. Although this proposal was much ridiculed as a utopian impossibility, many of the philosophes joined Saint-Pierre in spirit by praising princes for improving the lives of their subjects rather than for their bloody conquests. A number of the philosophes including Montesquieu and Voltaire, visited England and celebrated its virtues as a free society that had produced Francis Bacon, John Locke, and Isaac Newton—all major Enlightenment heroes. The Swiss-born Jean-Jacques Rousseau (1712–1778) contributed to the debate on the future of Poland, for which he proposed a constitution.

With branches in many countries, the Enlightenment had its headquarters in France. In part this was a result of the cultural resonance French civilization had enjoyed in the rest of Europe since the age of Louis XIV. What mattered in Paris mattered elsewhere. Works written by the Parisian-based philosophes were read in many foreign lands, sometimes in translation but often in French, which had become familiar to many educated people all over Europe. A good example was the *Encyclopédie*, a multivolume, multiauthor survey and critique of human knowledge that was published in France beginning in the 1750s, sold widely throughout Europe, and became the single most important engine of Enlightenment ideas. There were other reasons why the Enlightenment flowered most prominently in France. Like other European states, its government had produced a costly state administration, which intruded considerably on the lives of the people. But more than most other nations, it also developed a large reading public, who appreciated and could afford to buy works that in the name of freedom and public utility ridiculed the conspicuously inept government. As the government lurched from failure to failure, it made itself ever more vulnerable to the critiques of an increasingly energized public opinion. That opinion found some of its voice in the work of the philosophes, who claimed to speak in its name. An apparently immovable object—the Old Regime—was under attack from a seemingly irresistible force—public opinion—and the friction between them generated both heat and enlightenment.

Like other writers, the philosophes had to deal with state and church controls on their work that varied from country to country. In England, for example, the press was much freer than it was in France, where all publications had to be approved by government censors before they could be legally published. Authors and publishers who printed and circulated nonapproved work could be jailed and their presses and book inventories seized and destroyed. A number of philosophes spent time in prison, including Voltaire and Diderot, for publishing works considered immoral, insulting to the king, or contrary to church doctrine. The threat of imprisonment certainly made authors and publishers more cautious about publishing works illegally. But there was another strong reason to submit work for government approval: only a permission to publish provided legal protection from others republishing their work and reaping the profits—in other words, state approval was a primitive form of copyright. Even so, many Enlightenment works had no chance of official approval; and thus because of his controversial opinions, not a single major prose work by Voltaire was published legally in France during his lifetime. To evade government censorship, the philosophes often published anonymously or under false names. They sent their more controversial manuscripts to publishers abroad—mostly to Switzerland and the Netherlands, which enjoyed considerable press freedom. Some Dutch and

Swiss publishers specialized in prohibited books written by the philosophes and other authors, and, despite government efforts to prevent it, they conducted successful book-smuggling operations in France. A fair percentage of the prohibited books were gossipy scandal sheets, and some of the greatest bestsellers, including some works by the philosophes, were little more than pornography. But there were also major works by major authors, and even some of the pornographic books carried serious political and philosophical messages. Overall, contraband works constituted a large portion of the books and journals bought and read during the eighteenth century, and because of their generally critical slant they furthered the Enlightenment cause.

The Core Ideas

The Enlightenment never produced a coherent philosophy that all its members accepted, and the philosophes, who have been justly compared to a frequently feuding family, argued strenuously over many issues among themselves. But there were several common themes that recurred throughout their work.

One was "reason." Having rejected many commonly held opinions about God, nature, and society, the philosophes sought not to build highly abstract philosophical systems but to use "reason" to show how many of these opinions and systems rested on false foundations. Their notions about how "reason" worked came mostly from Locke. As the process was described by one of the most influential philosophes, the abbé de Condillac (1715–1780), the mind was a blank slate to begin with and received all its ideas from individual external sensations, which the mind combined to form mental pictures of the world. In applying "reason," the mind traced all ideas back to the sensations that gave rise to them. Ideas that could not be reduced to combinations of clear and distinct sensations were judged at best confused and at worst altogether false. To the philosophes, the more an idea was abstracted from sensation, the less likely it was true. For this reason, the philosophes distrusted large philosophical systems, which tried to explain the universe with a small number of grand principles. All truths might be reducible to a single equation in the mind of God, since God could perceive everything at once. But humans had only a restricted view of the world, and this meant that the sum of human knowledge could not have the same mathematical simplicity and elegance.

Despite their celebrated love of "reason," the philosophes were not unemotional rationalists, as they are often portrayed. Many of them, like many of their contemporaries, saw a key role for sentiment and even passion, which were necessary to energize the body and the mind. Without such emotions, they knew, life would be unbearable, if not impossible. Some of the philosophes were capable of weeping over and even writing maudlin, melodramatic novels that most people today would laugh at for their sentimentality. In general, the view of the philosophes was that reason ought to keep the passions under good control, but this did not mean repressing them altogether.

A second major theme was "progress." At the beginning of the eighteenth century a major intellectual controversy—sometimes called the "Battle of the Books," sometimes the "Quarrel of the Ancients and Moderns"—erupted over the question of whether contemporary culture was superior or inferior to that of classical antiquity. If the "ancients" successfully argued that antiquity had been superior in the fine arts, the "moderns" made the better case for the superiority of modern science. Inspired by the partial victory of the "moderns," many philosophes began to conceptualize human history in terms of the fitful march forward of "civilization," a term that was coined in the eighteenth century. Despite many setbacks, they argued, cultural—especially scientific and commercial—advances were gradually improving the human condition, making life more peaceful, humane, and comfortable. Such ideas were not nearly as naively presented as they have been later described. The philosophes were hardly unaware of the world's pain and suffering and of the ever-present possibility of temporary cultural reverses. In *Candide*—his most celebrated work—Voltaire took deadly aim at the optimistic doctrine that we live in the best of all possible worlds, and he once described history as the story of crime and error. But just as most of their contemporaries saw some providential pattern and direction in the flow of events, so, too, did most of the philosophes, who took the not entirely perverse view that life had been and could be improved through the cultivation of the human spirit.

A third outstanding theme was "nature." "Nature" had been an important focus of Western thought since the High Middle Ages, but it had a special meaning to the philosophes. To them, nature was not wild and tempestuous, but a rational, orderly, and elegant arrangement exemplified by the Newtonian model of the solar system and its predictable planetary orbits. The philosophes used this concept of a rational "nature" as a measure of the successes and failures of civilization. To illuminate the abuses of civilization, such as slavery, they contrasted the social conditions in their own age with those that had supposedly prevailed in a free and virtuous "state of nature," that is, in a period before the invention of government and social institutions. Some writers, most notably Jean-Jacques Rousseau, pushed this perspective so far that they denied that civilization had been a boon to humankind. A critic as much as he was a member of the Enlightenment, Rousseau portrayed the history of civilization as the story not of human progress, but of moral regress from a state of natural innocence, leading to increasing alienation and inequality.

The critique of civilization had a great impact on eighteenth-century thought, but it is important to note that most philosophes did not perceive "nature" and "civilization" as polar opposites. Much has been made of the eighteenth-century ideal of the "noble savage"—the individual uncorrupted by society—but in most Enlightenment scenarios this "savage" had many trappings of civilization, including language, arts, and a primitive form of government. Even Rousseau, who is most closely associated with the virtuous "noble savage" for his admiration of life in the state of nature, recognized that it was far too late to return to the forests. He never advocated such a return, nor did he think it was desirable. For even if Rousseau rejected the common view that people were naturally sociable, he agreed with the philosophes that humans were most completely fulfilled in a social state, and he shared their goal of reforming society, not destroying it.

A fourth major theme was "liberty." "Man is born free, but everywhere he is in chains," declared Jean-Jacques Rousseau. "No man has received from nature the right to command others," wrote Diderot. "Liberty is a gift of the heavens, and every individual of the species has the right to enjoy it as soon as he has reason." These influential statements have several profound implications. One is that liberty was not a right given to some privileged people by a sovereign ruler in some nations; it was a natural condition of all mature humans, irrespective of their nationality or social status. By the middle of the eighteenth century, liberty became routinely associated with the notion of "natural rights," as it had already been in the work of John Locke. In the view of most philosophes, the rights to life, liberty, and property were not alienable; that is, they could never be lost or even given away, and the role of government was to protect and preserve these rights. What remained unclear was to what extent these rights could be and had to be limited for purposes of good government.

Another implication is that no one has an inborn right to rule others. Although it is not specifically indicated, these statements clearly imply that political authority derives ultimately from the consent of the governed. Finally, these statements assert that the fundamental requirement of the right to exercise liberty is "reason." When guided by "reason," individuals will tend to act in a socially responsible way, argued the philosophes, since they will perceive their own self-interest in the good of society as a whole. Without "reason," the individual will not be able to make responsible choices and must be supervised by others. Thus children cannot be allowed to make their own decisions until they arrive at the "age of reason." Whether women have the same ability to reason as men and should enjoy equal political rights remained a debated question in the eighteenth century. Although some philosophes recognized an equality of capabilities, most assumed that women could never play as important a political role as men, since domestic responsibilities required them to devote their energies more to the private than to the public sphere.

The Program

Government

The philosophes' commitment to liberty did not entail a commitment to equality or democracy. Although the philosophes believed that all people should enjoy the basic civil rights to life, liberty, and property, they did not argue for an end to the nobility or for the equalization of all ranks and wealth in society. The philosophes assumed along with most members of the elite that the masses of the people were forever destined for agricultural labor and that they were too unreliable and uninformed to be entrusted with the vote. Until the French Revolution, they assumed that monarchy was here to stay. The real goal of enlightenment was to make monarchies work more efficiently for the general good.

One of the greatest concerns of the philosophes was the tendency of monarchies to degenerate into "despotisms," that is, states in which rulers acted on personal whim, not according to law and the interests of the people. The Ottoman Empire was frequently held up as an example of "despotism," and as governments grew in the eighteenth century, fears arose that "oriental despotism" on the Ottoman model would also take root in the West. To prevent "despotism" and to preserve liberty, the philosophes offered different prescriptions.

One of the more conservative programs to thwart the onset of "despotism" was put forward by the baron de Montesquieu in his celebrated *Spirit of the Laws* (1748). Montesquieu's solution was to reinforce the traditional social privileges that were enjoyed to a greater or lesser extent by all ranks of society. Although most governments in the world were "despotisms," Montesquieu argued, western Europe was blessed with law codes dating back to the Middle Ages that guaranteed privileges and thereby moderated the action of sovereign rulers. Moreover, in certain European nations—and here Montesquieu was thinking primarily of England—power was shared by kings and legislatures, and this separation of powers, too, protected against "despotisms." Needless to say, Montesquieu's solution appealed greatly to the nobility, who enjoyed the greatest privileges and the greatest influence within the representative assemblies of almost all European nations. At the same time, as a philosophe Montesquieu was no blind defender of tradition. In fact, he was highly critical of many contemporary practices, including the slave trade and the persecution of religious minorities.

Another program was put forward by philosophes like Saint-Pierre, Voltaire, and Turgot, who believed that the best way to tame monarchies was not to divide power or protect traditional privileges but to streamline governments so they operated more rationally and efficiently. Thus, the abbé de Saint-Pierre proposed to eliminate venality of office and replace it with a system of in-house elections, which was intended to improve the quality of state administrators. These "enlightened absolutists" argued that "public opinion" could enlighten a king upon the best way to serve his subjects. Turgot proposed that the monarchy create assemblies of local citizens who could advise the king on such matters as taxation and road building, without exercising direct power of their own. The chief question hanging over such solutions was whether by streamlining its operations the government would in fact become more "despotic," which is what the critics of enlightened absolutism frequently charged.

A much smaller group of radical philosophes, including Jean-Jacques Rousseau, argued that democracy was the only adequate defense of liberty. Rousseau believed not only that sovereignty derived from the people, or what he called the "general will," but also that in a properly constituted state, all male citizens would be convened to vote upon new laws. He even rejected the idea of democratic representation, that is, the election of representatives to vote for laws in an assembly, on the argument that representatives would follow their own, not their constituents', will and thereby become corrupted. As Rousseau recognized in *The Social Contract* (1762), direct democracy was impractical in a large nation like France, with its 25 million people and constant need for new legislation. In this, Rousseau followed the ideas of most philosophes, who thought that democracy was suited only for small, poor nations, not those with large populations and expanding economies. Even so, by reintroducing the concept of democracy into public debate, Rousseau and others like him widened Europe's political imagination, and over the next century, democracy in its representative form became common in western and central Europe through revolutions that even Rousseau did not foresee.

The list of specific political reforms advocated by the philosophes is nearly endless. Among the most notable were proposals to reform judicial procedure, modify tax policies, and develop a system of education. Cesare Beccaria (1738–1794), an Italian, wrote an influential critique of judicial torture, a common procedure during the Old Regime that he argued was not only inhumane but also ineffective for extracting reliable information. Impressed by Beccaria's work, Voltaire led a public campaign against the use of torture in France. Others argued for the introduction of a jury system, and there were many Enlightenment proposals for modernizing entire law codes, some of which influenced Catherine the Great. Tax systems came in for a great deal of philosophe criticism, on the grounds of both unfairness and inefficiency. The Physiocrats (discussed later in this chapter) contended that cumbersome contemporary tax systems were not only costly to run but also discouraged production, and they proposed that nearly all taxes be shelved in favor of a single tax that would fall exclusively on landholders, irrespective of social rank or geographical location. In Prussia and Austria, reformers were notably successful in establishing the rudiments of the first government-sponsored school system, hoping to teach subjects self-discipline in place of traditional laws and punishments.

Religion

The philosophes are perhaps best known as enemies of religion, especially Christianity. This characterization is inaccurate on several counts. First, while a very few philosophes were atheists, many of them were conventionally religious, particularly in central and eastern Europe. Voltaire, the most famous scoffer at traditional religion, was a strong believer in God and bitterly attacked the few atheists he knew. Second, most philosophes saw a definite social role for religion. One study of Enlightenment proposals for popular education shows that almost all these proposals recommended the teaching of religion as a means for maintaining morals and order among the people. Third, some of the philosophes derived their ideas from religious sources.

Thus, for example, Pietism, a German Protestant movement that emphasized inner spirituality, was critical in the development of Kant's moral theory, while Jansenism, a dissident movement within the Catholic Church, helped to inspire the philosophes' opposition to "despotism" in France.

It is true that the philosophes were critical of many traditional religious doctrines and practices, just as they were of other traditions. For them, religion was above all useful to inspire morality, and they believed that at the core of all the world's great religions lay the same basic moral code embodied in the Golden Rule. The rest of religion—its doctrines and rituals—was little more than the external packaging that should entice people to practice this moral code. Although the philosophes certainly did not escape all traditional prejudices—Voltaire, for example, made some horrendous statements against the Jews and the Jewish religion—in general, they counseled toleration of virtually all religions on the grounds that the different packaging of the central moral code was not a matter of public concern. What value did religion have, argued Montesquieu, if it was accepted only because of coercion? A multiplicity of religions, Voltaire argued, was desirable because each one checked the others from becoming too oppressive.

For the philosophes the main problem with religion was that over the course of history the real common purpose of religion—to teach basic morality—had been forgotten, as one sect or another had tried to impose one set of rituals and doctrines and suppress the others by force. Millions had died as a result of needless wars over these relatively unimportant aspects of religion, and thus the critique of traditional religious rituals and doctrines was necessary to refocus attention on religion's moral core. Of course, to traditional believers who saw their precious rituals and doctrines ridiculed by the philosophes, this critique was an outrage and an attack on some of their most cherished traditions. Indeed, it was seen as an attack on all religion.

The philosophes varied in their own religious beliefs, but many promoted a religious philosophy called "Deism." Deism was the belief that God created the world, set it in motion according to the rational natural laws he had prescribed, and then allowed the world to operate on its own. Clearly, this view represented an effort to reconcile traditional views of God with the new science. While it satisfied many philosophes, it hardly satisfied more traditional believers. First, it denied a continuing role for God in the affairs of this world, ruling out divine miracles, that is, violations of natural laws. The Scottish philosopher David Hume was widely acclaimed by the philosophes for his blistering attack on the belief in miracles reported in the Bible. He concluded that there were no valid rational reasons for believing in such miracles and that anyone who did so was at best a "dangerous friend" of Christianity. In his view, religion could only be accepted on faith. Second, Deism made prayer pointless and provided little consolation for the downtrodden—God was not going to help them by intervening in the natural order once he had created it. Third, Deism was emotionally sterile; it made religion more a rational philosophy than a practice capable of moving people at their inner core. Finally, Deism stripped Christianity of its notions of Heaven and Hell, which, according to the Enlightenment's critics, were necessary to make people act morally.

"The Sciences of Man"

As scientists and reformers, the philosophes were interested in the development of the social sciences (then called "the sciences of man") as a means for improving society. Montesquieu's *Spirit of the Laws* was one of the most influential books written for this purpose. A sprawling book in the area of what today would be called political sociology, it categorized societies according to various schemes, the most important being a breakdown into monarchies, republics, and despotisms. Montesquieu showed that these regimes differed not only in their forms of government, but also in their economies, social structures, educational systems, and motivating principles. Monarchies, he argued, operated on honor; republics on virtue; and despotisms on fear.

Fascinated by the possibility of improving the human condition through the application of science and technology, the philosophes were especially interested in economics and finance. Their general recommendation was to liberalize the economy, that is, to reduce government controls on wages, prices, and production and allow buyers and sellers to determine all three. This approach to economic problems was called *laissez faire*, meaning "let it operate on its own." In France, the most prominent school of laissez-faire economists were the Physiocrats ("physiocracy" meant "rule by nature") led by François de Quesnay (1694–1774). Believing that agriculture was the only source of wealth, the Physiocrats argued for the unobstructed circulation of grain within the nation as a means for increasing total output. By allowing prices to move higher, they contended, production would be stimulated, and as a result of greater production, grain prices would eventually move downward and supplies become more even.

Many similar ideas were advanced by the Scottish thinker Adam Smith (1723–1790), whose work *The Wealth of Nations*, published in 1776, was the single most influential book of economic theory of the eighteenth century. (In fact, the work dealt with much else besides economics.) Smith did not accept the Physiocratic notion that agriculture was the sole creator of wealth; instead, he put much more emphasis on the creative powers of labor. But Smith did endorse the notion that governments should let the market determine which goods were produced and at what price. He argued that in a free market an "invisible hand" encouraged individuals to be economically productive by rewarding with profit those who correctly judged the desires of buyers and produced goods at the most competitive prices. Smith attacked the policies of "mercantilism," which called upon the government to interfere in the decisions of the marketplace, since he believed the market was a much better judge of consumers' desires and a more efficient stimulus of production. In the nineteenth and twentieth centuries, the wealthy used Smith's ideas to argue against any expansion of government services. In fact, Smith

Voltaire was among the intellectual giants of the age. His contemplative, bemused skepticism is captured here in a remarkable statue by Jean Antoine Houdon (1741–1828). Houdon traveled widely, and in 1785 he went to America to create one of the most famous busts of George Washington. (Giraudon/Art Resource, NY)

was not an unbending apologist for laissez faire or for the wealthy. He bitterly attacked producers for constantly demanding special monopolies and other favors from governments, and he was not optimistic that these producers would ever allow the creation of a truly free market. Moreover, Smith recognized that the government in civilized countries had many social obligations that the market could not meet, among them, the duty to provide affordable education.

Enlightened Absolutism

Enlightened absolutism, or as it is sometimes called, "enlightened despotism," was a program adopted by some absolute rulers to apply the principles

The Written Record

ADAM SMITH'S *THE WEALTH OF NATIONS*, 1776

Smith advocated market-driven commerce, industry, and agriculture based on his
understanding of human nature, in which ambition was, on balance and for most
people, supreme. If unhindered, the general populace would contribute to the
common good, although this was not its chief goal. The division of labor was central to this rational process.

To take an example . . . from a very trifling manufacture, but one in which the
division of labor has been very often taken notice of, the trade of the pinmaker;
a workman not educated to this business (which the division of labor has rendered a distinct trade), nor acquainted with the use of the machinery employed
in it (to the invention of which the same division of labor has probably given
occasion), could scarce, perhaps, with his utmost industry, make one pin in a
day, and certainly could not make twenty. But in the way in which this business
is now carried on, not only the whole work is a peculiar trade, but it is divided
into a number of branches, of which the greater part are likewise peculiar
trades. One man draws out the wire, another straights it, a third cuts it, a fourth
points it, a fifth grinds it at the top for receiving the head; to make the head
requires two or three distinct operations; to put it on is a peculiar business, to
whiten the pins is another; it is even a trade by itself to put them into the paper;
and the important business of making a pin is, in this manner, divided into
about eighteen distinct operations, which in some manufactories are all performed by distinct hands, though in others the same man will sometimes perform two or three of them. I have seen a small manufactory of this kind where
ten men only were employed, and where some of them consequently performed two or three distinct operations. But though they were very poor, and
therefore but indifferently accommodated with the necessary machinery, they
could when they exerted themselves make among them about twelve pounds
of pins in a day. There are in a pound upwards of four thousand pins of a mid-
dling size. Those ten persons, therefore, could make among them upwards of
forty-eight thousand pins in a day. Each person, therefore, making a tenth part
of forty-eight thousand pins, might be considered as making four thousand
eight hundred pins in a day. But if they had all wrought separately and inde-
pendently, and without any of them having been educated to this peculiar business, they certainly could not each of them have made twenty, perhaps not one
in a day. . . .
   It is the maxim of every prudent master of a family, never to attempt to make
at home what it will cost him more to make than to buy. The taylor does not
attempt to make his own shoes, but buys them of the shoemaker. The shoemaker
does not attempt to make his own clothes, but employs a taylor. . . . What is
prudence in the conduct of every private family, can scarce by folly in that of a
great kingdom. If a foreign country can supply us with a commodity cheaper
than we ourselves can make it, better buy it of them with some part of the produce of our industry.

This division of labor, from which so many advantages are derived, is not originally the effect of any human wisdom, which foresees and intends that general opulence to which it gives occasion. It is the necessary, though very slow and gradual, consequence of a certain propensity in human nature which has in view no such extensive utility; the propensity to truck, barter, and exchange one thing for another.

Whether this propensity be one of those original principles in human nature, of which no further account can be given; or whether, as seems more probable, it be the necessary consequence of the faculties of reason and speech, it belongs not to our present subject to enquire. It is common to all men, and to be found in no other race of animals, which seem to know neither this nor any other species of contracts. Two grey-hounds, in running down the same hare, have sometimes the appearance of acting in some sort of concert. Each turns her towards his companion, or endeavors to intercept her when his companion turns her towards himself. This, however, is not the effect of any contract, but of the accidental concurrence of their passions in the same object at that particular time. Nobody ever saw a dog make a fair and deliberate exchange of one bone for another with another dog. Nobody ever saw one animal by its gestures and natural cries signify to another, this is mine, that yours; I am willing to give this for that. When an animal wants to obtain something either of a man or of another animal, it has no other means of persuasion but to gain the favor of those whose service it requires. A puppy fawns upon its dam, and a spaniel endeavors by a thousand attractions to engage the attention of its master who is at dinner, when it wants to be fed by him. Man sometimes uses the same arts with his brethren, and when he has no other means of engaging them to act according to his inclinations, endeavors by every servile and fawning attention to obtain their good will. He has not time, however, to do this upon every occasion. In civilized society he stands at all times in need of the co-operation and assistance of great multitudes, while his whole life is scarce sufficient to gain the friendship of a few persons. In almost every other race of animals each individual, when it is grown up to maturity, is entirely independent, and in its natural state has occasion for the assistance of no other living creature. But man has almost constant occasion for the help of his brethren, and it is in vain for him to expect it from their benevolence only. He will be more likely to prevail if he can interest their self-love in his favor, and shew them that it is for their own advantage to do for him what he requires of them. Whoever offers to another a bargain of any kind, proposes to do this. Give me that which I want, and you shall have this which you want, is the meaning of every such offer; and it is in this manner that we obtain from one another the far greater part of those good offices which we stand in need of. It is not from the benevolence of the butcher, the brewer, or the baker, that we expect our dinner, but from their regard to their own interest. We address ourselves, not to their humanity but to their self-love, and never talk to them of our own necessities but of their advantages. Nobody but beggar chooses to depend chiefly upon the benevolence of his fellow citizens. Even a beggar does not depend upon it entirely. The charity of well-disposed people, indeed, supplies him with the whole fund of his subsistence. But though this principle ultimately provides him with all the necessaries of life which he has occasion for, neither does nor can provide him with them as he has occasion for them. The greater part of his occasional wants are supplied in the same manner as those of other people, by treaty, by barter, and purchase. With the money which one man gives him he purchased food. The old clothes which another bestows upon him he exchanged for other old clothes which suit him better, or for lodging, or for food or for money, with which he can buy either food, clothes, or lodging as he has occasion. . . .

Capitals are increased by parsimony, and diminished by prodigality and misconduct. . . .

Parsimony, and not industry, is the immediate cause of the increase of capital. Industry, indeed, provides the subject which parsimony accumulates. But whatever industry might acquire, if parsimony did not save and store up, the capital would never be the greater. . . .

Whatever, therefore, we may imagine the real wealth and revenue of a country to consist in, whether in the value of the annual produce of its land and labor, as plain reason seems to dictate; or in the quantity of the precious metals which circulate within it, as vulgar prejudices suppose; in either view of the matter, every prodigal appears to be a public enemy, and every frugal man a public benefactor. . . .

It can seldom happen, indeed, that the circumstances of a great nation can be much affected either by the prodigality or misconduct of individuals; the profusion or imprudence of some, being always more than compensated by the frugality and good conduct of others. . . .

According to the system of natural liberty, the sovereign has only three duties to attend to; three duties of great importance, indeed, but plain and intelligible to common understandings: first, the duty of protecting the society from the violence and invasion of other independent societies; secondly, the duty of protecting, as far as possible, every member of the society from the injustice or oppression of every other member of it, or the duty of establishing an exact administration of justice; and, thirdly, the duty of erecting and maintaining certain public works and certain public institutions, which it can never be for the interest of any individual, or small number of individuals, to erect and maintain; because the profit could never repay the expense to any individual or small number of individuals, though it may frequently do much more than repay it to a great society.

Adam Smith, *Wealth of Nations* (New York: Modern Library, 1937), pp. 4–5, 13–14, 321, 324, 651.

and reforms of the Enlightenment in their respective nations. In fact, no ruler would completely bind himself or herself to the philosophes' program, and all the enlightened absolutists committed "despotic" acts that shocked the Enlightenment community. Even so, most historians now think that the enlightened absolutists acted with at least some regard to the Enlightenment program and that their associations with the philosophes were not mere window-dressing for otherwise unenlightened policies. Moreover, it is notable that none of the states with enlightened absolutist rulers boiled over in revo-

The Written Record

LOCKE'S THEORY OF KNOWLEDGE

In the age-old debate as to the most formative influences on an individual's life—heredity or environment—and the most significant tool for comprehending either—faith or reason—John Locke came down squarely in favor of environment and reason.

Let us then suppose the mind to be . . . white paper, void of all characters, without any ideas. How comes it to be furnished? Whence comes it by that vast store, which the busy and boundless fancy of man has painted on it with an almost endless variety? Whence has it all the materials of reason and knowledge? To this I answer, in one word, from experience. . . . Our observation, employed either about external sensible objects, or about the internal operations of our minds, perceived and reflected on by ourselves, is that which supplies our understandings with all the materials of thinking. These two are the fountains of knowledge, from whence all the ideas we have, or can naturally have, do spring.

John Locke, *Essay Concerning Human Understanding*, in *The English Philosophers from Bacon to Mill*, ed. Edwin A. Burtt (New York: Modern Library, 1939), p. 248.

lution at the end of the eighteenth century as France did. It is thus probable that in most cases their enlightened reforms did help to strengthen their regimes.

Frederick the Great, r. 1740–1786

Of all the eighteenth-century rulers, Frederick II, the Great, king of Prussia from 1740 to 1786, appeared best attuned to the Enlightenment. As a youth he had rebelled against the drill-sergeant methods of his father, Frederick William I. An attentive reader of the philosophes, he exchanged letters with them and brought Voltaire to live for a time as his pensioner in his palace at Potsdam, near Berlin.

Frederick conducted foreign and military affairs with cunning and guile. "The principle of aggrandizement is the fundamental law of every government,"* he wrote. Viewed as a general, diplomat, and the master mechanic of Prussian administration, Frederick the Great was efficient and successful, but, if enlightened, he was also quite clearly a despot.

No Physiocrat could have done more than Frederick to improve Prussian agriculture. From western Europe he imported clover, potatoes, crop rotation, and the iron plow. He drained the swamps of the lower Oder valley,

---

*Quoted in G. Ritter, *Frederick the Great: A Historical Profile* (Berkeley: University of California Press, 1968), p. 7.

Doing History

THE BEGINNING OF "MODERN HISTORY"

Identifying when modern history began is really only a matter of convenience. *Modern history* relates to the presence of activities and customs that seem less strange to us today than do certain very ancient customs. Consider the range of such changes. In the Renaissance astrology was an accepted branch of learning; religious objections to it, largely because its concept of human actions as being governed by the heavenly bodies threatened the doctrine of free will, lessened its significance, until Pope Sixtus V condemned it in 1586. The plague, which brought vast changes to the pattern of population, sets two major periods off from each other: the Black Death in 1347–1348 and the great Venetian outbreak of 1575–1577. Depending on the question one asks, both or either events are watersheds in science, medicine, or the environment.

Social historians find significance in the changing nature of slavery. Until about 1450 slaves were commonly used as domestic servants and might be of any race. After the Ottoman advance cut off the usual sources of non-European slaves, and the plantation economy of the New World gave rise to the need for large-scale slave labor, slavery began to change and was generally limited to only one race by the seventeenth century.

Historians of climate point to the crucial changes between 1500 and 1800 and to the environmental crisis in Scandinavia caused by overexploitation of forest and agricultural land. Still other historians note the growing emphasis during the Renaissance on individualism, while others find no less individualism in the Middle Ages, whether in William the Conqueror or Peter Abelard. Nor does a general theory of individuality necessarily apply to an entire society; an elite group may emphasize individualism for itself while repressing it among the lower classes. A shift in the meaning of "glory" also helps set the periods apart, though there can be no agreement on when this occurred. In the Middle Ages, glory was attached to the afterlife; modernity argues for the significance of having one's deeds recognized during one's lifetime (as Louis XIV so valued) and also commemorated posthumously—a shift reflected in literature, portraits, political rhetoric, and tombstones. Clearly changes in business methods, banking, taxation, industry, and the economy generally also set the periods apart, although these changes were gradual. Depending upon one's perspective, the primary determining date for modern history may turn on attitudes toward the environment, the status of women, or a scientific discovery that takes on new significance when reinterpreted by a future generation.

---

opened up farms in Silesia and elsewhere, and brought in 300,000 immigrants, mainly from other areas of Germany, to settle the new lands. After the ravages of the Seven Years' War, Frederick gave the peasants tools, stock, and seed to repair their ruined farms. Frederick, however, was hostile to the doctrine of laissez faire. His mercantilism stimulated the growth of Prussian industry, particularly the textiles and metals needed by the army, but it also placed a staggering burden of taxation on his subjects.

The religious and social policies of Frederick the Great combined the Age of Reason at its most reasonable with the Old Regime at its least enlightened.

The Parisian salons of this period taught writers precision and brought them together for elegant, stylized conversation. The salon was most often the reception room of a large, private home, where guests assembled under the guidance of a hostess, a wealthy woman from the nobility or the upper bourgeoisie. In the salon good conversation could flourish, and new ideas were encouraged. Pressure from the salons helped determine who was elected to the French Academy, which passed under the control of the philosophes in the 1760s, and thus the women who presided over the salons often became the arbiters of good taste. The salon shown here is from the year 1764.   (Réunion des Musées Nationaux/Art Resource, NY)

A deist, Frederick prided himself on religious tolerance. When the Jesuits were expelled from Catholic states, he invited them to seek refuge in predominantly Lutheran Prussia. He boasted that he would build a mosque in his capital if Muslims wanted to settle there. Yet Frederick alleged that Jews were "useless to the state"; he levied special taxes on the Jewish subjects and tried to exclude them from the professions and from the civil service.

Frederick rendered Prussians a great service by his judicial reforms, which freed the courts from political pressures. He put an end to the unusual custom of turning over appeals from the ordinary courts to university faculties, setting up a regular system of appellate courts instead. He mitigated the practice of bribing judges by insisting that gratuities received from litigants be placed in a common pool, from which each judge should draw only his fair share as a supplement to his meager salary.

Yet the same Frederick took a medieval view of the merits of social caste. Although he abolished serfdom on the royal domains, he did little to loosen the bonds of serfdom generally, except to forbid the sale of landless serfs in East Prussia in 1773. When he gave the peasants material assistance and urged them to become literate, his aims were utilitarian. Peasants were to learn nothing beyond the rudiments of reading and writing; otherwise, they might become discontented. He regarded the middle class, too, with disdain. At the close of the Seven Years' War he forced all bourgeois officers in the army to resign their commissions; business and professional men were to be exempt from military service but subject to heavy taxation. Even the favored Junkers did not escape Frederick's bureaucratic absolutism. Although he appointed only Junkers as army officers, he discouraged their marrying, so as to reduce the number of potential widows to whom the state would owe a pension.

Many historians pronounce Frederick's supposed enlightenment a mere propaganda device, an attempt to clothe the nakedness of his absolutism with the intellectual garments of the age. It is fairer to recognize that Frederick espoused two often-conflicting philosophies—the Spartan traditions of the Hohenzollerns and the humane principles of the Enlightenment. The grim overtones of the former kept him from sharing the latter's optimistic estimate of human nature and potentiality. Frederick was an enlightened despot in his general religious toleration and his reform of court procedure and criminal law, but he was also bent on centralization that enhanced the Prussian kingship.

Habsburgs, 1740–1792

Frederick's decisive victory in the War of the Austrian Succession had laid bare the basic weaknesses of the Habsburgs' dynastic empire. The empress Maria Theresa (r. 1740–1780), although not well versed in the philosophes, believed in the need for reform and often took as her model the institutions of her hated but successful rival, Frederick II of Prussia. The empress increased taxes, especially on the nobility, and strengthened the central government at the expense of local aristocratic assemblies, building up departments for central administration. She also took the first steps toward the eventual abolition of serfdom by placing a ceiling on the amount of taxes and of labor service that the peasants could be compelled to render. While personally devout, she subjected the church to heavier taxation, confiscated monastic property, and seized the property of the Jesuits when they were dissolved by the Pope in 1773. But she banned the works of Rousseau and Voltaire from her realm and even forbade the circulation of the Catholic Index. It was her eldest son, Joseph II, who instituted the major reforms associated with the enlightened despots.

Joseph (r. 1765–1790), who became emperor in 1765, ruled jointly with his mother until her death in 1780. Thwarted and restrained by Maria Theresa in her lifetime, the impatient emperor plunged into activity after his mother died. During his ten years as sole ruler (1780–1790), eleven thousand laws and six thousand decrees issued from Vienna.

For the first time, Calvinists, Lutherans, and Orthodox Christians gained full toleration. The emperor took measures to end the ghetto existence of the Jews, exempting them from the special taxes applied to them and lifting the requirement of wearing a yellow patch as a badge of inferiority. On the other hand, Joseph continued his mother's moves to increase state control over the church. He encouraged what he considered socially useful in Catholicism and dealt ruthlessly with what he judged superfluous or harmful. Thus he established hundreds of new churches while reducing the number of religious holidays. Calling monks "the most dangerous and useless subjects in every state," he suppressed seven hundred monasteries and nunneries. The government sold or leased the lands of the suppressed establishments, applying the revenue to the support of hospitals.

Unlike Frederick the Great, Joseph believed in popular education and social equality. His government provided teachers and textbooks for primary schools. More than a quarter of the school-age children in Austria actually attended school. Everyone in Vienna, high and low, was invited to visit the Prater, the great public park of the capital. The new Austrian legal code followed the recommendations of Beccaria in abolishing capital punishment and most tortures and in prescribing equality before the law. Aristocratic offenders, like commoners, were sentenced to stand in the pillory and, later, to sweep the streets of Vienna.

Joseph's policy toward the peasants marked the climax of his equalitarianism. He freed the serfs, abolished most of their obligations to manorial lords, and deprived the lords of their traditional right of administering justice to the peasantry. He also experimented with a single tax on land—a revolutionary innovation because the estates of the aristocracy were to be taxed on the same basis as the farms of the peasantry. These changes also had the effect of striking at Magyar privileges in particular.

Joseph's economic and political policies, however, often followed the paths of absolutism. In economics he practiced mercantilism, notably in the erection of high protective tariffs and in the government's close supervision of economic life. In politics he appointed commoners to high governmental posts. He also attempted to terminate the autonomous rights of his non-German possessions, notably Belgium, Bohemia, and Hungary.

Joseph's measures aroused mounting opposition. Devout peasants, almost oblivious to his attempts to improve their social and economic status, resented his meddling with old religious customs. The nobility clamored against his equalitarian legislation; their opposition to the single-tax experiment was so violent that he had to revoke the decree a month after it was issued. Hungary and Belgium rose in open rebellion against his centralizing efforts and forced him to confirm their autonomous liberties.

In foreign policy, too, his ambitious projects miscarried. By supporting Russian plans for the dismemberment of Turkey, Austria gained only a narrow strip of Balkan territory. Joseph also attempted to annex lands belonging to the neighboring south German state of Bavaria, where the death of the ruler opened another succession quarrel. But Frederick the Great was determined to check any advance of Habsburg power in Germany. In the half-hearted "Potato War" of the late 1770s, Austrian and Prussian troops spent most of their time foraging for food, and Joseph secured only a tiny fragment of the Bavarian inheritance.

Joseph died convinced that he had pursued the proper course, yet believing that he had accomplished nothing. In fact, his course was too insensitive to the feelings of others; but he attempted more in ten years than Frederick attempted in almost half a century, and not all of Joseph's attempts failed. Though some of his major reforms, such as the abolition of serfdom, were repealed soon after his death, others survived.

The reforms that survived profited from the conciliatory policies of Joseph's successor, his younger brother Leopold II (r. 1790–1792), who was an enlightened despot in his own right. As grand duke of Tuscany (1765–1790), he had improved the administration of his Italian duchy. He also introduced economic and judicial reforms. Unlike his brother, Leopold actively enlisted the participation of his subjects in affairs of state.

Spain, Portugal, Sweden, 1759–1792

As king of Spain (r. 1759–1788), Charles III energetically advanced the progressive policies begun under his father, Philip V. Though a pious Catholic, Charles forced the Jesuits out of Spain. He reduced the authority of the aristocracy, extended that of the Crown, and made Spain more nearly a centralized national state. He curbed the privileges of the great sheep ranchers. To give new life to the economy, he undertook irrigation projects, reclaimed waste lands, and established new roads, canals, textile mills, and banks. Spain's foreign commerce increased fivefold during the reign of Charles III. His successor, however, abandoned many of his policies.

In Portugal, the grand marques de Pombal, Sebastião de Carvalno (1699–1782), the first minister of King Joseph I (r. 1750–1777), secured his reputation by the speed and good taste with which he rebuilt Lisbon after the devastating earthquake of 1755. The Portuguese economy depended heavily on income from the colonies, especially Brazil, and on the sale of port wine to and the purchase of manufactured goods from Britain. Pombal tried to enlarge the economic base by fostering local industries and encouraging the growth of grain production. In an attempt to weaken the grip of clericalism, in 1759 he ousted the Jesuits and advanced religious toleration. To weaken the nobles, he attacked their rights of inheritance. But Pombal's methods were high-handed, and when José I died in 1777, Pombal fell from power and the prisons released thousands of men whom he had confined years earlier for their alleged involvement in aristocratic plots.

Equally high-handed in the long run was Sweden's benevolent despot, Gustavus III (r. 1771–1792), a nephew of Frederick the Great. He resolved not to be cramped by the noble factions that had run the country since the death

Francisco Goya (1746–1828) shows Charles III of Spain (1716–1788) in hunting costume. Goya sought to analyze character as shown by social position, and he became increasingly less subtle in intimating human capacity for evil through his canvases. Living at the royal court, he became disillusioned by the later corruption of Charles IV, and his work took a savage turn. Compare this hunting portrait with Van Dyck on Charles I of England (p. 25). (Scala/Art Resource, NY)

of Charles XII. While he distracted Swedish party leaders at the opera one evening, his soldiers staged a coup that enabled him to revive royal authority and to dissolve the factions. In economics and religion his enlightenment outdistanced that of his uncle in Prussia, for he removed obstacles to both domestic and foreign trade and extended toleration to both Jews and non-Lutheran Christians. Success, however, went to his head. As the king became more and more arbitrary, the nobles determined to recover their old power; in 1792 Gustavus was assassinated while organizing a league of princes to attack the French Revolution.

The Limitations of Enlightened Despotism

Enlightened despotism was impaired by the problem of succession. As long as monarchs came to the throne by the accident of birth, there was nothing to prevent the unenlightened or incapable from succeeding the enlightened and able. Even the least of the enlightened despots deserves credit for having reformed some of the bad features of the Old Regime; but not even the best of them could strike a happy balance between enlightenment and despotism. Joseph II was too doctrinaire, too inflexible in his determination to apply the full reform program of the Age of Reason. Pombal and Gustavus III were too arbitrary. Frederick the Great, obsessed with strengthening the Crown, entrenched the power of the Junkers, who were hostile to the Enlightenment. And in Russia events after the death of Peter the Great furnished another lesson in the difficulty of applying rational principles to political realities.

Russia, 1725–1825

Russia had two sovereigns who could be numbered among the enlightened despots: Catherine II, the Great (r. 1762–1796) and her grandson Alexander I (r. 1801–1825). For the thirty-seven years between the death of Peter the Great and the accession of Catherine the autocracy was without an effective leader as the throne changed hands seven times. More important than the individuals who governed during these years were the social groups contending for power and the social processes at work in Russia. The guards regiments founded by Peter came to exercise a decisive influence in the series of palace overturns, and the service nobility, no longer restrained by the czar, became dominant.

Nobles and Serfs, 1730–1762

In 1730 the gentry set out to emancipate themselves from the servitude placed upon them by Peter. By 1762 the nobles no longer needed to serve at all unless they wished to do so; simultaneously, the authority of noble proprietors over their serfs was increased. The former became the government's agents for collecting the poll tax; the latter could no longer obtain their freedom by enlisting in the army and could not engage in trade or purchase land without written permission from their masters.

To understand the revolutionary nature of the liberation of the nobles from the duty to give military service, one must remember that they had historically obtained their lands and serfs only on condition that they would serve. Now they could keep their lands and serfs with no obligations. Yet the service that had been hated when it was compulsory became fashionable when it was optional. There was really little else for a Russian noble to do except serve the state and to tighten controls over the serfs.

In these middle decades of the eighteenth century, successive waves of foreign influence affected the Russian nobility. German influence gave way to French, and with the French language came French literature. French styles of dress were copied by both men and women, and some gentlemen claimed that it would be impossible to fall in love with a woman who did not speak French. Quite literally, nobles and peasants no longer spoke the same language.

Catherine the Great, 1762–1796

Brought up in a petty German court, Catherine found herself transplanted to St. Petersburg as a young girl, living with a husband she detested, and forced to pick her way through the intrigues that flourished in the Russian capital. Catherine was particularly concerned that Western leaders think well of her and of the condition of Russia under her rule. When Diderot visited Russia in 1773, he reported that Catherine had the soul of Brutus and the charms of Cleopatra. Voltaire stayed out of Russia but accepted Catherine's bounty, in return for which he called her "the north star" and "the benefactress of Europe."

Catherine would perhaps have liked to reform conditions in Russia, but as a woman, a foreigner, and a usurper (she owed her throne to a conspiracy that deposed and murdered her husband, Peter III), she could not act upon her inclinations. Depending as she did upon the goodwill of the nobility, she could not interfere with serfdom. She had to reward her supporters with vast grants of state land, inhabited by hundreds of thousands of state peasants, who now became privately owned serfs who could be sold.

Once firmly established on the throne, however, Catherine decided to convoke a commission to codify the laws of Russia, for the first time since 1649. With the help of advisers, Catherine herself spent three years composing the *Instruction* to the delegates, full of abstract argument drawn from Montesquieu's *Spirit of the Laws* and Beccaria's *Crimes and Punishments*. The 564 delegates to the commission were elected by organs of the central government and by every social class in Russia except the serfs. Each delegate was charged to bring with him a collection of written documents from his neighbors presenting their grievances and demands for change.

Each class of representatives was eager to extend the rights of that class: The free peasants wanted to own serfs; the townspeople wanted to own serfs and be the only class allowed to engage in trade; the nobles wanted to engage in trade and have their exclusive right to own serfs confirmed. After 203 sessions of inconclusive debate, lasting over a year and a half, Catherine ended the labors of the commission in 1768. The commission was the last effort by czardom to consult the Russian people as a whole until the early twentieth century.

In 1773 Yemelyan Pugachev (d. 1775) roused the Cossacks to revolt against Catherine's cancellation of their special privileges. Pretending to be her murdered husband, Czar Peter III, and promising liberty and land to the serfs who joined his forces, Pugachev swept over a wide area of southeastern Russia and marched toward Moscow. Like the disturbances of the seventeenth century, Pugachev's revolt revealed the existence of bitter discontent in Russia.

Catherine took action. Her reorganization of local government (1775) created fifty provinces where there had been twenty before. She thus replaced a small number of unwieldly units with a larger number of small provinces, each containing roughly 300,000–400,000 inhabitants. While the reform of 1775 gave the nobles the lion's share of provincial offices, it also subjected them to the close direction of the central government. The revolt was brutally crushed.

In a charter of 1785 the nobles again received exemption from military service and taxation and secured absolute mastery over the fate of their serfs and their estates. A charter to the towns in the same year disclosed Catherine's sympathy with the tiny but growing urban middle class and established the principle of municipal self-government, although it remained a dead letter because of the rigorous class distinctions maintained in the urban centers of Russia. For the serfs, however, there was no charter.

Paul, r. 1796–1801, and Alexander I, r. 1801–1825

Catherine's son Paul succeeded her in 1796 at age forty-two. He appeared to be motivated chiefly by a wish to undo his mother's work. He exiled some of her favorites and released many of her prisoners. Paul's behavior, however, was unpredictable. On the one hand, he imposed a strict curfew on St. Petersburg and forbade the importation of sheet music. On the other hand, in a decree in 1797 he prohibited the requirement of labor on Sunday.

What was probably fatal to Paul was his policy of toughness toward the nobility. He restored compulsory service from the nobles and curtailed their powers in the provinces. Nobles were forced to meet the bills for public buildings and to pay new taxes on their lands; they were also subjected to corporal punishment for crimes. Paul wanted to develop in the army's officers a sense of responsibility for their men. The guards regiments detested his programs, and a conspiracy of guardsmen resulted in the murder of Paul and the succession of Alexander in 1801.

Educated by a liberal Swiss tutor, Alexander I (r. 1801–1825) had absorbed much of the new eighteenth-century teachings. Yet the application of liberal principles in Russia would directly challenge the most powerful forces in society and would also require the czar to relinquish some of his own power. Alexander compromised and in the end accomplished very little. He did sponsor a law creating a new category of free farmers—serfs who had been freed by their masters—and prescribing that if a proprietor freed an entire village of serfs, he must also confer their lands upon them. This mild initiative depended on the voluntary cooperation of the proprietors, however, and it resulted in the freeing of fewer than forty thousand of the many millions of serfs.

Alexander had as his chief mentor Michael Speransky (1772–1839), son of a Russian priest, intelligent, well educated, and conscientious. Speransky drafted a constitution that would have made Russia a limited monarchy. A series of locally elected assemblies would culminate in a national assembly, the Duma, which would have to approve any law proposed by the czar and would act as a Russian parliament. Because it would have enormously favored the nobility and excluded the serfs, Alexander balked at implementing the project he had commissioned. A council of state was created to advise the czar, but since he appointed and dismissed its members and was not obliged to take its advice, the effect was simply to increase imperial efficiency, not to limit imperial authority. Further efficiency was achieved through the reorganization of the ministries, whose duties were set out clearly for the first time, eliminating overlapping.

During the last decade of Alexander's reign, 1815–1825, the most important figure at court was Count Alexsey Arakcheev (1769–1834), an efficient and brutal officer who reformed the army and organized a hated system of "military colonies," drafting the population of whole districts to serve in the regiments quartered there. When not drilling or fighting, these soldiers were to work their farms, and their entire lives often were subject to the whims of their officers. By the end of Alexander's reign, almost 400,000 soldiers were living in these harsh military camps.

Although Alexander gave Russia no important reforms, he did act as the "liberal czar" in his dominions outside Russia proper. Made king of a partially restored Poland in 1815, he gave the Poles an advanced constitution, with their own army and officials and the free use of their own language. After the annexation of Finland from Sweden in 1809, he allowed the Finns to preserve their own law codes and the system of local government introduced during the long period of Swedish rule.

Foreign Policy, 1725–1796

Between the death of Peter the Great and that of Catherine, Russian foreign policy still pursued the traditional goals of expansion against Sweden, Poland, and Turkey. But Russia found that these goals increasingly involved it with the states of central and western Europe. In the War of the Polish Succession (1733–1735) Russian forces were allied with those of Austria. The Russians and Austrians then became allies in a new war against the Turks from 1735 to 1739. Although the Russians invaded the Crimea successfully, their territorial gains were limited to Azov. The Austrians failed to cooperate in an invasion of the Danubian principalities and made it clear that they did not relish a Russian advance toward the Habsburg frontiers. Prussian influence, which was anti-Austrian, manifested itself with the designation of the German grandson of Peter the Great (the future Peter III) as heir and with the selection of the German Catherine, whose father was a Prussian general.

The Russians remained loyal to Austria and fought the Prussians in the Seven Years' War. Russian forces invaded East Prussia and in 1760 entered Berlin; the accession of the pro-Prussian Peter III early in 1762 led the Russians to change sides and join the Prussians briefly against the Austrians and the French. When Catherine, on her accession, withdrew Russian forces, Russia was excluded from the peace conferences of 1763.

In foreign policy Catherine the Great was vigorous and unscrupulous in pursuing Russia's traditional goals. When the throne of Poland fell vacant,

Catherine secured the election of her former lover, Stanislas Poniatowski, who became Stanislas II (r. 1764–1795). Frederick the Great then joined with Catherine in a campaign to win rights for the Lutheran and Orthodox minorities in Catholic Poland. One party of Polish nobles, offended at foreign intervention, secured the aid of France and Austria, which adopted the stratagem of pressing Turkey into war with Russia to distract Catherine from Poland.

In the Russo-Turkish War (1768–1774) the Russian Baltic fleet sailed into the Mediterranean and destroyed the Turkish fleet in the Aegean (1770). While Russians and Turks were discussing peace terms, Frederick the Great concluded that Russia's success with the Turks might lead it to seize most of Poland unless he acted quickly; he therefore arranged the first partition of Poland (1772), which lost to Russia, Prussia, and Austria almost one third of its territory and one half of its population. Russia received a substantial area of what became Belorussia, or White Russia. Two years later, in the treaty of Kutchuk Kainardji, Catherine annexed much of the formerly Turkish stretch of the Black Sea coast; the Crimea was separated from the Ottoman Empire and annexed by Russia in 1783. She also obtained something the Russians had long covered—freedom of navigation on the Black Sea and the right of passage through the Bosporus and the Dardanelles.

Now Catherine began to dream of expelling the Turks from Europe and reviving the Byzantine Empire under Russian protection. She had her younger grandson christened Constantine and imported Greek-speaking nurses to train him in the language. She also proposed to set up a kingdom of Dacia (the Roman name for "Romania"). By way of preparation, in 1783 Catherine built a naval base at Sebastopol in the newly annexed Crimea. To achieve these grandiose designs, Catherine sought the consent of Austria and took Joseph II on a boat tour of the recently acquired territories of the Russian southwest. However, in a Second Russo-Turkish War (1787–1791) Catherine's Austrian allies again provided feeble assistance and soon became embroiled in a conflict of interest with Russia over the European lands of the sultan. In the end Catherine contented herself with acquiring the remaining Turkish lands along the northern coast of the Black Sea.

Before her death Catherine participated in two more partitions of Poland. The second partition came as the result of a Polish constitutional movement, supported by the Prussians in opposition to Russian interests. Catherine intervened on the pretext of defending the established order in Poland and fighting revolution. In 1793 both the Russians and Prussians took large slices of Polish territory. An attempted Polish revolution was followed by the third partition, in 1795, by which Poland disappeared from the map. This time Austria joined the other two powers and obtained Krakow; Prussia got Warsaw, and Russia got Lithuania and other Baltic and east Polish lands.

The spectacular successes of Catherine meant the transfer to Russia of millions of people—Poles, Lithuanians, Belorussians, Tatars—who hated the Russians, and it left a legacy of instability and insecurity. It also meant that Russia had destroyed the useful buffers of the Polish and Tatar states, and now had common frontiers with its potential enemies, Prussia and Austria.

George III and American Independence

Although Catherine the Great failed to apply the ideas of the Age of Reason, her name often appears on lists of enlightened despots. Another name is at times added to the list—George III, king of Great Britain (r. 1760–1820). George III tried to wrest control of the House of Commons from the long-dominant Whig oligarchy and retain it through patronage and bribery. Virtuous as a person and devoted to his family, George as a monarch was stubborn, shortsighted, and in the long run unsuccessful. It was easy for him at first to exploit the factional strife among the Whigs, maneuver William Pitt out of office in 1761, and make his tutor Lord Bute (1713–1792) head of the cabinet. Bute and the king, however, found it hard to justify their failure to deprive France of its sugar-rich West Indian islands in the Peace of Paris, which concluded the Seven Years' War. The Commons approved the treaty, but George dismissed Bute.

The harshest criticism came from John Wilkes (1727–1797), a member of Commons. Wilkes's attack on the treaty in his paper the *North Briton* infuriated the king; bowing to royal anger, the Commons ordered the offending issue of the paper burned. Later, Wilkes ran for Parliament three times, and each time the Commons, under royal pressure, threw out his election. When Wilkes finally took his seat again in 1774, he was a popular hero.

A wiser king would have reconsidered his course, but George III did not relax his determination to manage both Parliament and cabinet. After seven years of short-lived, unstable ministries (1763–1770), George finally found a man to fill Bute's old role and do the king's bidding—Lord North, who headed the cabinet until 1782. Under North royal intervention in domestic politics at first stiffened, then wavered, and at length collapsed in the face of a revolt.

Background of the American Revolt, 1760–1776

The breach between the colonies and Britain first became serious after the Seven Years' War, when Britain began to interfere more directly and frequently in colonial matters. By 1763 the colonies had become accustomed to regulating their own affairs, although the acts of their assemblies remained subject to the veto of royally appointed governors or of the king himself. The vast territories acquired in 1763 in Canada and west of the Allegheny Mountains brought Britain added opportunities for profitable exploitation and added responsibilities for government and defense. When an uprising of Indians under Pontiac (c. 1720–1769) threatened frontier posts in the area of the Ohio Valley and the Great Lakes, colonial militias failed to take effective action, and British regulars were brought in. The continuing threat prompted the royal proclamation of October 1763 forbidding "all our loving subjects" to settle west of a line running along the summit of the Alleghenies. To His Majesty's "loving subjects" in the seaboard colonies, however, the proclamation seemed deliberately designed to exclude them from the riches of the West.

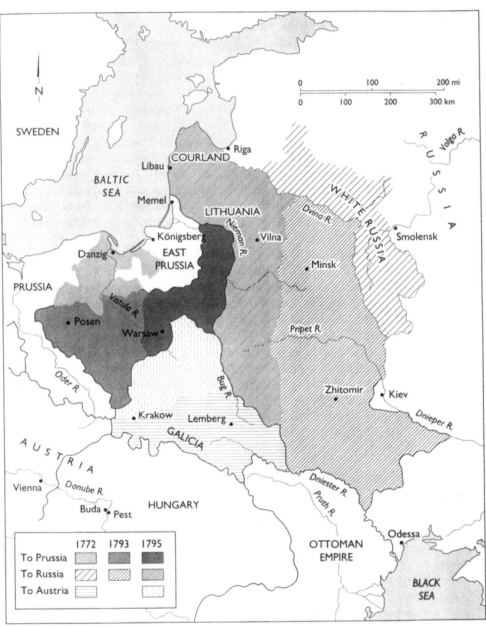

Partitions of Poland, 1772, 1793, 1795

The colonies resented still more keenly the attempt by Parliament to raise revenue in North America. The British government had very strong arguments for increasing colonial taxes: The national debt had almost doubled during the Seven Years' War; the colonies' reluctance to recruit soldiers and raise taxes themselves had increased the cost of the war to British taxpayers; now the mother country faced continued expense in protecting the frontier. Surely the Americans would admit the reasonableness of the case for higher taxes, the members of Parliament thought.

That, however, was precisely what the Americans did not admit. The first of the new revenue measures, the Sugar Act of 1764, alarmed the merchants of the eastern seaboard because the customs officers actually undertook to collect duties on molasses, sugar, and other imports. Here was a threat to the colonial economy, for the import duties had to be paid out of the colonies' meager supply of coins. The second revenue measure, the Stamp Act of 1765, imposed levies on a wide variety of items, including legal and commercial papers, liquor licenses, playing cards, dice, newspapers, calendars, and academic degrees. These duties further drained the supply of coins.

The revenue measures touched off a major controversy. Indignant merchants in the New World boycotted all imports rather than pay the duties, and in October 1765 delegates from nine of the colonies met in New York City as the Stamp Act Congress. The Congress, complaining that the new duties had "a manifest tendency to subvert the rights and liberties of the colonists," proclaimed the principle that there was to be no taxation without representation. Britain surrendered on the practical issue, but did not yield on the principle. The appeals of London merchants, nearly ruined by the American boycott against British goods, brought about the repeal of the Stamp Act in 1765. In 1766, however, Parliament passed a Declaratory Act asserting that the king and Parliament could indeed make such laws affecting the colonies.

For the next decade Britain adhered firmly to the principles of the Declaratory Act, and colonial radicals just as firmly repeated their opposition to taxation without representation. Parliament again tried to raise revenue, this time by the Townshend duties (1767) on colonial imports of tea, paper, paint, and lead. Again the merchants of Philadelphia, New York, and Boston organized boycotts. In 1770 Lord North's cabinet withdrew the Townshend duties except for a three-penny tariff on a pound of tea. Three years later the English East India Company attempted to sell surplus tea in North America, hoping to overcome American opposition to the hated duty by making the retail price of East India tea, duty included, far cheaper than that of Dutch tea smuggled by the colonists. The result was the Boston Tea Party. On December 16, 1773, to the cheers of spectators lining the waterfront, a group of Bostonians who had a large financial stake in smuggled tea disguised themselves as Native Americans, boarded three East India ships, and dumped chests of tea worth thousands of pounds into the harbor.

Britain answered defiance with force and the colonists met force with resistance. The Quebec Act (1774), incorporating the lands beyond the Alleghenies into Canada, bolted the door to the westward expansion of colonial frontiers. The Intolerable Acts (1774)—so called because taken together the colonists found them intolerable—closed the port of Boston to trade and suspended elections in Massachusetts. At Lexington and Concord in April 1775 the farmers of Massachusetts fired the opening shots of what became the War of Independence. At Philadelphia on July 4, 1776, delegates to a Continental Congress formally declared thirteen of the fourteen American mainland colonies independent of Great Britain.

Implications of the Revolution

For the mother country the American Revolution implied more than the secession of thirteen colonies. It involved Britain in a minor world war that jeopardized its dominance abroad and weakened the power and prestige of King George III at home. The most crucial battle in North America came early in the war—the surrender at Saratoga in 1777 of the British forces under General John Burgoyne (1722–1792). Burgoyne's surrender convinced the French that support of the American colonists would give them an excellent chance to avenge the humiliation of 1763. Entering the war in 1778, France soon gained the alliance of Spain and eventually secured the help or friendly neutrality of most other European states.

French intervention prepared the way for eventual victory. In the peace signed at Paris in 1783, Britain recognized the independence of the former colonies. To Spain it handed back Florida, which it had taken in 1763, and the strategic Mediterranean island of Menorca. But it kept Gibraltar, which the Spanish had also hoped to recover, and it ceded only minor territories to France.

During the early years of the war, the British public was intensely anti-American; but the temper of opinion changed as the strength of American resistance became evident. Instances of British mismanagement piled up, while most of Europe rallied to the rebellious colonies. By 1780 George III and his policies were so unpopular that the House of Commons passed a resolution declaring that "the influence of the Crown has increased, is increasing, and ought to be diminished." In 1782 Lord North stepped down. In the next year the post of prime minister fell to William Pitt the Younger (1759–1806), son of the heroic Pitt of the Seven Years' War. With the advent of Pitt, control of British politics shifted away from the king and back to professional politicians.

Support of the revolution in the colonies was by no means unanimous. Many well-to-do colonists, including southern planters and Pennsylvania Quakers, either backed the mother country or took a neutral position in the struggle; New York supplied more recruits to George III than to George Washington. However, revolutionary sentiment ran particularly high in Virginia and New England and among social groups who had the habit of questioning established authority—many merchants, pioneers living on the frontier, and the numerous religious groups who had come to the New World in protest against the Old.

The Written Record

THE STAMP ACT CONGRESS ASSERTS THE RIGHT OF LOCAL REPRESENTATION

The Stamp Act Congress met in New York City in October 1765 and declared:

That His Majesty's liege subjects in these colonies are entitled to all the inherent rights and liberties of his natural born subjects within the kingdom of Great Britain.

That it is inseparably essential to the freedom of a people, and the undoubted right of Englishmen, that no taxes be imposed on them but with their own consent, given personally or by their own representatives.

That the people of these colonies are not, and from their local circumstances cannot be, represented in the House of Commons in Great Britain.

That the only representatives of these colonies are persons chosen therein by themselves, and that no taxes ever have been, or can be constitutionally imposed on them, but by their respective legislatures.

From *Documents of American History,* 9th ed., ed. Henry S. Commager (Englewood Cliffs, N.J.: Prentice Hall, Inc., 1973), p. 58.

At the heart of the draft composed by the delegates to the Constitutional Convention at Philadelphia in 1787 was the separation of the executive, legislative, and judicial arms of government. Each of the branches of government had the power to check the other two. The Founding Fathers of the American republic sought guidance not only from Montesquieu's *The Spirit of the Laws* but also from the constitutions of the thirteen original states and from English precedents. The first ten amendments to the United States constitution (1791), guaranteeing freedom of religion, freedom of the press, and other basic liberties, were taken mainly from the English Bill of Rights of 1689.

Challenges to the Enlightenment

The philosophes expected people to see reason when it was pointed out, to give up the habits of centuries, and to revise their behavior in accordance with natural law. But the rationalism of the Enlightenment tended to omit from its calculations the unpredictable complexities of human nature. A minor philosophe, the abbé de Mably (1709–1785), got at this central problem when he asked: "Is society, then a branch of physics?" Most of the philosophes and their followers believed that it was, and they applied to unpredictable people the mathematical methods used in the physical sciences. The Physiocrats, for

Paul Revere's drawing of "the bloody Massacre" in Boston.   (Courtesy of the Library of Congress)

example, tried to reduce the complexities of human economic activities to a few simple agricultural laws.

A few outspoken critics, however, disagreed. The Italian philosopher Giovanni Vico (1668–1744) published in 1725 *Scienza Nuova* (New Science), which looked at the state not as a piece of machinery subject to natural laws but as an organism with a pattern of growth, maturity, and decay imposed by its own nature. A Scottish philosopher, David Hume (1711–1776), dramatized his opposition to mercantilism and his advocacy of free international trade by avowing that he prayed for the prosperity of other nations. Yet his profound skepticism and his corrosive common sense caused him to make short work of the philosophes' appeals to nature and reason. To Hume the laws of justice, for instance, were not unalterable but varied with circumstances and, in an emergency, might yield entirely to "stronger motives of necessity and self-preservation. Is it any crime, after a shipwreck, to seize whatever means or instrument of safety one can lay hold of, without regard to former limitations of property?"*

Immanuel Kant (1724–1804), who taught philosophy at the University of Königsberg in East Prussia, raised the debate to the level of metaphysics. While advocating many of the doctrines of the Enlightenment, Kant also believed in a higher reality reaching ultimately to God. He called the eternal verities of the higher world *noumena* (from a Greek word meaning "things thought"), in contrast to the *phenomena* of the material world that are experienced through the senses. Knowledge of the noumenal realm, Kant believed, reached us through reason—reason, however, not as the Enlightenment used the term, not as common sense, but as intuition. The highest expression of the Kantian reason was the "categorical imperative." This was the moral law within the conscience implanted by God. Kant's redefinition of reason and his rehabilitation of conscience exemplified the growing philosophical reaction against the dominant rationalism of the Enlightenment. The Jesuits, too, argued against seeing man as a machine.

Pietists and Methodists

The popular reaction, on the other hand, was an evangelical revival that began with the German Pietists. The Pietists asserted that religion came from the heart, not the head, and that God was far more than a watchmaker, more than the remote creator of the world-machine. One of the chief leaders of Pietism was Count Nikolaus Zinzendorf (1700–1760), founder of the Moravian Brethren, who set up a model community based on Christian principles. Moravian emigrants to America established a colony at Bethlehem, Pennsylvania, helping to create the reputation for thrift, hard work, and strict living enjoyed by the Pennsylvania Dutch ("Dutch" meaning *Deutsch*, German).

In England John Wesley (1703–1791), ordained in the Church of England, at first stressed the ritualistic aspects of religion but then felt his own faith evaporating. Pietism converted Wesley to the belief that he would find faith through inner conviction. For more than fifty years Wesley labored to share his discovery, preaching throughout the British Isles in churches, in the fields, at the pitheads of coal mines, and in jails. When Wesley died, his movement had already attracted more than 100,000 adherents, called "Methodists" because of their methodical devotion to piety and to plain dress and plain living. Although Wesley always considered himself an Anglican, the Methodists eventually set up a separate organization. The new sect won its following almost entirely among the lower and middle classes, among people who sought the religious excitement and consolation they did not find in deism or in the Church of England.

Although their beliefs diverged entirely from those of the Enlightenment, the Methodists, too, worked to improve the condition of society. Where the

---

*David Hume, *Enquiries Concerning the Human Understanding and Concerning the Principles of Morals*, 1751, ed. L.A. Selby-Bigge, 3rd ed. (Oxford: Clarendon Press, 1975), p. 186.

philosophes advocated public reform, the Methodists favored private charity; where the philosophes attacked the causes of evils, the Methodists accepted these evils as part of God's plan and sought to mitigate their symptoms. They began agitation against drunkenness, the trade in slaves, and the barbarous treatment of prisoners, the insane, and the sick. Wesley established schools for coal miners' children and opened dispensaries for the poor. The Methodists' success derived in part from their social programs and in part from the magnetism of Wesley and his talented associates. In America, Methodist missionaries flourished under the dynamic leadership of Francis Asbury (1745–1816). The number of colleges called Wesleyan and the number of churches and streets called Asbury testify to the significance of methodism in North American social history.

Literature and the Arts: The Beginnings of Romanticism

The literary landmarks of the century included both the classical writings of the French philosophes and the English Augustans, and new experiments in the depiction of realism and "sensibility," that is, the life of the emotions. In England the Augustan Age of letters took its name from the claim that it boasted a group of talents comparable to those of Vergil, Horace, and Ovid, who had flourished under the emperor Augustus in Rome.

The greatest of the Augustans was Jonathan Swift (1667–1745), a pessimistic and sometimes despondent genius. In his great work *Gulliver's Travels* (1726), the broad and savage satirization of scientific endeavors and the startling contrast between the noble and reasonable horses, the Houyhnhnms, and the brutish and revolting human Yahoos were intended as attacks on easy assumptions of rational human behavior.

Much closer to the classical temper were Edward Gibbon's *History of the Decline and Fall of the Roman Empire* (1788) and Dr. Johnson's *Dictionary*. Gibbon (1737–1794) made history the excuse for a sustained attack on Christian fanaticism while elucidating his theories of decline in magisterial prose. The lexicographer Samuel Johnson (1709–1784) expressed another concern of the age in the preface to his *Dictionary:*

> When I took the first survey of my undertaking, I found our speech copious without order and energetic without rules; wherever I turned my view, there was perplexity to be disentangled and confusion to be regulated; choice was to be made out of a boundless variety, without any established principle of selection; adulterations were to be detected, without a settled test of purity; and modes of expression to be rejected or received, without the suffrages of any writers of classical reputation or acknowledged authority.*

Meantime, the rapid development of the novel greatly increased the popularity of more down-to-earth and emotional reading. Two of the earliest

---

*Samuel Johnson, *A Dictionary of the English Language* (London: William Stralan, 1755), p. 4.

examples of the new type of fiction were by Daniel Defoe—*Robinson Crusoe* (1719) and *Moll Flanders* (1722). Both were far removed from the refinements and elevated feelings of classicism. Realism was also evident in two celebrated midcentury novels: In *Roderick Random* (1748), Tobias Smollett (1721–1771) drew an authentic picture of life in the British navy, with its cruelty and hardship; *Tom Jones*, by Henry Fielding (1707–1754), published in 1749, was the first truly great social novel, with convincing portraits of the toughs of London slums and the hard-riding, hard-drinking country squires.

Fielding also delighted in parodying the sentimental fiction of Samuel Richardson (1689–1761), who created three giant novels cast in the form of letters by the hero or heroine. An example was *Clarissa Harlowe* (1748), which described in 2400 pages the misfortunes of Clarissa, whose lover was a scoundrel and whose greedy relatives were scheming to secure her property. With all Richardson's excessive emotionalism and preachiness, his descriptions of passion and conscience carried such conviction to a growing reading public that his novels did much to establish the tradition of moral earnestness in English fiction and public discussion.

In France the novel of sensibility came into its own with the very popular *Manon Lescaut* (1731) of Antoine François Prévost, which related the adventures of a young woman sent to the colony of Louisiana. Much closer to Richardson in style and tone was Rousseau's long novel about the conflict of love and duty, *La Nouvelle Héloïse* (1761). Increasingly readers were turning to such fiction, rather than to the church, for guidance on moral and especially sexual questions.

In Germany the most important literary works were the dramas of Lessing and the outpourings of writers associated with the *Sturm und Drang* (storm and stress) movement. Lessing (1729–1781) combined the sensibility of Richardson and the tearful sentimentality of French comedies with an enlightened devotion to common sense and toleration. In *Nathan the Wise* (1779) he dramatized the deistic belief that Judaism, Christianity, and Islam are all manifestations of a universal religion.

Yearning, frustration, and despair characterized the most successful work of the Sturm and Drang period *The Sorrows of Young Werther* (1774), a short novel, made the youthful Johann Wolfgang von Goethe (1749–1832) famous overnight. Napoleon claimed to have read it seven times, weeping copiously at each reading when the hero shoots himself because the woman he loves is already married. The themes of self-pity and self-destruction were to be prominent in the romantic movement that swept over Europe at the close of the eighteenth century. Such essential sentimental art and literature stood in clear contrast to the dominant insistence on Reason as a guide associated with the Enlightenment.

The classicism of the century more strongly affected its art. Gibbon's history, the research of scholars and archaeologists, and the discovery in 1748 of the ruins of Roman Pompeii, well preserved under lava from Vesuvius, raised interest in antiquity to a high pitch. For the scholars of the Enlightenment, the balance and symmetry of Greek and Roman temples represented, in effect, the natural laws of building. Architects adapted classical models with great artistry and variety.

In painting, neoclassicism had an eminent spokesman in Sir Joshua Reynolds (1723–1792), president of the Royal Academy. Beauty, Sir Joshua told the academy, rested "on the uniform, eternal, and immutable laws of nature," which could be "investigated by reason, and known by study." This was the golden age of English portraiture, the age of Reynolds, Thomas Gainsborough (1737–1788), George Romney (1734–1802), and Sir Thomas Lawrence (1769–1830). But it was also the age of William Hogarth (1697–1764), who created a mass market for the engravings that he turned out in thousands of copies, graphic sermons on the vices of London—*Marriage à la Mode*, *The Rake's Progress*, *The Harlot's Progress*, and *Gin Lane*.

In France the decorative style called *rococo* prevailed during the reign of Louis XV. It was even more fantastic than the baroque, but lighter, airier, more delicate and graceful, addicted to the use of motifs from bizarre rock formations and from shells. The style captured the social graces of the period, for it was elegant while superficial, elaborate while stereotyped, and, at its best, cheerfully playful while, at its worst, florid and self-conscious.

Meanwhile, three artistic fashions that were to figure significantly in the age of romanticism were already catching on—the taste for the oriental, for the natural, and for the Gothic. Rococo interest in the exotic created a vogue for things Chinese—Chinese wallpaper, the "Chinese" furniture of Thomas Chippendale (c. 1718–1779), and the delicate work in porcelain or on painted scrolls that is called *chinoiserie*. Eighteenth-century gardens were bestrewn with pagodas and minarets.

But music was the queen of the arts in the eighteenth century. A German choirmaster, Johann Sebastian Bach (1685–1750), mastered the difficult art of the fugue, an intricate version of the round in which each voice begins the theme in turn while other voices repeat it and elaborate upon it. Bach composed fugues and a wealth of other material for the organ; for small orchestras he created numerous works, including the Brandenburg Concertos, in which successive instruments are given a chance to show off their potential. His sacred works included many cantatas, the Mass in B minor, and two gigantic choral settings of the Passion of Christ.

Bach's quiet provincial life contrasted sharply with the stormy international career of his countryman George Frederick Handel (1685–1759). Handel spent most of his adult years in London trying to run an opera company. He wrote more than forty operas and used themes from the Bible for *The Messiah* and other vigorous oratorios arranged for large choruses and directed at a mass audience.

Although Bach and Handel composed many instrumental suites and concertos, it was not until the second half of the century that orchestral music really came to the fore. New instruments were invented, notably the piano, which greatly extended the limited range of the harpsichord. New forms of instrumental music—the sonata and the symphony—were also developed, largely by an Austrian, Franz Joseph Haydn (1732–1809). Haydn wrote more than fifty piano pieces in the sonata form, in which two contrasting themes are started in turn, developed, interwoven, repeated, and finally resolved in a *coda* (Italian for "tail"). Haydn also arranged the sonata for the orchestra, grafting it onto the Italian operatic overture to create the first movement of the symphony.

Still, the operatic landmark of the early century was John Gay's (1685–1732) *Beggar's Opera* (1728), a tuneful work caricaturing the London underworld. Later, the German Christoph Gluck (1714–1787) made opera a well-constructed musical drama, not just a vehicle for the display of vocal skill. He kept to the old custom of taking heroes and heroines from classical mythology, but he tried to invest these figures with new vitality.

Opera, symphony, concerto, and chamber music all reached a climax in the works of another Austrian, Wolfgang Amadeus Mozart (1756–1791). As a boy Mozart was exploited by his father, who carted him all over Europe to show off his virtuosity on the harpsichord and his amazing talent for composition. Overworked throughout his life, and in his later years burdened with debts, he died a pauper at the age of thirty-five. Yet his youthful precocity ripened steadily into mature genius, and his facility and versatility grew ever more prodigious.

The Enlightenment also saw a flowering of women as writers, especially on social issues. They were leaders in the movement to abolish slavery, played significant roles as hostesses of *salons* where writers met to debate the issues of the day, and founded new religious movements. The concept of romantic love and of marriage as not only a contract but also companionship for life changed attitudes toward the family. One early feminist writer stood above all others: Mary Wollstonecraft (1759–1797). A rebel against society's conventions in dress and behavior, she wore trousers, championed the poor, and left home at an early age. An essayist and novelist, she called for sexual liberation, openly spoke of woman's sexual passion, and compared women to slaves. Her *A Vindication of the Rights of Woman* (1792) is often used to date the beginning of the modern women's rights movement. Her work would be forgotten, however, because she seemed too radical and shocking: she had a child out of wedlock, lived openly with a leading anarchist, William Godwin (1756–1836), and scandalized British society. She would not be rediscovered until the end of the nineteenth century.

SUMMARY

French cultural leadership in the eighteenth century was preeminent. The key concepts of the eighteenth-century philosophes, or intellectuals, were reason, natural law, and progress. Philosophes, who expressed optimism in human abilities to apply reason, owed a debt to John Locke for their ideas on government and human psychology. Under the direction of Diderot, philosophes produced the thirty-three-volume *Encyclopédie*, advancing views of progress and reason, exposing superstition and ignorance, and denouncing inequality in the light of natural law and science.

François Quesnay and Adam Smith summed up the economic principles of those philosophes known as Physiocrats. The Physiocrat's program of laissez faire, or "let nature take its course," clashed with traditional mercantilist doctrines.

In justice and education, philosophes sought reforms based on reason and natural law. They championed tolerance and attacked superstition. The well-known philosophe Voltaire professed belief in God but rejected intolerance and furthered deist doctrine.

Like many other philosophes, Montesquieu in *The Spirit of the Laws* (1748) expressed admiration for British ideas on government. In *The Social Contract* (1762), Jean-Jacques Rousseau set out his theory of the general will to reconcile the needs of the individual and the institution of government. Rousseau's ideas have formed the basis of radical political doctrines ever since.

Enlightened despots of the period displayed a mix of Enlightenment ideas and absolute monarchy. Frederick the Great read the works of philosophes and promoted Physiocratic ideas in agriculture. But he rejected laissez-faire ideas. In religion and social policy, he inaugurated a measure of tolerance and supported judicial reforms but did not move to reduce social inequality.

Joseph II of Austria, Charles III of Spain, as well as rulers in Portugal and Sweden instituted enlightened reforms. However, the successors of these enlightened rulers did not continue their programs.

In Russia, Catherine was an absolute autocrat who liked the idea of reform. She tried to codify laws based on enlightened ideas, reorganized local government, and introduced some municipal reform. But under Catherine, serfdom grew as the nobility gained increased authority over their serfs.

Czar Alexander I had absorbed enlightened ideas but was hesitant and accomplished little despite good intentions. Russia continued its expansionist foreign policy. Catherine annexed the Crimea and participated in the partitions of Poland.

In Britain, George III, stubborn and shortsighted, tried to reassert royal prerogative. After the Seven Years' War, a breach divided Britain and its North American colonies. Colonists' resistance to Britain's attempt to raise revenue in North America resulted in the issuing of the Declaration of Independence on July 4, 1776.

With French help, the colonists won their independence, which was recognized in 1783 at the Peace of Paris. The successful revolt of the American colonists weakened the power and prestige of George III. The Declaration of Independence appealed to the laws of nature described by Locke, while the new Constitution of the United States reflected Montesquieu's ideas on the separation of powers.

Philosophes failed to take into account the complexities of human nature. Their appeals to the laws of nature and reason did not reform states. David Hume and Immanuel Kant reflected the philosophic reaction to rationalism.

Popular reaction to the Enlightenment was expressed in German Pietism and the Methodist movement in England.

A new type of fiction appeared in the works of Daniel Defoe and the social novels of Henry Fielding. In Germany, Goethe's *Sorrows of Young Werther* embodied the frustration of the Sturm and Drang movement. Neoclassicism influenced the arts, but the age of romanticism was foreshadowed in the growing taste for the oriental, natural, and Gothic.

FOUR

The French Revolution and Napoleon

∞

After nearly a century of relative political stability, Europe was shaken by a wave of revolutionary movements in the 1780s and 1790s. Most of these revolutionary movements were limited in their scope and failed in the short run, but in the long run they did foster fundamental changes in the European political system. In the next century, Europe had to contend with the coming of democracy, increasing equality before the law, and the ever present possibility of popular revolution. The very vocabulary of modern politics took shape in this period. "Revolution" acquired new meaning, as did "liberty," "equality," "citizen," "patriot," "nation," "rights," and "constitution."

The causes of this revolutionary wave were many, and they differed somewhat from country to country. One of the most important was the financial burden of war imposed on governments by the War of the Austrian Succession, the Seven Years' War, and the American Revolution. Although wealthier economies and state borrowing—which soared in this period—cushioned the impact, governments were eventually forced to impose significantly heavier taxes on their citizens, which caused widespread resentment. Britain is a prime example. In 1790, the British national debt was fifteen times what it had been in 1707, but even so, the government had to increase yearly tax loads from about 5 million pounds to about 18 million pounds to cover its escalating military expenses. Under the new political conditions of the late eighteenth century, revolution became an ever more likely response. Thus although Britain managed to escape state bankruptcy and revolution at home, it did not escape the revolt of thirteen of its North American colonies when it tried to force these colonies to pay a greater share of the tax burden after 1763.

Several factors brought about this revolutionary response to tax increases in the later eighteenth century.

First was the emergence of a larger, wealthier middle class that lacked the financial and other privileges enjoyed by the nobility and other privileged orders. Although most wealthy middle-class people wanted to join these orders, not destroy them, resentments were bound to bubble up when issues of tax assessments were raised. It is thus not surprising that the largest number of revolutionary leaders came from middle-class professional backgrounds. In the past, peasants had participated in tax revolts, but they had lacked the means and the program to carry off full-scale changes of regime. The middle class, by contrast, had the wealth, organization, communication skills, and vision to bring about true revolutions. The result was the formation of committees of correspondence, primitive party structures, and militias to enact revolutionary agendas, usually with the use of violence.

Second, the philosophes and their allies had revealed a vast number of cracks in the old system that needed to be fixed. As reformers, the philosophes did not advocate revolution. But the impact of their work was to make the Old Regime seem at best inefficient and at worst wholly illegitimate. Not only did the Enlightenment point out failings in the old system, but it also raised expectations about the possibility of correcting them, thereby making full-scale revolution appear feasible.

Third, rising literacy rates and an expanded press—in the form of books and newspapers—had given "public opinion" fresh means to express itself. Dissenters, in particular, had new tools to generate groundswells of discontent. They were particularly clever at fomenting a sense of "crisis" by raising the imminent threat of "despotism," one of the surest signs of which was the heavier tax burden imposed by the state.

Finally, even though local conditions dictated different revolutionary agendas, revolution was contagious. The American Revolution set a powerful example for Europeans to study and to imitate, first, because it was successful, and second, because it was justified by Locke's theory of universal "natural rights," which could be adjusted to validate demands almost anywhere. According to Locke, the sole purpose of government was to protect the rights of life, liberty, and property that all humankind enjoyed as gifts from God and nature; if a government did not adequately protect these rights or violated them, it could be legitimately replaced. Under this theory, discontents of many kinds in many national contexts could be objected to as violations of natural rights—most importantly tax increases, which were represented as an assault on the right to property and a threat to liberty in general. Once the French Revolution began, revolution was given a further boost, especially when French armies advanced into central Europe.

Among the first places in Europe that witnessed the formation of revolutionary movements were the United Provinces and Austrian Netherlands. In the United Provinces, a Dutch "Patriot" movement emerged during the 1780s that clashed with the ruling house of Orange over demands for a more democratic government and a less pro-British foreign policy. The movement managed to raise a militia backed by the French government, but the revolution was snuffed out when the king of Prussia, aided by the British, intervened militarily and easily crushed the Patriots for the time being. In the Austrian Netherlands, an insurgent coalition managed to expel Austrian troops by 1789, also in the name of "liberty." But weakened by internal divisions, this uprising collapsed, and the Austrians returned in 1790. By then it had become clear that the revolutionary cause was not going to be won without a struggle.

The French Revolution

Unquestionably, the European revolution with the greatest impact was the French Revolution, which was also the most radical of all. As in the case of many revolutions at this time, the immediate cause was financial. In the late 1780s, the French state faced bankruptcy and tried to do something about it. By doing so, however, it touched off the French Revolution in 1789 for reasons that have been hotly debated. Some historians have argued that the Revolution was a result of social tensions, while others have contended that the crisis was chiefly political in nature. Over the last quarter-century, the second view has prevailed. Even so, many social forces helped shape the course of the Revolution once it began, making it necessary to examine both the French political system and French society in order to explain the Revolution's genesis and history.

The French State in the Later Eighteenth Century

The French state was not so much overthrown at the end of the eighteenth century as it collapsed. Problems began at the top. Louis XV (1710–1774) was not an unintelligent or irresponsible ruler, but he was distant, secretive, and often indecisive. Many French people, as well as foreigners, concluded that he was not acting in accordance with the needs of the French nation, but upon the demands of his many mistresses, most notably Madame de Pompadour (1721–1764). When Louis XV died in 1774, his reputation was at a low point. Far from mourning his death, the French people celebrated it with a round of insulting jokes. Hopes ran high that his successor, Louis XVI (1754–1793), would clean house and restore luster to France's tarnished image. But Louis XVI provided no sense of strength and direction. Socially awkward and apparently slow-witted, he was unable to have normal sexual relations with his wife for seven years into their marriage, an incapacity that made him appear weak in public eyes and a target of coarse humor. Worse, he was widely thought to be dominated by his wife, the Austrian-born Marie Antoinette (1755–1793). Although she was admired at first, the queen quickly acquired a reputation—most of it undeserved—as a callous, sexually perverse agent of a hated foreign power, and her unpopularity inevitably rubbed off on Louis XVI. That the kings seemed to be spineless creatures of their women for nearly a century was especially damaging politically in an absolutist regime like France's, since the king was the symbol of the entire state. Weakness in the king was yet another sign that France was falling into a "despotism," since it was assumed that a weak king could be manipulated more easily by backstairs interest groups seeking their own advantage at the expense of the nation.

Another factor in the collapse of the state was France's fall in international standing. The outcome of the Seven Years' War was devastating to France, since it brought the loss of most of France's overseas empire. Much of the blame was directed at the alliance France had signed with its old enemy, Austria, in 1756, but the regime refused to abandon this unpopular arrangement. On the contrary, it reinforced it with the marriage of the future Louis XVI to Marie Antoinette. During Louis XVI's reign (1774–1792), there was only one notable foreign policy success: France helped thirteen American colonies gain their independence and bloody their common enemy, Britain. But this victory hardly reversed an overall diplomatic decline. The American Revolution imposed enormous debts on France that it could not afford, making it hard for France to act effectively elsewhere. Moreover, it was preceded and followed by Austrian, Russian, and Prussian power-grabs in eastern Europe that upset the stability France desperately wanted to maintain in order to save its dwindling resources for the fight against Britain. When in 1787 Russian and Austria went to war with the Ottoman Empire—an old French diplomatic partner—the French response was negligible and showed the extent of French decline. Another humiliation was the collapse of the Dutch Patriot movement in the same year, which also advertised France's inability to protect its foreign allies. For a nation that prided itself on being the "first power in the world," this was a poor showing indeed, and the French people clearly considered the decline of French fortunes abroad to be a major sign of the Old Regime's failure.

At home, the regime also lost its grip. Battles over Jansenism and fresh taxes needed for war erupted again in the early 1750s and culminated in the abolition of the Parlement in 1771, which in turn unleashed a flood of pamphlets—many of them Jansenist inspired—denouncing the alleged arrival of "despotism." Partly to regain the support of public opinion, Louis XVI reinstated the Parlement shortly after he became king in 1774, and relations between the Crown and the Parlement improved until the eve of the French Revolution. But the debate over the extent and nature of royal power hardly ended, and accusations of "despotism" continued to flow in regard to other issues, such as state censorship of the press and the antiquated judicial system. There were some reform experiments: the military was streamlined, and Protestants gained limited toleration. But reform did not keep pace with the high expectations fanned by the Enlightenment.

The most urgent problem was finances. The American Revolution added more than a billion livres to a debt that had already risen to more than 2 billion livres. As a result, the state's credit rating fell so low that lenders began charging the monarchy a whopping 10 percent on loans, and eventually the government had trouble securing loans even at this extraordinary rate. (Because of its greater reliability, the English government paid only 3 to 4 percent on loans, which greatly lowered the annual cost of servicing its enormous debt.) The French government was obliged to spend an increasing percentage of its budget on interest payments, which in turn forced increases in taxes to cover spending. Already in 1774, Turgot, the reform minister who was also a philosophe close to the Physiocrats, sought to break out of this vicious cycle by increasing tax revenues through expansion of the economy. The key to this expansion was removal of state controls on the grain trade and the elimination of the guilds. But his experiments were spoiled by a temporary famine, and Turgot was dismissed after only two years because he alienated the king and other ministers with his undisguised personal ambition.

Turgot was followed by Jacques Necker (1732–1804), a Swiss banker, as chief financial officer. Necker intended to fix state finances by making the state's financial institutions work more efficiently through reforms in tax collection and the treasury. In the meantime, Necker was forced to continue heavy borrowing, but he hoped to attract loans at lower interest by persuading lenders of the government's financial health. To achieve this goal, Necker published a misleadingly optimistic account of state finances in 1781. An effort to win "public opinion" to the monarchy's side, this document became an instant bestseller, because, however sanitized, it provided the French people with their first full view of state finances. Other ministers were shocked by this revelation of what they regarded as state secrets. Necker's many rivals conspired to get Necker fired in 1781, and most of his reforms were undone by his successors.

In 1783, Charles Alexandre de Calonne (1734–1802) became chief finance minister. Calonne initially tried to stimulate the economy through extra state spending. But this policy added so much to the already inflated debt that by 1786 he changed direction and produced another version of Turgot's plan. Its main provisions included the elimination of controls on the grain trade, the implementation of a general land tax to replace others, and the calling of an Assembly of Notables (deputies handpicked by the crown) to validate his package and approve new loans. Calonne's program was supported by the king, and the Assembly met in early 1787. Little did anyone realize that it was the overture to the French Revolution.

French Economy and Society

In the eighteenth century, France, like other countries, was still a nation in which legally defined privileges divided subjects into separate and unequal groups, and there were few demands to eliminate these privileges outright. But the Enlightenment had made privileges appear less justifiable than before, and the philosophes' demand that all social institutions prove their usefulness had forced the French nobility, in particular, to be on the defensive. The monarchy, too, helped to discredit privileges by turning noble status into a purchasable commodity rather than a reward for merit, thereby stripping privileges of their ancient prestige. Moreover, by eroding the tax exemptions that went with noble status in order to expand its tax base, the government made it easier to imagine the nation functioning without privileges. The French Revolution eventually suppressed privileges altogether in favor of universal rights.

The weakening case for maintaining privileges interacted with other developments that exacerbated social tensions, most notably the uneven expansion of the economy. Growth of population from about 23 million in 1715 to 28 million in 1789 stimulated production in many sectors. The demand for grain rose most dramatically, but there was also a growing market for goods that made life more comfortable—from underwear to medical devices—and diets more interesting—from sugar to coffee. Colonial trade experienced the greatest growth—1000 percent over the eighteenth century—and there were also significant increases in manufacturing. Yet the new wealth did not reach everyone. Sectors of the economy connected to foreign trade and the manufacture of new commercial goods generally did well in the period of 1730–1770, but other sectors enjoyed much less prosperity. Whereas enclosure allowed England to become a nation of large, efficient farms, France retained a large number of small farms, and the number of poor landless peasants rose. Wage increases did not keep pace with the rise in prices, and the gap between the wealthy and the poor widened, leading to increasing discontent. Moreover, by the 1770s, the general economic picture darkened. An Anglo-French treaty of 1786 that lowered tariffs on imported goods resulted in widespread unemployment and misery in the crucial textile industry because English goods were produced more cheaply.

In the midst of this unbalanced economic expansion, the size of the middle classes increased as a percentage of the population over the eighteenth century—doubling or tripling while the population overall grew only by about a third. Many middle-class people hoped to convert their wealth into noble status. Indeed, in France it was easier to climb into the nobility than it was in England, mainly because in France one could purchase an expensive venal office that conferred noble status on an entire family within as little as twenty years. As a result of the natural extinction of older noble families and of venal ennoblement, by 1789 few French noble families could legitimately claim to have enjoyed noble status for more than two centuries. Ironically, this situation caused more resentment than satisfaction: resentment among the nobles that ennoblement was too easy and allowed newcomers to dilute the prestige of noble titles, and resentment among the middle classes that ennoblement still took too long and was too expensive. In their education, investments, outlook, and even social background, the nobility and the middle classes were becoming increasingly alike, which made noble privileges appear unfair and arbitrary.

The peasants also saw that in many respects the legal system of privilege was working against their interests. Although it is not clear if the amount paid in feudal dues (customary payments owed to landlords) was increasing during the eighteenth century, landlords certainly became more efficient at collecting them, even when peasants received little or nothing in return. Peasants were probably more concerned about royal taxes, but they became increasingly resentful of attempts to revive these antiquated rights. In a number of instances, peasants even took their landlords to court to prevent them from reimposing feudal dues that had not been collected for many years. In this cause, the peasants received help from powerful allies. Attacks on the

inefficiency and unfairness of "feudalism" poured from the pens of the Physiocrats and philosophes. Some of these attacks were subsidized by the
monarchy, which hoped to reduce or eliminate feudal dues so that it could
squeeze the peasantry more heavily itself. Reversing the charges of "despotism" directed against the Crown, writers working for the state argued that
feudal dues were vestiges of the landlords' medieval "tyranny" and should
be abolished. Indeed, the king set an example by abolishing the remnants of
serfdom in his personal domain as a violation of natural law on the eve of the
French Revolution. Once again, the old order stood condemned, even by
those who were its outstanding representatives and stood to lose the most if
the Old Regime crumbled.

It is unlikely that these social tensions would have produced the French
Revolution on their own, and it is possible that a wiser monarchy could have
avoided the collapse of government finances. But clearly France was overdue
for some serious structural reforms, and once the crisis of the state burst into
political revolution, a host of socioeconomic issues arose as well—ranging
from the status of women to the social role of government—thereby adding
to the revolutionaries' burden of rebuilding the nation.

The Outbreak of the Revolution

The Assembly of Notables was convened early in 1787 to consider the package of financial proposals put together by Calonne with the backing of the
king. Contrary to Calonne's and Louis XVI's expectations, the Assembly
balked at the new tax proposals. Although it did approve other parts of
Calonne's plan, including deregulation of the grain trade, this was not
enough to resolve the financial crisis. Fully discredited, Calonne was
replaced by one of the leaders of the opposition in the Assembly, Loménie de
Brienne (1724–1794), who wound up proposing a plan similar to Calonne's.
But the Assembly also refused to approve Brienne's plan, leading to its dissolution in May 1787. Brienne was left trying to strike a deal with the Parlements, whose approval was a political necessity. But the Parlements
refused to agree to Brienne's proposals, insisting that only an Estates General
(a defunct assembly of deputies elected from the three estates throughout the
realm) could ratify them. The monarchy at first refused to agree to this
demand, and in May 1788 it abolished the Parlements and instituted a new
court system. The result was a nationwide outpouring of protests that perceived in this measure a clear sign of encroaching "despotism." After a summer of angry discontent, the monarchy relented in August 1788, mostly
because it was now virtually bankrupt. The king fired Brienne, recalled
Necker as chief finance minister, and agreed to call a meeting of the Estates
General. Relief and joy greeted this fateful decision.

But the calling of the Estates General only opened up a new debate—this
one on voting procedures. In the last Estates General of 1614, representatives
of the three estates (clergy, nobility, commoners) had voted separately, and all
estates had to approve proposals put before them. This time, however, there

were hopes that the representatives of a now seemingly united nation should meet in one large assembly. In September, the Paris Parlement rejected this idea. In the belief that custom should be maintained to prevent the king from manipulating the upcoming meeting, it recommended that the estates vote separately. To many leaders of the commoners (or third estate) and their allies, the decision was a signal that certain members of the privileged orders were plotting to dominate the Estates General. In response, a fresh outpouring of pamphlets indicted the nobility and clergy for their desertion of the common front against "despotism." Indeed, some pamphleteers, most notably the abbé Emmanuel Sieyès (1748–1836), now claimed that the nobility should no longer be counted as part of the "nation," a term that in Sieyès's view included only the third estate. Although in December 1788 the monarchy allowed the third estate to double the customary number of its representatives, this decision did not settle the question of whether all the deputies would vote in one large assembly or in separate estates. It was in an atmosphere of heightened confusion, fear, and suspicion in early 1789 that the nation elected representatives for the first time in nearly two centuries and drew up lists of grievances to guide their voting.

A final difficulty was the weather. Hail and drought had reduced the wheat harvest in 1788, and the winter of 1788–1789 was so bitter that the Seine froze over at Paris, blocking arrivals of grain and flour by barge, the usual way of shipping bulky goods. Half-starved and half-frozen, Parisians huddled around bonfires provided by the municipal government. By the spring of 1789 the price of bread had almost doubled—a very serious matter, for bread was the mainstay of the diet, and workers normally spent almost half their wages on bread for their families. Now they faced the prospect of having to lay out almost all their wages for bread alone.

France had survived bad weather and poor harvests many times in the past without experiencing revolution; this time, however, the economic hardships were the last straw. Starving peasants begged, borrowed, and stole, poaching on the hunting preserves of the great lords and attacking their game wardens. The concern over meat and bread in Paris erupted in a riot in April 1789 at the establishment of Réveillon, a wealthy wallpaper manufacturer who, it was rumored, intended to cut his workers' wages.

The method of electing the deputies aided the champions of reform. In each district of France the third estate made its choice indirectly, at the public meeting, by choosing electors who later selected a deputy. Since this procedure greatly favored the articulate, middle-class lawyers and government administrators won control of the commoners' deputation. The reforming deputies of the third estate found some sympathizers in the second estate and many more in the first, where the discontented poorer priests had a large delegation.

Upon the Estates General's convocation on May 5, 1789, the monarchy immediately lost the initiative when it presented no coherent program to solve the financial crisis and refused to settle the voting controversy. After weeks of argument, the third estate met on June 17, voted to transform itself

Marie Antoinette's sense of regal isolation from the larger problems of the French nation is illustrated unintentionally by this flattering portrait of her and her children at Versailles. The artist, Elisabeth Vigée-Lebrun (1755–1842), was a leading court painter who emphasized the sense of grace so important to royalty at the time. After the Revolution she emigrated to Italy and then to Russia. The painting hangs today in the Musée de Versailles.   (Réunion des Musées Nationaux/Art Resource, NY)

into the National Assembly—an institution that did not, like the Estates General, meet at the pleasure of the king—and invited deputies of the other estates to join them. Finding its chamber locked because of preparations for a royal address, the representatives of the third estate met in an emergency session at an indoor tennis court. On June 20 they took what became known as the "Tennis Court Oath," in which they swore not to disband until France had a new constitution. Although on June 27 the king finally consented to voting in one grand body, it was clear that events were spinning beyond his control, and reform was rapidly turning into revolution.

The Dissolution of the Monarchy

The National Assembly had barely settled down to work when a new wave of rioting swept over France, further undermining the position of the king. Economic difficulties grew more severe in the summer of 1789. Unemployment increased, and bread seemed likely to remain scarce and expensive, at least until after the harvest. Meanwhile, the commoners feared that the king and the privileged orders might attempt a counterrevolution. Large concentrations of troops appeared in the Paris area early in July—to preserve order and protect the National Assembly, the king asserted. But the Parisians suspected that Louis was planning the forcible dissolution of the Assembly. Suspicion deepened into conviction after Louis dismissed Jacques Necker.

Popular Uprisings, July–October 1789

Reaction to Necker's dismissal was immediate. On July 12 and 13 the Parisian electors formed a new municipal government and a new militia, the National Guard, both loyal to the National Assembly. Paris was forging the weapons that made it the leader of the Revolution. Crowds were roaming the streets, demanding cheaper bread and parading busts of Necker draped in black. On July 14 they broke into government buildings in search of arms. They found one arsenal in the Invalides, the great military hospital, and they hoped to find another in the Bastille, a fortress-prison in the eastern part of the city.

An armed group several hundred strong stormed the Bastille, killing part of the garrison and suffering many casualties themselves. The legend, cherished by defenders of the Old, Regime, that participants in the assault were simply "rabble" or a "mob" is untrue. An official list of participants compiled some time after the event showed that most were neighborhood merchants and artisans, especially woodworkers. The fall of the Bastille was of enormous symbolic significance. Although there were only seven prisoners to be released, an aroused people had demonstrated what it could accomplish. The capture and subsequent demolition of the Bastille did much to ensure the destruction of the Old Regime, as rioting spread throughout France in July 1789. Thus the Fourteenth of July became the great French national holiday, the counterpart of the American Fourth of July.

Parts of the countryside, meantime, were experiencing the Great Fear, an extraordinary attack of mass delusion. From village to village word spread that "brigands" were coming, aristocratic hirelings who would destroy the now ripe crops and force the National Assembly to preserve the status quo. There were in fact no bands of brigands, only an occasional starving farmhand and, on some occasions, foraging national guardsmen trying to steal food. But the peasants in several districts went berserk, grabbing hoes and

This contemporary work shows the march of the fishwives and other women to Versailles in October 1789.   (New York Public Library Picture Collection)

pitchforks, anything resembling a weapon, and driving many of the nobility to flight and ultimately to emigration. They attacked châteaux and broke into other buildings that might house a hoard of grain or the hated documents justifying collection of manorial dues. Some nobles voluntarily gave the peasants what they wanted; others saw their barns and archives burnt; a few were lynched.

The October Days, the last crisis of a tumultuous year, again demonstrated the impotence of Louis XVI and the power of his aroused subjects. The harvest of 1789 had been good, but a drought crippled the operation of water-mills for grinding flour from the wheat. Thus, as autumn drew on, Parisians still lined up for bread and still looked suspiciously at the royal troops stationed near their city. Rumors of the queen's behavior at Versailles further incensed them: Marie Antoinette made a dramatic appearance at a banquet of royal officers, clutching the heir to the throne in her arms, striking the pose that her mother, Maria Theresa, had employed to win the support of the Hungarians in the 1740s. And on hearing that the people had no bread, she was reported to have remarked callously, "Let them eat cake." This story was false, but it was repeated in the lively new Paris papers that delighted in denouncing the queen.

The climax came on October 5, when an array of determined market-women and fishwives, neatly dressed milliners, and even middle-class "ladies with hats" marched from Paris to Versailles in the rain to demand bread. They disrupted the National Assembly and penetrated the palace, where they might have lynched Marie Antoinette if she had not taken refuge with the king. The next day the women marched back to Paris, escorting the royal family, who took up residence in the Tuileries Palace. More important, the National Assembly also moved to Paris.

Forging a New Regime

The outlines of the new regime were already starting to take shape before the October Days. The Great Fear prompted the National Assembly to abolish in law what the peasants were destroying in fact. On the evening of August 4, 1789, the deputies voted that taxation would be paid by all inhabitants of the kingdom in proportion to their revenues, and that public expenses would be borne equally by all. The clergy also gave up tithes, and the liberal minority of the second estate surrendered the nobility's game preserves and manorial dues and courts. The Assembly abolished the remnants of serfdom, forbade the sale of justice or of judicial office, and decreed that "all citizens, without distinction of birth, can be admitted to all ecclesiastical, civil, and military posts and dignities." The Old Regime was effectively dead.

Three weeks later, on August 26, the National Assembly approved a Declaration of the Rights of Man. "Men are born and remain free and equal in rights," it asserted. "These rights are liberty, property, security, and resistance to oppression." It called property "an inviolable and sacred right" and liberty "the exercise of the natural rights of each man" within the limits "determined by law." "Law," the Declaration stated, "is the expression of the general will." Further, "Every society in which the guarantee of rights is not assured or the separation of powers not determined has no constitution."*

The Declaration of the Rights of Man mirrored the economic and political attitudes of the middle class, although it was also attractive to many aristocrats. It insisted on the sanctity of property, and it proclaimed that "social distinctions may be based only on usefulness," thus implying that some social distinctions were to be expected. It incorporated the key phrases of the philosophes: natural rights, general will, and separation of powers. The National Assembly made a resounding statement of the ideals of the Enlightenment; yet, as the subsequent history of the Revolution demonstrated, it found no formula by which to translate these ideals into practice.

The economic legislation of the National Assembly provided a case in point. Belief in the theory of equal taxation did not solve urgent financial problems, for the new and just land tax imposed by the deputies could not be collected. Tax collectors had vanished in the general liquidation of the Old Regime, and peasants now assumed that they owed the government nothing. Once again, the French state borrowed until its credit was exhausted, and

---

*Quoted in Georges Lefèbvre, *The Coming of the French Revolution,* trans. R. R. Palmer (Princeton, N.J.: Princeton University Press, 1976), pp. 221–23.

| *A Closer Look* |

THE DECLARATION OF THE RIGHTS OF MAN AND THE CITIZEN, 1789

Here is the full text:

The representatives of the French people, organized in National Assembly, considering that ignorance, forgetfulness, or contempt of the rights of man are the sole causes of public misfortunes and of the corruption of governments, have resolved to set forth in a solemn declaration the natural, inalienable, and sacred rights of man, in order that such declaration, continually before all members of the social body, may be a perpetual reminder of their rights and duties; in order that the acts of the legislative power and those of the executive power may constantly be compared with the aim of every political institution and may accordingly be more respected; in order that the demands of the citizens, founded henceforth upon simple and incontestable principles, may always be directed towards the maintenance of the Constitution and the welfare of all.

Accordingly, the National Assembly recognizes and proclaims, in the presence and under the auspices of the Supreme Being, the following rights of man and citizen.

1. Men are born and remain free and equal in rights; social distinctions may be based only upon general usefulness.

2. The aim of every political association is the preservation of the natural and inalienable rights of man; these rights are liberty, property, security, and resistance to oppression.

3. The source of all sovereignty resides essentially in the nation; no group, no individual, may exercise authority not emanating expressly therefrom.

4. Liberty consists of the power to do whatever is not injurious to others; thus the enjoyment of the natural rights of every man has for its limits only those that assure other members of society the enjoyment of those same rights; such limits may be determined only by law.

5. The law has the right to forbid only actions that are injurious to society. Whatever is not forbidden by law may not be prevented, and no one may be constrained to do what it does not prescribe.

6. Law is the expression of the general will; all citizens have the right to concur personally, or through their representatives, in its formation; it must be the same for all, whether it protects or punishes. All citizens, being equal before it, are equally admissible to all public offices, positions, and employments, according to their capacity, and without other distinction than that of virtues and talents.

7. No man may be accused, arrested, or detained except in the cases determined by law, and according to the forms prescribed thereby. Whoever solicit, expedite, or execute arbitrary orders, or have them executed, must be punished; but every citizen summoned or apprehended in pursuance of the law must obey immediately; he renders himself culpable by resistance.

8. The law is to establish only penalties that are absolutely and obviously necessary; and no one may be punished except by virtue of a law established and promulgated prior to the offense and legally applied.

9. Since every man is presumed innocent until declared guilty, if arrest be deemed indispensable, all unnecessary severity for securing the person of the accused must be severely repressed by law.

10. No one is to be disquieted because of his opinions, even religious, provided their manifestation does not disturb the public order established by law.

11. Free communication of ideas and opinions is one of the most precious of the rights of man. Consequently, every citizen may speak, write, and print freely, subject to responsibility for the abuse of such liberty in the cases determined by law.

12. The guarantee of the rights of man and citizen necessitates a public force; such a force, therefore, is instituted for the advantage of all and not for the particular benefit of those to whom it is entrusted.

13. For the maintenance of the public force and for the expenses of administration a common tax is indispensable; it must be assessed equally on all citizens in proportion to their means.

14. Citizens have the right to ascertain, by themselves or through their representatives, the necessity of the public tax, to consent to it freely, to supervise its use, and to determine its quota, assessment, payment, and duration.

15. Society has the right to require of every public agent an accounting of his administration.

16. Every society in which the guarantee of rights is not assured or the separation of powers not determined has no constitution at all.

17. Since property is a sacred and inviolable right, no one may be deprived thereof unless a legally established public necessity obviously requires it, and upon condition of a just and previous indemnity.

As presented and translated in Isaac Kramnick, ed., *The Portable Enlightenment Reader* (New York: Penguin Books, 1995), pp. 466–68.

then, in desperation, the National Assembly ordered the confiscation of church lands (November 1789).

The government thus acquired assets worth at least 2 billion livres. On the basis of this collateral it issued *assignats*, paper notes used to pay the government's debts, which temporarily eased the financial crisis. Unfortunately, the Revolution repeated the mistake of John Law at the time of the Mississippi Bubble: It did not know when to stop. As the state sold parcels of confiscated land—that is, as it reduced the collateral securing its paper money—it was expected to destroy the same amount of assignats. But the temptation not to reduce the number of assignats proved too great to resist, and inflation resulted. The assignats, progressively losing their solid backing, depreciated until in 1795 they were worth less than 5 percent of their face value.

The state sold at auction the property seized from the church and from aristocratic *émigrés* (those who had left the country). Some peasants profited by the opportunity to enlarge their holdings, and many bourgeois also bought up land, sometimes as a short-term speculation. The poor and landless, however, gained nothing, since they could not afford to buy, and the National Assembly made no move to help them. Following laissez-faire doctrines, the Assembly abolished the guilds and the tariffs and tolls on trade within France. And deeming the few simple organizations of labor unnatural restrictions on economic freedom, it abolished them, too. In June 1791, after an outbreak of strikes, it passed the Loi de Chapelier, banning strikes, labor unions, and many guilds.

Reforming the Church

Since the suppression of tithes and the seizure of ecclesiastical property deprived the church of its revenue, the National Assembly agreed to finance ecclesiastical salaries. The new arrangement made the French church subject to constant government regulation. Few difficulties arose from the Assembly's prohibition of monastic vows or from the liquidation of some monasteries and convents, since many of these establishments were already far gone in decay, but an uproar arose over legislation altering the status of the secular clergy.

The Civil Constitution of the Clergy (June 1790) redrew the ecclesiastical map of France. It reduced the number of bishoprics by more than a third, making the remaining dioceses correspond to new civil administrative units. It transformed bishops and priests into civil officials, paid by the state and elected by the population of the diocese or parish. A new bishop was required to take an oath of loyalty to the state.

These provisions ran counter to the tradition of the Roman church as an independent ecclesiastical monarchy. Naturally the pope denounced the Civil Constitution. When the National Assembly then required that every member of the French clergy take a special oath supporting the Civil Constitution, only a few bishops and fewer than half the priests complied. Thus a breach was opened between the leaders of the Revolution and a large segment of the population. From Louis XVI down to humble peasants, Catholics rallied to the nonjuring clergy, as those who refused the special oath were termed. The Counter-Revolution now had a cause to represent.

After the summer of 1789, alarmed prelates and nobles fled France, leaving behind more rich estates to be confiscated. Many émigrés gathered in the German Rhineland to intrigue for Austrian and Russian support of a counterrevolution. The king's misgivings about the Civil Constitution of the Clergy prompted his disastrous attempt to join the émigrés on the Franco-German frontier. In June 1791, three months before the completion of the new constitution, Louis and Marie Antoinette left the Tuileries disguised as a valet and governess. But a local official along the route recognized Louis; the alarm was sent ahead, and a detachment of troops forced the royal party to make a

A Closer Look

WOMEN'S RIGHTS IN THE FRENCH REVOLUTION

Olympe de Gouges (1748–1793) was a leading female revolutionary. A butcher's daughter and actress, she believed that women had the same inalienable rights as men. In 1791 she addressed her *Declaration of the Rights of Woman* and for the next two years demanded that the revolutionary government act upon it. In November 1793, the National Convention, worried that her feminist demands would threaten the revolution by losing supporters for it and determined to close all revolutionary women's clubs in Paris, charged her with treason. Found guilty, she was sent to the guillotine.

Following are the first ten of the basic rights set forth in the Declaration:

1. Woman is born free and remains equal to man in rights. Social distinctions can be founded only on general utility.

2. The goal of all political association is the preservation of the natural and imprescriptible rights of Woman and Man: These rights are liberty, property, security, and above all resistance to oppression.

3. The source of all sovereignty resides in the nation, which is nothing but the union of Woman and Man: No body, no individual, may exercise any authority not emanating expressly therefrom.

4. Liberty and justice consist of returning all that belongs to another; thus, the only limits on the exercise of woman's natural rights are the perpetual tyranny wielded by men; these limits must be reformed by the law of nature and the law of reason.

5. The laws of nature and of reason prohibit all actions harmful to society: Anything not forbidden by these wise and divine laws, cannot be forbidden, and no one can be forced to do that which the law does not require.

6. The law should be the expression of the general will; all female and male citizens should concur either personally or by their representatives in its formulation; it should be the same for all: All female and male citizens are equal in its eyes, and equally entitled to all honors, places and public employments according to their abilities without any other distinction than that of their virtues and their talents.

7. No woman is an exception; she is accused, arrested, and detained in cases determined by law. Women, like men, obey this rigorous law.

8. The law should only impose those penalties which are strictly and absolutely necessary, and one may be punished only by a law that has been established and promulgated prior to the offense and legally applied to women.

9. Once a woman has been declared guilty, the law should be applied rigorously.

10. No one is to be harassed for their fundamental beliefs; a woman has the right to mount the scaffold; she also has the right to mount the rostrum, providing that her actions do not threaten lawful public order.*

---

*Olympe de Gouges, *La Nation à la Reine: Les Droits de la Femme* (Paris: Momoro, 1791), as translated by and quoted in *The Global Experience: Readings in World History since 1500*, 2nd ed., ed. Philip F. Riley et al. (Englewood Cliffs, N.J.: Prentice Hall, 1992), pp. 94–95.

hot, dusty, dispirited journey back to Paris. After the abortive flight, the revolutionaries viewed Louis XVI as a potential traitor and kept him closely guarded in the Tuileries.

Revolutionary Culture

The French Revolution gave rise to a new republican culture that in its forms and themes reflected the increasingly more democratic politics of the age. The collapse of censorship meant that almost anything could be published legally. In the early years of the Revolution, the nation was flooded with hundreds of new newspapers and thousands of pamphlets representing political viewpoints ranging from those of extreme left (radical revolutionaries) to those of the extreme right (resolute counterrevolutionaries). These publications were often used as springboards for political careers; thus it is not surprising that many of the Revolution's outstanding leaders were also journalists. Revolutionaries used the new unregulated press to debate current issues and to demonize their enemies, sometimes in vulgar ways. In a deliberate effort to offend polite sensibilities, the radical Jacques Hébert (1757–1794) peppered his widely read, popular journal *Father Duchesne* with obscenities. Among his favorite targets was Marie Antoinette. The unpopular queen was vilified by many other writers as well, some of whom pornographically depicted her alleged sexual perversions.

Altogether different in tone and taste were revolutionary festivals, such as those commemorating the anniversary of the storming of the Bastille. Attended by tens of thousands of spectators, these festivals—featuring statues of liberty, ceremonial mountains, cascading waterfalls, patriotic dancing, stirring music, and dramatic speeches—were intended to raise revolutionary awareness and teach citizenship to ordinary citizens. Relying upon a rich symbolism that identified the regenerated nation with the purity of nature, they sought to provide a substitute for the ancient emblems of the monarchy and church. Although Christian elements did appear prominently in the early festivals, these elements gradually disappeared as the Revolution became more radical.

Other rallying points for political action included political clubs that mushroomed throughout the nation almost overnight at the beginning of the Revolution. Among other activities, these clubs conducted debates on outstanding political issues, reported suspicious behavior to the authorities, and lobbied the National Assembly and regional governments on matters of concern. The most successful were the clubs that became associated with the faction known as the Jacobins, radical Republicans of the left. Although they originally admitted only people with property, the Jacobins established more than four hundred such clubs by 1791, and this number increased to over a thousand during the next two years, as membership requirements were gradually lowered. In addition to the Jacobin clubs were groups with more specialized agendas. Among them were more than sixty women's political associations, which flourished until they were closed down by the Terror in late

1793, a time when revolutionaries regarded female political activity with increasing suspicion.

The Constitution of 1791

The major undertaking of the National Assembly was the Constitution of 1791. To replace the bewildering complex of provincial units that had existed under the Old Regime, the Assembly divided the territory of France into eighty-three departments of approximately equal size; the departments were subdivided into *arrondissements*, or "districts," and the districts into communes—that is, municipalities. In the communes and departments, elected councils and officials enjoyed considerable self-government.

The Constitution established an independent, elected judiciary to replace the parlements and other courts of the Old Regime. It vested legislative authority in a single elected chamber. Although the king still headed the executive branch, his actions now required the approval of his ministers. The ministers, in turn, were responsible only to the king and not to the legislature, as they generally are in a parliamentary or cabinet government. Although the king received the power of veto, it was only a suspensive veto that could block legislation for a maximum of four years. The new constitution undertook to give France a uniform code of law, declared marriage a civil contract rather than a religious sacrament, and promised free public education.

While the constitution of 1791 went a long way toward popular government, implementing slogans of popular sovereignty and social equality, it stopped well short of full democracy. It created two classes of citizens—active and passive—and limited the right of voting to those male citizens who annually paid in taxes an amount equal to at least three days' wages for unskilled labor in their locality. The passive citizens, numbering about a third of the male population, enjoyed the full protection of the law but did not receive the vote. Moreover, the new legislature was chosen by indirect election. Active citizens voted for electors, who were required to be men of substantial wealth and who ultimately elected the deputies.

The Legislative Assembly

On October 1 the first and only Legislative Assembly elected under the new constitution began deliberations. No one faction commanded a majority in the new Assembly, although the Center had the most seats.* Since they occupied the lowest seats in the assembly hall, the deputies of the center received the derogatory nickname of the Plain or Marsh. The capable politicians of the left soon captured the votes of the Plain, following the leadership of a loose grouping of Jacobins known in time as *Girondins*. Their chief spokesman was

---

*In the practice followed by most Continental European assemblies, the right sat to the right of the presiding officer as he faced the assembly, the left to his left, and the center in between; thus the common usage of *left* for radical and *right* for conservative parties.

Jacques Brissot (1754–1793), an ambitious lawyer, journalist, and champion of reform causes. The Girondins were held together by their patriotic alarm over France's situation at home and abroad.

Accordingly, the Girondins specialized in fervent nationalist oratory. They pictured revolutionary France as the intended victim of a reactionary conspiracy—a conspiracy engineered by the émigrés, aided at home by the nonjuring clergy and the royal family, and abetted abroad by a league of monarchs under Leopold II, the Austrian emperor and brother of Marie Antoinette. The sudden death of Leopold in March 1792 and the accession of his inexperienced and less cautious son, Francis II (r. 1792–1835), increased the Austrian threat. On April 20 the Legislative Assembly declared war on Austria; the war was to continue, with a few brief intervals of peace, for the next twenty-three years.

The war went badly for France at the outset. Prussia soon joined Austria, and morale sagged on the home front when Louis dismissed the Girondin ministers because they had proposed to banish nonjuring priests and appointed more conservative replacements. Spirits began to rise in July, especially with a great celebration of the third anniversary of the assault on the Bastille. Paris was thronged with national guardsmen from the provinces on the way to the front, and the contingent from Marseilles introduced to the capital a patriotic hymn which became the national anthem of republican France.

Through the early summer of 1792 the Jacobins of Paris had been plotting an insurrection. They won the support of a formidable following—army recruits, national guardsmen, and the rank-and-file Parisians who were angered by the depreciation of assignats and by the high price and short supply of food and other necessities. One by one the forty-eight wards into which the city was divided came under the control of Jacobins. The climax came on the night of August 9–10, when the regular municipal authorities were ousted from the Paris city hall and the Jacobins installed a new and illegal commune.

The municipal revolution had immediate and momentous results. On the morning of August 10 the forces of the new commune, joined by national guardsmen, attacked the Tuileries and massacred the king's Swiss guards, while the royal family took refuge with the Legislative Assembly. With most of the deputies of the Right and the Plain absent, the Assembly voted to suspend the king from office, to imprison the royal family, and to order the election of a constitutional convention. Until this new body should meet, the government was to be run by an interim ministry staffed largely by Girondins, but in which the strong-man was Georges Danton (1759–1794), a radical and an exceptional orator.

The First Republic

The weeks between August 10 and the meeting of the Convention on September 21 were a time of extreme tension. The value of the assignats depreci-

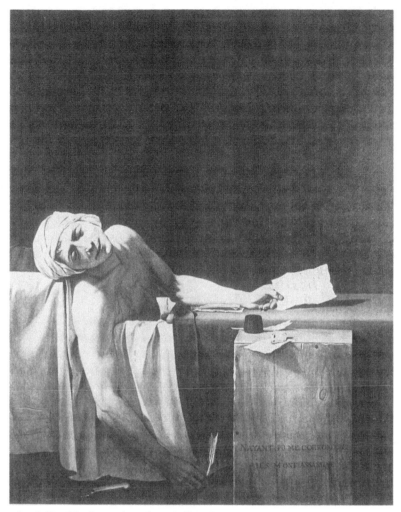

Jacques Louis David's dramatic and symbolic painting The Death of Marat *(1793) hangs in the Royal Museum of Fine Arts in Brussels. David drew upon the conventions of classical art while imposing a sense of dramatic realism on his work. The details of the composition provide narrative drive to the scene. Marat, David's friend, is seen as a betrayed hero. He lies in his bath, stabbed to death by a political enemy, Charlotte Corday (1769–1793), who was admitted to Marat's bath chamber on the basis of a letter he still holds.* (Erich Lessing/Art Resource, NY)

ated by 40 percent during August alone. Jacobin propagandists, led by Jean Paul Marat (1743–1793), an embittered Swiss physician turned journalist, continually excited the people of Paris. Excitement mounted still higher when the news arrived that Prussian troops had invaded northeastern France. In the emergency, Danton, the minister of justice, won immortality by urging patriots to employ "boldness, more boldness, always boldness."

In Paris, boldness took the form of the September Massacres, mass killings of supposed traitors and enemy agents made possible by the collapse of normal police authority. For five days, beginning on September 2, mobs moved from prison to prison; at each stop they held impromptu courts and summary executions. Neither the new Paris commune nor the national ministry could check the hysterical wave of killings. The number of victims exceeded a thousand and included ordinary criminals and prostitutes as well as aristocrats and nonjuring priests, who were often innocent of the treason with which they were charged. The September Massacres foreshadowed the terror to come.

On September 20 a rather minor French victory, grandly styled "the miracle of Valmy," turned the enemy forces back from the road to Paris; more solid French successes in Belgium, Savoy, and the Rhineland followed in late 1792. Then the tide turned again, washing away the conquests of the autumn. By the summer of 1793 a half-defeated France faced a hostile coalition including almost every major power in Europe. An atmosphere of perpetual emergency surrounded the Convention.

Gironde and Mountain, 1792–1793

In theory the election of deputies to the National Convention in 1792 marked the beginning of political democracy in France. Virtually all male citizens were invited to the polls. Yet less than a quarter of the potential electorate actually voted, the rest abstained or were turned away from the polls by the watchdogs of the Jacobin clubs, ever on the alert against "counterrevolutionaries." The Convention was numerically dominated by the Center, or the Plain, but again, as in the Legislative Assembly, the Plain was politically irresolute, although now sympathetic to a republic. Many ties existed between the Gironde on the right and the Mountain (so named because its deputies sat high up in the meeting hall), who made up the left.

Gironde and Mountain united to declare France a republic on September 21, 1792. The Girondins wanted a breathing spell in revolutionary legislation; they also defended provincial interests against possible encroachments by Paris. The Gironde, therefore, favored a large measure of federalism—which in the revolutionary vocabulary meant decentralization and a national government limited by many checks and balances. The details were set forth in a draft constitution completed early in 1793 by the marquis de Condorcet: The executive and the legislature would be independent of each other and separately elected; the results of elections would be adjusted according to proportional representation; laws would be submitted to a popular referendum; and voters could recall unworthy officials. But the leaders of the Mountain denounced federalism and advocated an all-powerful central government.

The chief spokesman for the Mountain was Maximilien Robespierre (1758–1794). This earnest young lawyer did not look like a revolutionary. He powdered his hair neatly and wore the knee breeches of the Old Regime. Yet Robespierre was a political extremist whose speeches were lay sermons couched in the language of a new faith. Apparently Robespierre was sure that he knew the general will, and that it demanded a Republic of Virtue. If the French would not act in a free and virtuous fashion voluntarily, then, as Rousseau had recommended, they should be "forced to be free."

Robespierre and the Republic of Virtue triumphed. The Mountain won out over the Gironde in the Convention. The first step came when, after one hundred hours of continuous voting, the Convention declared the king, "Citizen Louis Capet," guilty of treason, and by a narrow margin sentenced him to the guillotine without delay. Louis XVI died bravely on January 21, 1793.

In February the Convention rejected Condorcet's draft constitution and declared war on Britain, Spain, and the Netherlands. France now faced a formidable coalition of opponents, including Austria and Prussia. In March the French army suffered a series of defeats in the Low Countries. These defeats were largely blamed on the army generals. Their loyalty had been in doubt ever since the former marquis de Lafayette (1757–1834), a major political figure and the commander of the Army of the North, had defected to the Prussians in August 1792, when his political ambitions were frustrated by the rise of more radical factions. Now there was a new desertion to arouse concern among the revolutionaries. In April 1793 it was revealed that Charles-François Dumouriez (1739–1823), Lafayette's replacement, was plotting to march on Paris to overturn the revolutionary government. Instead, he deserted his post and passed over to the Austrians, sending a shock wave that deepened fears of a counterrevolutionary conspiracy throughout the country.

Marat now loudly denounced many Girondists as traitors; the Girondin deputies countered by calling for the impeachment of Marat, who was brought before a special tribunal and triumphantly acquitted. In July, Marat was assassinated in his bath by Charlotte Corday, a young woman wielding a butcher's knife who was convinced that she was a new Joan of Arc called to deliver France from Jacobin radicalism.

By then, however, the Girondins had been completely vanquished. In the face of unemployment, high prices, and shortages of food, soap, and other necessities, they had little to prescribe except more laissez faire. The sections, or wards, of Paris demanded price controls and food requisitioning; they also pressed for the expulsion of Girondins from the Jacobin clubs and the Convention. Finally, on June 2, 1793, a vast crowd of armed sansculottes from the sections, following the precedent of August 1792, invaded the hall and forced the arrest of twenty-nine Girondin deputies. Backed by these armed Parisians, the Mountain intimidated the Plain, and the Convention consigned the arrested Girondins to the guillotine. The Reign of Terror had begun.

The Reign of Terror, 1793–1794

How was it that the advocates of democracy now imposed a dictatorship on France? Let Robespierre explain:

> To establish and consolidate democracy, to achieve the peaceful rule of constitutional laws, we must first finish the war of liberty against tyranny.... We

must annihilate the enemies of the republic at home and abroad, or else we shall perish.

   If virtue is the mainstay of a democratic government in time of peace, then in time of revolution a democratic government must rely on virtue and terror. . . . Terror is nothing but justice, swift, severe, and inflexible; it is an emanation of virtue. . . . It has been said that terror is the mainstay of a despotic government. . . . The government of the revolution is the despotism of liberty against tyranny.*

The Convention duly voted a democratic constitution, drawn up by the Mountain, granting universal manhood suffrage and giving supreme power, unhampered by Girondin checks and balances, to a single legislative chamber. The constitution of 1793 was approved by a large majority, but its operation was deferred, and it never came into force.

The actual government of the Terror centered on a twelve-man Committee of Public Safety, composed of Robespierre and other stalwarts largely from the Mountain. Although nominally responsible to the Convention, the Committee of Public Safety acted as a kind of war cabinet. Never under the dominance of a single member, it really functioned as a committee—"The Twelve Who Ruled." A second committee, that of General Security, supervised police activities and turned suspected enemies of the republic over to the new Revolutionary Tribunal.

The Mountain scrapped much of the local self-government inaugurated under the constitution of 1791. It also whittled away steadily at the prerogatives assumed by the Paris sections. Local Jacobin clubs purged department and commune administrations of members considered politically unreliable. Special local courts supplemented the grim labors of the Revolutionary Tribunal. To make provincial France toe the line, the Mountain sent out trusted "deputies on mission."

The "swift, severe, and inflexible justice" demanded by Robespierre was administered in an increasingly arbitrary manner. To give the government a free hand, the Convention passed a vaguely worded "law of suspects" that indiscriminately criminalized many activities and ultimately allowed political considerations to outweigh matters of evidence and law in obtaining convictions. The number of victims who died as a result of the Terror remains open to debate. In the western region of the Catholic Vendée, where the government put down a violent counterrevolutionary insurgency with great force, upward of a quarter-million people may have perished. Elsewhere, it is estimated that thirty thousand to forty thousand people died through guillotining, shooting, drowning, hanging, and mistreatment in prison. Among those most vulnerable to the Terror were ex-nobles, the clergy, and conspicuous representatives of the Old Regime, including prominent women suspected of misusing their influence. Thus, the dethroned queen, Marie Antoinette, who in fact had corresponded and plotted with her Austrian relatives to relieve her increasingly desperate situation, was tried and guillotined on October 16, 1793, as a traitor. Shortly thereafter, Madame Jeanine

---

*Le Moniteur Universel, February 7, 1794. Our translation.

Dubarry, one of Louis XV's most sexually and financially notorious mistresses, was also tried and executed. Yet although their cases usually commanded less attention, the vast majority of those executed during the Terror were commoners who, because of insufficiently patriotic behavior, political revenge, or bad luck, were branded as counterrevolutionaries—as, no doubt, some actually were.

The wartime hysteria that helped to account for the excesses of the Terror also inspired a very practical patriotism. The army drafted all bachelors and widowers between the ages of eighteen and twenty-five. Hundreds of open-air forges were installed in Paris to manufacture weapons. By the close of 1793 the forces of the republic had driven foreign troops from French soil.

Credit for this new shift in the tide of battle did not rest solely with the Jacobins. The military successes of the republic reflected in part the improvements made in the army during the dying years of the Old Regime; they resulted still more from the weaknesses of the coalition aligned against France. Yet they could scarcely have been achieved without the new democratic spirit that allowed men of the third estate to become officers.

Total mobilization demanded equality of economic sacrifice. To combat inflation and scarcity, the Terror issued "maximum" legislation, placing ceilings on prices and wages. In theory, wages were held at a maximum 50 percent above the wage rate of 1790, and prices were halted at 33 percent above the price level of 1790. The government rationed meat and bread, forbade the use of the more expensive white flour, and directed all patriots to eat *pain d'é-galité* (equality bread), a loaf utilizing almost the whole of the wheat. Finally, early in 1794 the Convention passed the Laws of Ventôse, named for the third winter month in the new revolutionary calendar. These laws authorized seizure of the remaining properties of the émigrés and other opponents of the republic and recommended their distribution to landless French citizens.

Attempts by the government to enforce wage ceilings enraged Parisian workers. And although the "maximum" on prices temporarily checked the depreciation of the assignats, many price-controlled articles were available only on the black market, which even the government had to patronize. Moreover, the redistribution of property permitted by the Laws of Ventôse was never implemented.

The Terror presented its most revolutionary aspect in its drastic social and cultural reforms. The Convention abolished slavery in the colonies (although it was to be reintroduced by Napoleon a decade later). At home, clothing, the arts, amusements, the calendar, religion, all were changed, for the Republic of Virtue could tolerate nothing that smelled of the Old Regime. Even the traditional forms of address, "Monsieur" and "Madame," gave way to "Citizen" and "Citizeness." The Convention also introduced the metric system as more in keeping with the Age of Reason; a special committee, devised new weights and measures based on the decimal system rather than on the haphazard accumulations of custom.

Sometimes the forces of tradition resisted the Terror, which tried to destroy the old religion but never succeeded in legislating a new faith. Many churches were closed and turned into barracks or administrative offices.

The guillotine was the symbol of the Reign of Terror. As crowds watched, prisoners were decapitated and their heads held up for display. Popular engravings were sold to townspeople unable to witness the executions so that they could be reminded of them. In this illustration Louis XVI is executed, his head ceremonially held out to the assembled revolutionary army.   (New York Public Library Picture Collection)

Some of the Jacobins launched a "de-Christianization" campaign to make Catholics into philosophes and their churches into "Temples of Reason." Robespierre, however, disliked the cult of Reason; the Republic of Virtue, he believed, should acknowledge an ultimate author of morality. The Convention therefore decreed in May 1794 that "the French people recognize the existence of the Supreme Being and the immortality of the soul."

The France of Robespierre demanded superhuman devotion to duty and inhuman indifference to hardship and bloodshed. During the first half of

The Written Record

THE DEATH OF A KING

There were many eyewitnesses to the events of the French Revolution. The English, of course, followed its destructive path with fascination. The following is an account (no doubt biased) by one such eyewitness. Henry Essex Edgeworth de Finmont (1745–1807), a Catholic who went to Paris to be spiritual director to the Irish who lived in the capital and became Louis XVI's confessor.

The carriage proceeded thus in silence to the Place de Louis XV,* and stopped in the middle of a large space that had been left round the scaffold: this space was surrounded with cannon and beyond an armed multitude extended as far as the eye could reach. . . . As soon as the King had left the carriage, three guards surrounded him, and would have taken off his clothes, but he repulsed them with haughtiness: he undressed himself untied his neckcloth, opened his shirt, and arranged it himself. The guards, whom the determined countenance of the King had for a moment disconcerted, seemed to recover their audacity. They surrounded him again, and would have seized his hands. What are you attempting, said the King, drawing back his hands. "To bind you," answered the wretches. To bind *me*, said the King with an indignant air. "No! I shall never consent to that: do what you have been ordered, but you shall never bind me. . . ."

Many voices were at the same time heard encouraging the executioners. They seemed reanimated themselves, in seizing with violence the most virtuous of Kings, they dragged him under the axe of the guillotine, which with one stroke severed his head from his body. All this passed in a moment. The youngest of the guards, who seemed about eighteen, immediately seized the head, and showed it to the people as he walked round the scaffold; he accompanied this monstrous ceremony with the most atrocious and indecent gestures. At first an awful silence prevailed; at length some cries of "Vive la République!" were heard. By degrees the voices multiplied, and in less than ten minutes this cry, a thousand times repeated, became the universal shout of the multitude, and every hat was in the air.

From *English Witnesses of the French Revolution*, ed. J. M. Thompson (Oxford: Basil Blackwell, 1938), pp. 230–31.

*Now the Place de la Concorde.

1794 Robespierre pressed the Terror so relentlessly that even the members of the Committees of Public Safety and General Security began to fear that they would be the next victims. The Law of the 22 Prairial, Year II (that is, June 10, 1794) enormously expanded the definition of "enemies of the people" who were subject to punishment by the Revolutionary Tribunal so as to include the following: "Those who have sought to disparage the National Convention . . . to have sought to impede the provisioning of Paris . . . to inspire discouragement . . . to mislead opinion, to deprave morals," and "those who, charged with public office, take advantage of it in order to serve the enemies of the Revolution, to harass patriots, or to oppress the people."*

Thus Robespierre began to lose his following both in the Convention and in the two powerful committees. More and more of his former supporters favored moderation and argued that the growing French success in the war called for less, not more, terror. The crucial day was the Ninth of Thermidor (the month of Heat, or July 27, 1794), when shouts of "Down with the tyrant!" and the refusal of the presiding officer to give Robespierre the floor blocked his efforts to address the Convention. The Convention ordered his arrest, and on the next day he went to the guillotine.

Why had Robespierre fallen so quickly? He lost control because of the very situation he had created. An idealist who believed that a political society must guarantee the natural rights of humanity, he also believed that a Supreme Being protects the oppressed and punishes their oppressors. He had concluded that it was temporarily necessary to suspend the institutions in which he believed in order to break the chains imposed by tradition, to return in time to a life based on the principles he espoused. He sought, therefore, to destroy each faction systematically as it arose against him. But the charges he brought against others who could be considered as idealistic as he, and the summary justice meted out by his followers angered and frightened opposition groups in his own party. They united to fight back, both to protect the principles they felt he had abandoned and to protect their own lives.

The Thermidorean Reaction and the Directory, 1794–1799

The leaders of the Thermidorean Reaction, or the move toward moderation, many of them former Jacobins, now dismantled the machinery of the Terror. They disbanded the Revolutionary Tribunal, recalled the deputies on mission, and deprived the Committees of Public Safety and General Security of their independent authority. They closed the Paris Jacobin club and invited the surviving Girondin deputies to resume their old seats in the Convention. They took the first step toward restoring Catholicism by permitting priests to celebrate Mass, although under state supervision and without state financial support.

But instability, personal insecurity, and class and caste hatred were by now rife. In Paris long-haired young bourgeois calling themselves the *jeunesse dorée* (gilded youth) went about dressed like dandies and carrying long sticks, which they used to attack suspected Jacobins. They organized the destruction of busts of Marat and forced the removal of his remains from their burial place. The leaders of Thermidor caused an acute inflation by can-

---

*From *A Documentary Survey of the French Revolution*, ed. J. H. Stewart (New York: Macmillan, 1951), pp. 528–29.

celing the economic legislation of the Terror; no longer checked by the "maximum," the prices of some foods rose to a hundred times the level of 1790, and the assignats sank so low in value that businesses refused to accept them. Popular suffering became more intense than it had ever been under the Terror. Desperate, half-starving Parisians staged several demonstrations against the Thermidoreans during 1795, clamoring for bread and lower prices.

The Thermidorean Reaction concluded with the passage of the constitution of 1795, the last major act of the Convention. The Thermidoreans wanted both to retain the republic and to assure the dominance of the propertied classes. The new constitution therefore denied the vote to the poorest quarter of the nation and required that candidates for public office possess considerable property. It established two legislative councils, the Five Hundred and the Elders. The Council of Five Hundred nominated and the Elders chose five persons who headed the executive Directory, which otherwise was almost totally independent of the legislative councils.

The constitution of 1795 demonstrated that the most radical phase of the Revolution had passed. But three weeks before it was to go into operation, more trouble broke out in Paris. The counterrevolutionary insurgents were put down in the massacre of Vendémiaire (October 5, 1795), dispersed in part by the young Napoleon Bonaparte, who commanded troops loyal to the Thermidorean Convention. The first winter of the Directory (1795–1796) brought France the most intense popular suffering of the revolutionary period as a consequence of inflation, chronic shortage of food, and extreme cold. Thereafter, the situation steadily improved, thanks to good harvests and the Directory's vigorous attack on economic problems.

The new regime levied high protective tariffs, both as a war measure against England and as a concession to French business. Again responding to business pressure, it destroyed the plates used to print the assignats and in 1797 withdrew paper money from circulation. The return to hard money required stringent government economies, which the Directory instituted. Tax collection was made more efficient, and France enjoyed considerable loot from victorious wars. The Directory eased the crushing burden of the national debt by repudiating two thirds of it and gave the old unit of currency, the livre, a new and lasting name, the franc.

The Directory easily suppressed the amateurish (and betrayed) Conspiracy of the Equals, sponsored by François Gracchus Babeuf (1760–1797), who has come down in socialist teachings as the first modern communist. The Directory experienced much greater difficulty, however, in steering a cautious middle course between the two extremes of restoring the monarchy and reverting to Jacobin terrorism. The constitution of 1795 was repeatedly violated, as the directors and the legislative councils clashed, each seeking to shift the political balance in its own favor. The councils fired directors before their terms were finished, and directors refused to allow duly elected council members to take their seats. Disgruntled politicians and apprehensive moderates, fearing the collapse of the regime, began to maneuver for the help of the increasingly successful army. The result was the coup d'état of Brumaire (that is, October) in 1799 and the dictatorship of Napoleon.

Napoleon and France

As late as 1792 Catherine the Great predicted that ten thousand soldiers would suffice to douse the "abominable bonfire" in France. The war that broke out in the spring of 1792 soon destroyed such illusions. Almost all the European powers eventually participated, and the fighting ranged far beyond Europe. By the time the war was a year old, Austria and Prussia had been joined by Holland, Spain, and Great Britain. By 1794 the French had definitely gained the advantage, and in 1795 French troops occupied Belgium, Holland, and the Rhineland.

One reason for French success was the Convention's energetic mobilization of national resources, which enabled France to have the unprecedented total of a million men under arms by the spring of 1794. Another reason lay in the weakness of the first coalition, which lacked a first-rate commander. Moreover, the partitions of Poland in 1793 and 1795 greatly assisted the French because they kept Russia out of the war and greatly distracted Austria and Prussia. By 1795 mutual mistrust had reached the point where the Prussians dared not attack the French for fear of being attacked themselves by their nominal allies, the Austrians.

Prussia was the first member of the coalition to make peace. In the Treaty of Basel (1795), Prussia yielded to France the scattered Hohenzollern holdings west of the Rhine. Spain, which ceded to France the western part of the island of Santo Domingo (today the Dominican Republic), soon deserted the coalition, as did the Netherlands. Besides Belgium and the Rhineland, France had also annexed Savoy and Nice, thereby extending its southeastern border to the crest of the Alps. These conquests, however, belied the ideals of the Revolution. In declaring war on Austria in 1792, France had sworn to uphold a promise of the constitution of 1791: never to undertake a war of conquest. This was to be "not a war of nation against nation, but the righteous defense of a free people against the unjust aggression of a king." But the conquering armies of the First Republic brought closer the day when nation would fight nation—when the other European nations would invoke "the righteous defense of a free people against the unjust aggression," not of a king, but of revolutionary France.

Bonaparte's Rise

By the close of 1795 only Britain and Austria remained officially at war with France. To lead the attack against Habsburg forces in northern Italy, the French Directory picked a youthful general who was something of a philosophe and revolutionary, as well as a ruthless, ambitious adventurer. He was born Napoleone Buonaparte on Corsica in 1769, soon after the French acquisition of that Mediterranean island from Genoa, and he retained

The Written Record

NAPOLEON RALLIES HIS TROOPS

In the Italian campaign Major General Bonaparte, still only in his twenties, cleared the Austrians out of their strongholds in one year and made them sue for peace. He showed a remarkable ability to strike quickly and to surprise his opponents before they could consolidate their defenses. He also showed a gift for propaganda and public relations, as this proclamation from the early phases of the campaign illustrates:

Soldiers! In two weeks you have won six victories; you have made fifteen-thousand prisoners; you have killed or wounded more than ten-thousand men.

Deprived of everything, you have accomplished everything. You have won battles without cannon, negotiated rivers without bridges, made forced marches without shoes, encamped without brandy, and often without bread. Only the phalanxes of the Republic, only the soldiers of Liberty, would have been capable of suffering the things that you have suffered.

You all burn to carry the glory of the French people; to humiliate the proud kings who dared to contemplate shackling us; to go back to your villages, to say proudly: "I was of the conquering army of Italy!"

Friends, I promise you that conquest; but there is a condition you must swear to fulfill: to respect the people whom you are delivering; to repress horrible pillaging.

Peoples of Italy, the French army comes to break your chains; greet it with confidence; your property, religion and customs will be respected.

Abridged from *Le Moniteur Universel*, May 17, 1796. Our translation.

throughout his life an intense family loyalty and a view of public affairs that was essentially anti-French.

As a boy of nine Napoleon began to attend military school in France and, although he now spelled his name in the French style, was snubbed as a foreigner by some of his fellow cadets. He immersed himself in reading Rousseau and dreamed of the day when he might liberate Corsica from French control.

When the Revolution broke out, the young artillery officer helped to overthrow the Old Regime in Corsica and then returned to France to resume his military career. He commanded the artillery in December 1793, when the forces of the Convention recaptured the Mediterranean port of Toulon, which had fallen to the British earlier in the year. After Thermidor he fell under a cloud as a suspected "terrorist" and settled for a desk job in Paris. He was available to rescue the Thermidorean Convention in Vendémiaire. He married Josephine de Beauharnais, a widow who was an intimate of the ruling clique of the Directory. The combination of Josephine's connections and Napoleon's talent gained him the Italian command in 1796.

In the Treaty of Campo Formio (1797), ending the Italian campaign, Austria acknowledged the loss of Belgium and recognized two puppet states that Napoleon set up in northwestern Italy: the Ligurian Republic (Genoa) and the Cisalpine Republic (the former Austrian possession of Lombardy). In return, the Habsburgs received the Italian territories of the Venetian Republic.

Only Britain remained at war with France. Napoleon decided to attack it indirectly through Malta and Egypt, the latter a semi-independent vassal of the Ottoman Empire. He invited more than a hundred archaeologists, geographers, and other scholars to accompany his army and thereby helped to found the study of Egyptology. Napoleon's experts established in Egypt an outpost of French culture that lasted into the twentieth century. From the military standpoint, however, the campaign failed. Having eluded the British Mediterranean fleet commanded by Horatio Nelson (1758–1805), Napoleon landed in Egypt in July 1798 and routed the Mamluks, the ruling oligarchy. Then disaster struck. On August 1, 1798, Nelson discovered the French fleet moored at Abukir Bay along the Egyptian coast and destroyed it before its captains could weigh anchor. Nelson's victory deprived the French of both supplies and reinforcements. After a year of futile campaigning in the Near East, Napoleon suddenly left Egypt in August 1799 and returned to France.

Napoleon found the situation in France ripe for a decisive political move, for the Directory was shaken by a strong revival of Jacobinism. Several hundred deputies in the legislative councils belonged to the Society of the Friends of Liberty and Equality, essentially the old Jacobin club. Under their influence, the councils in 1799 decreed a forced loan from the rich and passed a Law of Hostages, designed to make the émigrés stop plotting against the Directory by threatening their relatives in France with reprisals.

Abroad, the Directory had established four new satellite republics with classical names: the Batavian (Holland), the Helvetian (Switzerland), the Roman, and the Parthenopean (Naples). But this new success of French imperialism provoked the formation of the second coalition, headed by Britain, Austria, and Russia. Czar Paul I (r. 1796–1801) was head of the Knights of Malta, which Napoleon had expelled from its headquarters on the island of Malta. In the campaign of 1799 Russian troops fought in Italy and Switzerland, and the Russian general Alexander Suvorov (1729–1800), who defeated the French repeatedly, became the hero of western Europe. By August 1799 the French had been expelled from Italy.

In these circumstances, Napoleon was given a rousing reception on his return from Egypt. Soon he was plotting to overthrow the Directory, with the complicity of two of the five directors. On November 9 and 10, 1799 (18 and 19 Brumaire by the revolutionary calendar), the plot was executed. The three directors not in the plot resigned, and the two legislative councils named Napoleon military commander of Paris. He then barely persuaded the councils to entrust to the two remaining directors and himself the task of drafting a new constitution, and a detachment of troops loyal to Napoleon expelled the hostile deputies.

Consulate and Empire

The constitution of the Year VIII was the fourth attempt by revolutionary France to provide a written instrument of government, its predecessors being the constitutions of 1791, 1793, and 1795. The new document erected a very strong executive, the Consulate. Although three consuls shared the executive, Napoleon as first consul left the other two only nominal power. Four separate bodies had a hand in legislation: The Council of State proposed laws; the Tribunate debated them but did not vote; the Legislative Corps voted them but did not debate; the Senate had the right to veto legislation. The members of all four bodies were either appointed by the first consul or elected indirectly by a process so complex that Bonaparte had ample opportunity to manipulate candidates. The core of this system was the Council of State, staffed by Bonaparte's hand-picked choices, which served both as a cabinet and as the highest administrative court. The three remaining bodies were intended merely to go through the motions of enacting whatever the first consul decreed. Even so, they were sometimes unruly, and the Tribunate so annoyed Napoleon that he finally abolished it in 1807.

Meantime, step by step, Napoleon increased his own authority. In 1802 he persuaded the legislators to make him first consul for life, with the power to designate his successor and to amend the constitution at will. France was now a monarchy again in all but name. In 1804 Napoleon prompted the Senate to declare that "the government of the republic is entrusted to an emperor." A magnificent coronation took place at Notre Dame in Paris on December 2. The pope consecrated the emperor, but, careful to avoid following Charlemagne's example, Napoleon placed the crown on his own head.

Each time Napoleon revised the constitution in a nonrepublican direction, he made the republican gesture of submitting the change to the electorate. Each time the results were overwhelmingly favorable: In 1799–1800 the vote was 3,011,107 for Napoleon and the constitution of the Year VIII, and 1,562 against; in 1803 it was 3,568,885 for Napoleon and the life consulate, and 8,374 against; in 1804 it was 3,572,329 for Napoleon and the empire, and 2,579 against. Although the voters were exposed to considerable official pressure and the announced results were perhaps rigged a little, the majority in France undoubtedly supported Napoleon. His military triumphs appealed to their growing nationalism, and his policy of stability at home ensured them against further revolutionary crises and changes.

Men of every political background now staffed the highly centralized imperial administration. Napoleon cared little whether his subordinates were returned émigrés or ex-Jacobins, so long as they had ability. Besides, their varied antecedents reinforced the impression that narrow factionalism was dead and that the empire rested on a broad political base. Napoleon paid officials well and offered the additional inducement of high titles. With the establishment of the empire he created dukes by the dozen and counts and barons by the hundred. He rewarded outstanding generals with the rank of marshal and other officers with admission to the Legion of Honor, which also paid its members an annual pension. "Aristocracy always exists," Napoleon remarked. "Destroy it in the nobility, it removes itself to the rich and powerful houses of the middle class."

Law and Justice

Napoleon revived some of the glamor of the Old Regime but not its glaring inequalities. His series of law codes, the Code Napoléon (1804–1810), declared all men equal before the law without regard to rank and wealth. It extended to all the right to follow the occupation and embrace the religion of their own choosing. It gave France the single coherent system of law that the philosophes had demanded and that the revolutionary governments had been unable to formulate.

The Code Napoléon did not, however, embody the full judicial reform program of the Enlightenment. It favored the interests of the state over the rights of the individual, and it permitted some use of torture in trial procedure. Judges were appointed by the emperor; jurors were selected by his prefects. Although Napoleon confirmed the revolutionary legislation permitting divorce by mutual consent, the code canceled other revolutionary laws protecting wives, minors, and illegitimate children, and restored the man of the family to his former legal superiority. It also restored slavery in French colonies.

Ambiguity also clouded Napoleon's attitude toward civil liberties. Although he prided himself on welcoming former political heretics into his administration, his generosity always stemmed from expediency, never from fundamental belief in liberty. If he failed to get his way by conciliation, he used force. In the western departments, where royalist uprisings had become chronic, he massacred rebels who declined his offer of amnesty in 1800. In 1804 he kidnapped a Bourbon prince from the neutral German state of Baden because the prince was believed to be the choice of monarchist conspirators for the throne of France. Although Napoleon immediately discovered the prince's innocence, he had him executed nonetheless.

Religion and Education

Political considerations generally colored Napoleon's decisions on religion. Since French Catholics loathed the anticlericalism of the Revolution, Napoleon sought to appease them by working out a reconciliation with Rome. The Concordat (a treaty with the Vatican), negotiated with Pope Pius VII (r. 1800–1823), accomplished this reconciliation when it was ratified in 1802. While it canceled only the most obnoxious features of the Civil Constitution of the Clergy, the French state agreed to end the popular election of bishops and priests. The bishops were to be nominated by the government and then consecrated by the pope; the priests were to be appointed by the bishops. But by declaring that Catholicism was the faith of the "great majority of Frenchmen," rather than the state religion, the Concordat implicitly admitted the toleration of Protestants and Jews, both of whom were expected to accept state supervision of their governing councils.

Finally, the Concordat made the activities of the church in France subject to the "police regulations" of the state. The French government was to supervise the publication of papal bulls, the establishment of seminaries, the content of catechisms, and a host of other details. Despite all this, the anticlericals opposed the Concordat, and it took all Napoleon's influence to obtain its ratification by the legislative bodies of the Consulate.

The Concordat, then, made the church a ward of the French state. Although it antagonized anticlericals, it conciliated many Catholics, and it remained in force until 1905. The Concordat, however, did not bring complete peace between France and the Vatican. When Pius VII objected to Napoleon's making a French satellite of the Papal States, the "new Caesar" lectured him on the proper division of authority between the spiritual and temporal powers. Pius passed the last years of the Napoleonic regime as a prisoner, in northern Italy and then in France.

The Revolution and Napoleon also cost the church its monopoly over education. The constitution of 1791 had promised France a system of state schools. The Thermidorean Convention established a "central school" in each department of France to provide secondary education of good quality at relatively low cost to students. Napoleon abolished these central schools in 1802 and replaced them with a smaller number of central *lycées* open only to the relatively few pupils who could afford the tuition or who received state scholarships. The students wore uniforms and marched to military drums, and the curriculum, too, served the ends of patriotic indoctrination. Napoleon neglected primary schooling almost completely, yet he did advance the construction of secular schools. The way was open for bitter educational competition between church and state in nineteenth-century France.

Economics

Political aims also governed the economic program of an emperor determined to promote national unity. French peasants wanted to be left alone to enjoy the new freedom acquired in 1789. Napoleon did little to disrupt them, except to raise army recruits. He continued the hard money policy of the Directory and, unlike the Directory, balanced the budget, thanks in part to the plunder that he gained in war. He greatly improved the efficiency and honesty of tax collectors and established the semiofficial Bank of France (1800) to act as the government's financial agent. He strengthened the curbs placed on strikes and labor unions and obliged every worker to carry a *livret* (booklet), in effect an identity card recording the worker's jobs and general reputation. Although seaports suffered from the decline of overseas trade, rich war contracts and subsidies kept employment and profits generally high. As the war went on and on, however, Napoleon found it increasingly difficult to keep the peasantry and the bourgeoisie contented, and the seaport populations suffered grievously. Despite the levies on conquered countries, he had to draft more soldiers from the peasantry and increase the already unpopular taxes on salt, liquor, and tobacco.

In summary, Napoleon paid lip service to the republic while subverting republican institutions; he used prefects to impose centralized authority, and he scorned free speech. Yet Napoleon was an enlightened despot. His law code and some of his educational reforms would have delighted the philosophes. He ended civil strife without sacrificing the redistribution of land and the equality before the law gained in 1789 and the years following. Abandoning some revolutionary policies, modifying others, and completing still others, Napoleon regimented the Revolution without wholly destroying it.

Napoleon and Europe

To many in France, Napoleon was and remains the most brilliant ruler in French history. To many Europeans, on the other hand, Napoleon was a foreigner who imposed French control and French reforms. Napoleonic France succeeded in building up a vast and generally stable empire, but only at the cost of arousing the enmity of other European nations.

The War, 1800–1807

Napoleon had barely launched the Consulate when he took to the field again. The second coalition was falling to pieces. Czar Paul of Russia alarmed Britain and Austria by his interest in Italy, and Britain offended him by retaining Malta, the headquarters of his Knights. Accordingly, the czar formed a Baltic League of Armed Neutrality linking Prussia, Sweden, and Denmark with Russia against Britain. He even contemplated joining with France to drive the British out of India; this scheme collapsed when he was murdered in 1801 and succeeded by his son, Alexander I. The Baltic League disintegrated in the same year after Nelson violated Denmark's neutrality to bombard its fleet in port at Copenhagen. Napoleon defeated the Austrians in Italy and negotiated the Treaty of Lunéville (1801), whereby Austria recognized the reconstituted French satellites in Italy and agreed that France should have a hand in redrawing the map of Germany.

After Lunéville, Britain again remained alone at war with France. British taxpayers, however, wanted relief from their heavy burden; British merchants longed to resume trading with the Continental markets partially closed to them since 1793. Although Britain had been unable to check Napoleon's expansion in Europe, it had very nearly won the colonial and naval war by 1801. The British had captured former Dutch and Spanish colonies, and Nelson's fleet had expelled the French from Egypt and Malta. The British cabinet was confident that it held a strong bargaining position and could obtain favorable terms from Napoleon. Yet in the Peace of Amiens (1802) the British promised to surrender part of their colonial conquests and

This romantic portrait of Napoleon, by Jacques-Louis David, shows him pausing after work-ing early into the morning (note the clock behind him) on his famous Code Napoléon. He appears to be exceeding even his own demand for "two-o'clock-in-the-morning courage." He wears the insignia of the Legion of Honor (which he created in 1802) and the epaulettes of a general. Upon seeing this flattering portrait, Napoleon said to David, "You have understood me. By night I work for the welfare of my subjects and by day for their glory." (Photograph ©2002 Board of Trustees, National Gallery of Art, Washington; Samuel H. Kress Collection)

got nothing in return. The French failed either to reopen the Continent to British exports or to relinquish Belgium.

The one-sided Peace of Amiens provided only a year's truce in the world-wide struggle of France and Britain. Napoleon soon aroused British exporters by a more stringent tariff law and jeopardized British interests in the Caribbean by a grandiose project for a colonial empire based on Haiti and on the vast Louisiana territory ceded back to France in 1800 by Spain. In Haiti, the blacks revolted against the efforts of the Consulate to reimpose slavery. Stub-born black resistance under Francois-Toussaint L'Ouverture (c. 1744–1803) and Jean-Jacques Dessalines (c. 1758–1806), ex-slaves, and an outbreak of yellow fever took a fearful toll of French troops and forced Napoleon to abandon the American project. In 1803 he sold to the United States for 80 million francs (about $16 million) all of the Louisiana territory.

When the Louisiana Purchase was completed, France and Britain were again at war. From 1803 through 1805 Napoleon actively prepared to invade England. He assembled more than 100,000 troops and a thousand landing barges on the French side of the Straits of Dover. In 1805 he sent Admiral Pierre de Villeneuve (1763–1806) and the French fleet to the West Indies to lure the British fleet away from Europe. Villeneuve was to slip back to Europe to escort the French invasion force across the Channel while Nelson was still combing the Caribbean in search of the French fleet.

Villeneuve failed to give Nelson the slip; back in European waters, he put in at a friendly Spanish port instead of heading directly for the Channel, as Napoleon had ordered. Nelson engaged the combined French and Spanish fleets off Cape Trafalgar at the southwest corner of Spain (October 1805). He lost his own life, but not before he had destroyed half of his adversaries' ships without sacrificing one of his own. The battle of Trafalgar gave the British undisputed control of the seas and blasted French hopes of a cross-Channel invasion.

By the time of Trafalgar, Austria and Russia had joined with Britain in a third coalition. Austria in particular had been alarmed by Napoleon's efforts to promote a major revision of the political map of Germany by abolishing more than a hundred German city-states and small ecclesiastical principalities. The chief beneficiaries of this readjustment were south German states that Napoleon clearly intended to form into a bloc dominated by France, as opposed to Austria and Prussia.

Napoleon routed the Continental members of the coalition in the most dazzling campaign of his career. At Ulm, he captured thirty thousand Austrians who had moved westward without waiting for their Russian allies. He met the main Russian force and the balance of the Austrian army near the village of Austerlitz. The ensuing battle (December 2, 1805) fittingly celebrated the first anniversary of Napoleon's coronation as emperor. Bringing up reinforcements secretly and with great mobility and speed, Napoleon completely surprised his opponents; their casualties were three times greater than his own. Within the month he forced the Habsburg emperor, Francis II, to sign the humiliating Treaty of Pressburg, giving the Austrian Tyrol to Bavaria and Venetia to the Napoleonic puppet kingdom of Italy.

A still harsher fate awaited the Prussians, brought back into the war for the first time since 1795 by Napoleon's repeated interventions in German affairs. In October 1806 the French smashed the main Prussian contingents in the twin battles of Jena and Auerstädt and occupied Berlin. But Napoleon postponed a final settlement with Prussia until he had beaten his only remaining Continental opponent, Russia, at Friedland in June 1807.

Even though Napoleon's great string of victories against the third coalition resulted partly from the blunders of his enemies, the French army was now the most seasoned and feared force in Europe. New recruits were furnished by conscription, which raised an average of eighty-five thousand men a year under Napoleon, and they were quickly toughened by being assigned in small batches to veteran units. French officers were promoted on the basis of ability rather than seniority or influence, and they were, on the whole, more concerned with maintaining the morale of their men than with imposing strict discipline. Napoleon seldom risked an engagement unless his forces were the numerical equal of the enemy's; then he staked everything on a dramatic surprise. Yet even his seemingly invincible French army had defects. The medical services were poor, so that most deaths on campaigns were from disease or improperly treated wounds. Pay was low and irregular, and supplies were also irregular, since it was French policy to have men and horses live off the land as much as they could.

Napoleon reached the pinnacle of his career when he met Czar Alexander I on the "neutral ground" of a raft anchored in the Niemen River at Tilsit, on the frontier between East Prussia and Russia. There, in July 1807, the two emperors drew up a treaty dividing Europe between them. Alexander acknowledged France's hegemony over central and western Europe and secured in return the recognition of eastern Europe as the Russian sphere. Napoleon pledged Russia a share in the spoils of the Ottoman Empire if it were dismembered. He demanded no territory from the defeated czar, only a commitment to cease trade with Britain and to join the war against it.

While the two emperors negotiated on the raft, Frederick William III (r. 1797–1840), the Prussian king, nervously paced the banks of the Niemen. He had good cause to be nervous, for Tilsit cost him almost half his territory. Prussia's Polish provinces formed a new puppet state, the grand duchy of Warsaw. Prussian territory west of the Elbe River went to Napoleon to dispose of as he wished.

Thus all Europe was divided into three parts: first came the French Empire, including France proper and the territories annexed since 1789; second were the satellites, ruled in many cases by relatives of Napoleon; and third came Austria, Prussia, and Russia, forced by defeat to become allies of France. The only powers remaining outside the Napoleonic system were Britain, Turkey, and Sweden.

In central Europe Napoleon decreed a further reduction in the number of German states, and in 1806 he aided the formal dissolution of the Holy Roman Empire. Francis II, the reigning Habsburg, now called himself emperor of Austria. To replace the vanished empire, Napoleon created the Confederation of the Rhine, which included almost every German state except Austria and Prussia. At the heart of this confederation Napoleon carved out for his brother Jerome the kingdom of Westphalia, which incorporated the Prussian holdings west of the Elbe seized at Tilsit.

Napoleon longed to give dignity and permanence to his creations. It was not enough that his brothers and his in-laws should sit on thrones; he himself must found a dynasty, must have the heir so far denied him in fifteen years of childless marriage. He divorced Josephine, therefore, and in 1810 married Marie-Louise, the daughter of the Habsburg Francis II. In due time Marie-

Louise bore a son, called "the king of Rome" but destined never to rule in
Rome or anywhere else.

The Continental System

Nowhere was Napoleon's imperialism more evident than in the Continental
System. This was an attempt to regulate the economy of the whole Continent.
It had a double aim: to build up the export trade of France and to cripple that
of Britain. The Berlin Decree, issued by Napoleon in November 1806, forbade
all trade with the British Isles and all commerce in British merchandise. It
ordered the arrest of all Britons on the Continent and the confiscation of their
property. Britain replied by requiring that neutral vessels wishing to trade
with France put in first at a British port and pay duties. Napoleon retaliated
with the Milan Decree (December 1807), ordering the seizure of all neutral
ships that complied with the new British policy. The neutrals, as neutrals
often are, were caught in the middle; the two decrees effectively instituted a
Continental blockade.

Napoleon's vassals and allies had to support the Continental System or
suffer the consequences. Of all the "un-French" activities countenanced in
Holland, the worst, in Napoleon's view, was toleration of Dutch smuggling
of English contraband. The emperor also expected the satellites to feed
French industrial prosperity.

The Continental System failed almost totally. Only a few French industries
benefited; the cessation of sugar imports from the West Indies, for example,
promoted the cultivation of native sugar beets. But the decline of overseas
trade depressed Bordeaux and other French Atlantic ports, and the increasing difficulty of obtaining such raw materials as cotton caused widespread
unemployment and produced a rash of bankruptcies. Since the new French
markets on the Continent did not compensate for the loss of older markets
overseas, the value of French exports declined by more than a third between
1805 and 1813.

The Continental System did not ruin Britain, although it did confront the
British with a severe economic crisis. Markets abroad for British exports were
uncertain; food imports were reduced; while prices rose sharply, wages
lagged behind; and because of hoarding, coins were in such short supply that
not enough could be minted to keep pace with the demand. Both farm and
factory workers suffered acutely. Yet Britain rode out the storm. More land
was brought under the plow. Factory owners improvised substitute payments for their workers when coins were unavailable. Exporters not only
developed lucrative new markets in the Americas, the Ottoman Empire, and
Asia but also smuggled goods to old customers on the Continent. Napoleon
lacked the naval force to seize smugglers at sea, and he lacked a staff of incor-
ruptible customs inspectors to control contraband in the ports.

The Continental System antagonized both the neutral powers and Napoleon's allies. French seizure of United States merchant vessels in European
ports under the terms of the Milan Decree put a dangerous strain on Franco-

American relations. But British restrictions also weighed heavily on the Americans. British impressment of American seamen on the pretext that they were deserters from the Royal Navy, together with the designs on Canada of expansionists in the United States, produced an indecisive and minor Anglo-American war in 1812–1814.

The Peninsular War, 1808–1813

In Europe the political and military consequences of the Continental System formed a decisive and disastrous chapter in Napoleonic history, a chapter that opened in 1807 when the emperor decided to impose the system on Britain's traditional ally, Portugal. The Portuguese expedition furnished Napoleon with an excuse for the military occupation of neighboring Spain. In 1808 he overthrew the Spanish royal family and made his brother Joseph his puppet king of Spain. But every measure taken by Napoleon–the installation of a foreign monarch, the attempted enforcement of the Continental System, the suppression of the Inquisition, and the curtailment of noble and clerical privileges–violated Spanish customs and offended Spanish pride. The population of Madrid rose in revolt on May 2, 1808.

Although the uprising in Madrid was brutally repressed, the Peninsular War (named after the Iberian peninsula) rapidly grew. The Spaniards employed ambushes and poisoned wells and used other guerrilla devices. It became impossible to tell combatants from civilians. At the same time, the expedition that Britain sent to assist the Spaniards was ably commanded and generously supplied. Napoleon poured more than 300,000 troops into the campaign, but his opponents gained the upper hand in 1812, when he unwisely detached part of his forces for an invasion of Russia.

German National Awakening

German intellectuals launched a campaign to check the great influence that the French language and French culture had gained over their divided lands. Jacob Grimm (1785–1863) and his brother Wilhelm (1786–1859) contributed not only their very popular *Fairy Tales* (published 1812–1815) but also research designed to prove the superiority of the German language. The philosopher J. G. Fichte (1762–1814) delivered at Berlin the highly patriotic *Addresses to the German People* (1807–1808), claiming that German was the *Ursprache*—the fountainhead of language. The Germans themselves, Fichte continued, were the *Urvolk*—the oldest and most ethical of nations.

The new German consciousness was evident even when Austria had reentered the war against France in 1809. While the new spirit enabled the Austrians to make a better showing, they were narrowly defeated at Wagram (1809) and for the fourth time in a dozen years submitted to a peace dictated by Napoleon. The Treaty of Schönbrunn (1809) stripped them of their coastline on the Adriatic and assigned their Polish territory of Galicia to the grand duchy of Warsaw. Francis II gave his daughter to Napoleon in marriage, and

Napoleonic Europe, and After

The Spanish artist Francisco de Goya (1746–1828) had the deepest sympathy for victims of war and none at all for royalty—including Spain's. It was said that he made his initial sketches in the blood of executed Spanish patriots. Here he shows the point-blank execution of Spaniards by the French in Madrid on May 3, 1808. The painting hangs in the Prado in Madrid; Goya painted it in 1814, in continued protest against the war.   (Erich Lessing/Art Resource, NY)

his defeated land became the unwilling ally of France. Leadership in the German revival passed to Prussia.

The shocks of Jena and Tilsit jarred Prussia out of the administrative lethargy that had overtaken it since the death of Frederick the Great in 1786. The University of Berlin attracted Fichte and other prophets of German nationalism, and there they began to lay down the theories of a new German national state. Able generals and statesmen, most of them non-Prussian, came to power. General Gerhard von Scharnhorst (1755–1813) headed a group of officers who reorganized the army on more democratic principles and improved its efficiency. The ceiling of forty-two thousand soldiers imposed by Napoleon was evaded by the simple device of assigning recruits to the reserve after a fairly brief period of intensive training and then inducting another group of recruits. By 1813 Prussia had more than 150,000 trained men available for combat duty.

The social and administrative reorganization of the Prussian state was inspired by the energetic Baron Karl von und zum Stein (1757–1831), an enlightened aristocrat from the Rhineland. Stein conciliated the middle class by granting towns and cities some self-government. He granted some civil rights to Jews. To improve the status of the peasantry, he sponsored an edict of October 1807 abolishing serfdom in Prussia. The edict, however, did not break up the large Junker estates or provide land for the liberated serfs, many of whom thereafter led a difficult existence as day laborers. Nor did it terminate the feudal rights of justice the Junkers exercised over their peasants. Stein and others eliminated only the worst abuses of the Old Regime and left authority where it had traditionally rested—with the king, the army, and the Junkers.

The Russian Campaign, 1812–1813

The event that defeated Napoleon's great designs was the French debacle in Russia. French actions after 1807 soon convinced Czar Alexander that Napoleon was not keeping the Tilsit bargain and was intruding on Russia's sphere in eastern Europe. When Alexander and Napoleon met again at the German town of Erfurt in 1808, they could reach no agreement. For Alexander, French acquisitions from Austria in 1809 raised the unpleasant prospect of French domination over the Balkans, and the transfer of Galicia from Austria to the grand duchy of Warsaw suggested that this Napoleonic vassal might next seek to absorb Russia's acquisitions from the partitions of Poland. Meanwhile, Napoleon's insistent efforts to make Russia enforce the Continental System increasingly angered Alexander. These grievances caused a break between the czar and the emperor and led to the invasion of Russia by the French in the early summer of 1812.

For the invasion Napoleon assembled nearly 700,000 men, most of whom were unwilling conscripts and only about half of whom were French. The supply system for so distant a campaign broke down almost immediately, and the Russian scorched-earth policy made it hard for soldiers to live off the land and impossible for horses to get fodder, so that many of them had to be destroyed. As the army marched eastward, one of Napoleon's aides reported:

> There were no inhabitants to be found, no prisoners to be taken, not a single straggler to be picked up. We were in the heart of inhabited Russia and yet we were like a vessel without a compass in the midst of a vast ocean, knowing nothing of what was happening around us.*

Napoleon had hoped to strike a quick knockout blow, but the battle of Borodino in September was indecisive. Napoleon entered Moscow and remained in the burning city for five weeks, until October 19, in the vain hope of bringing Czar Alexander to terms. But Russian stubbornness, typhus, the onset of winter, and the shortage of supplies forced Napoleon to begin a nightmare retreat. Ill-fed, inadequately clothed and sheltered, without medical help, the retreating soldiers suffered horribly. Less than a quarter of the army survived the retreat from Moscow; the rest had been taken prisoner,

---

*Armand Augustin Louis, Marquis de Caulaincourt, *With Napoleon in Russia: The Memoirs of General de Caulaincourt, Duke of Vicenza* (New York: Morrow, 1935), p. 62.

had died of wounds, starvation, or disease, or had frozen to death. General Winter had defeated him.

Napoleon's Fall, 1813–1815

The British had been the first to resist Napoleon successfully, at Trafalgar and on the economic battlefields of the Continental System. Then had come Spanish resistance, followed by Russian. Now in 1813 almost every nation in Europe joined the final coalition against the French. Napoleon raised a new army, but he could not so readily replace the equipment lost in Russia. In October 1813 he lost the "Battle of the Nations," fought at Leipzig in Germany, necessitating his retreat into France. The German troops in his army were deserting, the Confederation of the Rhine collapsed, Italian support was increasingly unreliable, and the mystique of Napoleon was blighted. By April 1814 the well-organized forces of the coalition occupied Paris. Faced also with mounting unrest and conspiracy at home, the emperor abdicated when his marshals refused to continue the war. Napoleon was sent into exile as ruler of the island of Elba, off the western coast of Italy.

The statesmen of the victorious coalition gathered in the Congress of Vienna to draw up the terms of peace. The Bourbons returned to France in the person of Louis XVIII, a younger brother of Louis XVI. Realizing that he could not revive the Old Regime intact, the new king issued the Charter of 1814 establishing a constitutional monarchy. Then, on March 1, 1815, Napoleon pulled his last surprise: He landed on the Mediterranean coast of France.

For a hundred days, from March 20, when Napoleon reentered Paris, the French empire was reborn. Once again the emperor rallied the French people, this time by promising a truly liberal regime with a real parliament and genuine elections. He never had time, however, to show whether his promise was sincere, for on June 18 the British under Sir Arthur Wellesley, the duke of Wellington (1769–1852), and the Prussians under General Gebhard von Blücher (1742–1819) delivered the final blow at Waterloo, near Brussels. Again Napoleon was sent into exile, this time to the remote British island of St. Helena in the South Atlantic. There, on May 5, 1821, he died, perhaps from arsenic poisoning. Bonapartism, however, did not die with him. A Napoleonic legend arose, glossing over the faults and failures of the emperor, depicting him as a champion of liberalism and patriotism, and paving the way for the advent of another Napoleon in 1848.

Conclusion

The French Revolution was a blinding event that has sometimes obscured the fact that most countries of Europe did not experience full-scale revolutions during the 1790s. Indeed, although the French Revolution imposed some progressive reforms abroad—for example, the liberation of some Jewish ghettos—by means of arms, the Revolution also delayed more serious restructuring in many nations by associating reform with French occupation.

After 1815, the revolutionary wave was succeeded by a powerful wave of reaction, even in areas, such as Russia, where democratic revolution had posed no significant threat to the established regime. During the Restoration and for some time thereafter, conservatives were able to forestall even the mildest reform by pinning the damning label of "Jacobin" on their advocates.

Yet if the French Revolution, like almost all great leaps forward, was followed by efforts to reverse direction, it had changed so much in the old order of things that after 1815 all the kings' horses and all the kings' men could no more put the Old Regime back together again than they could, as in the nursery rhyme, Humpty Dumpty. To be sure, nobilities did reacquire special rights and exercise disproportionate power in most parts of Europe throughout the nineteenth century. But with the passage of time, noble privileges, especially in western Europe, eroded, as a growing middle class, capitalizing on the new wealth produced by the Industrial Revolution, thrust its way into the upper reaches of society and the state. It is likely that this development would have occurred eventually without the French Revolution. But at the very least, the French Revolution contributed to this process by providing the first working model of a legal system and society in which citizens, enjoying roughly equal legal rights, participated in a project to create a new nation based on the ideals of the Enlightenment. Other efforts drawing inspiration from the French Revolution would soon follow, with greater success, thereby contributing to the rise of a far more inclusive "nationalism" than had prevailed until that time.

Another process of "inclusion" accelerated by the Revolution was the coming of democracy. In the eighteenth century, even radicals such as Rousseau had considered monarchy to be the only workable form of government in large, commercially advanced countries like those of western Europe. Refusing to accept this verdict, the French revolutionaries conducted the first European experiment with democracy on a national scale. In retrospect, it is clear that this experiment, despite its failures, opened the door to others. Thus, by the 1830s, enlightened aristocrats, such as the French historian and politician Alexis de Tocqueville, concluded that the arrival of democracy in Europe was an inevitable development, which his generation had no choice but to face and accept. By the end of the nineteenth century, democracy and its instruments—constitutions, bills of rights, parties, and so on—were common fixtures of most European political systems. In short, the French Revolution proved to be the first major breakthrough into the age of mass politics.

Finally, the French Revolution gave the world its most influential model of revolution. Although it had some forerunners, such as the Puritan and American revolutions, the French Revolution was far more systematic in its efforts to uproot old institutions and to create wholly new ones. (The American nation, too, was new, but it continued to rely heavily on the precedents of English law.) The shattering of the cake of custom was so explosive and its violence so intense that some conservative historians have argued that the French Revolution was more a forerunner of twentieth-century totalitarian regimes than of liberal democracy. Without denying the similarities, it is important not to lose sight of the critical differences. Perhaps the most important difference is that, however imperfect the realization, the French revolutionaries set out as their goal the securing of individual liberty through the exercise of the ballot—a goal that was scorned by totalitarian rulers on the extreme left and right.

Over the nineteenth century, "liberty" was defined over and over again in light of the new opportunities and threats posed by industrialization. Among the many lessons the French revolutionaries taught later generations of radicals was that in the modern world popular revolutions were not only possible, but also inevitable, as long as "liberty," however understood, was denied. Could they have foreseen it, this prospect would hardly have been comforting to those who in 1648 had hoped and tried to put a lid on disorder, nor would it have been entirely pleasing even to those "progressives" of the eighteenth century who had sought to liberalize the Old Regime. But, however unintended, such was their legacy, proving once again that even if it is people who make history, they do not make it exactly as they please.

SUMMARY

Years of fiscal mismanagement contributed to the severe financial crisis that precipitated the French Revolution. Louis XVI, irresolute and stubborn, was unable to meet the overwhelming need for reform. The third estate, which constituted over 97 percent of the population, held some land, but rural poverty was widespread. Moreover, this estate bore the heavy burden of taxation. Discontent was rife among urban workers. The bourgeoisie helped focus this discontent against the privileged estates and called for an end to the abuses of the Old Regime, especially the inequalities of tax assessments.

The financial emergency of the heavily indebted monarchy forced the king to summon the Estates General. Bad weather and poor harvests in the winter of 1788–1789 led to demands for drastic change. When the Estates General met, the third estate successfully challenged the king over procedure, transforming the Estates General into a National Assembly charged with writing a constitution.

Popular uprisings pushed the Revolution along at an increasing pace. The National Assembly abolished the abuses of the Old Regime and in August 1789 issued the Declaration of the Rights of Man, embodying the ideals of the Enlightenment.

By 1791 the National Assembly had completed its task and established a government based on a separation of powers. The activities of French émigrés and of Louis XVI and the outbreak of war in 1792 opened a gulf between moderates and extremists. In Paris the Jacobins led a municipal revolution that resulted in the abolition of the monarchy.

In 1793 Robespierre, an advocate of democracy, imposed a dictatorship on France. During the Reign of Terror twenty thousand were killed. Calling for total mobilization and economic sacrifice, Robespierre and the Committee of Public Safety organized a drive to push foreign invaders from France.

The excesses of the Terror created the conditions for Robespierre's downfall in July 1794. A new Constitution of 1795 established the Directory, which assured the dominance of the propertied classes.

In 1799 Napoleon engineered a coup d'état ending the Directory and establishing the Consulate. Napoleon became first consul for life in 1802 and emperor in 1804. He moved quickly to centralize imperial administration and appointed talented ministers to office.

The Code Napoléon embodied some ideas of the Old Regime as well as revolutionary principles such as the equality of all citizens before the law.

In religion, Napoleon made peace with the church in the Concordat of 1802. Education was subservient to the state, with lycées established to train administrators. Napoleon established the Bank of France and improved tax collection.

In Europe, Napoleon built a vast empire. He forced Prussia, Russia, and Austria to accept peace terms, leaving only Britain in the war against France. The French Empire was divided into three parts: France and the territories it annexed; French satellite states; and Austria, Prussia, and Russia. In Germany, Napoleon formally dissolved the Holy Roman Empire and created the Confederation of the Rhine.

Napoleon's effort to wage economic warfare against Britain backfired, hurting France and antagonizing neutral powers. Nationalist movements in Spain and Prussia threatened the French Empire after 1808.

When Napoleon's Russian campaign of 1812 ended in disaster for his Grand Army, the nations of Europe formed a new coalition that presided over Napoleon's downfall. In 1814 the Bourbons were restored to power. The Napoleonic legend, however, would haunt France, as would the revolutionary goals of liberty, equality, and fraternity.

Chronology

1648	Treaties of Westphalia
1649–1660	The Interregnum in England
1651	Hobbes, *Leviathan*
1660–1685	Reign of Charles II in England
1661–1715	Personal reign of Louis XIV in France
1665–1700	Reign of Charles II in Spain
1687	Newton, *Principia Mathematica*
1682–1725	Reign of Peter the Great in Russia
1685	Revocation of Edict of Nantes in France
1685–1750	Johann Sebastian Bach in Germany
1685–1759	Georg Friedrich Handel in Germany and England
1688–1689	Glorious Revolution in England
1689	Bill of Rights in England
1689–1702	Reign of William and Mary in England
1689–1697	War of League of Augsburg
1690	Locke, *Second Treatise on Government*
1697–1718	Reign of Charles XII in Sweden
1700–1721	Great Northern War
1701	Act of Settlement in England
1701–1714	War of the Spanish Succession
1701–1746	Reign of Philip V in Spain
1702–1714	Reign of Anne in Great Britain
1711–1740	Reign of Charles VI in the Holy Roman Empire
1713	Treaties of Utrecht
1713	*Unigenitus*
1713–1740	Reign of Frederick William I in Prussia
1714–1727	Reign of George I in Great Britain
1715–1774	Reign of Louis XV in France
1715–1723	Regency of Duke d'Orléans in France

1718–1720   Royal Bank of John Law in France

1720   South Sea Bubble in Great Britain

1721–1745   Administration of Robert Walpole in Great Britain

1726–1743   Administration of Cardinal Fleury in France

1727–1760   Reign of George II in Great Britain

1733–1738   War of the Polish Succession

1740–1786   Reign of Frederick the Great in Prussia

1740–1780   Reign of Maria Theresa in Austrian Territories

1740–1748   War of the Austrian Succession

1745–1764   "Reign" of Madame de Pompadour in France

1748   Montesquieu, *Spirit of the Laws*

1751   Diderot and D'Alembert, *Encyclopedia* (volume I)

1751   Samuel Johnson, *Dictionary*

1755–1756   Diplomatic Revolution

1756–1763   Seven Years' War

1756–1791   Wolfgang Amadeus Mozart in Germany

1759   Voltaire, *Candide*

1760–1820   Reign of George III in Great Britain

1762–1796   Reign of Catherine the Great in Russia

1762   Rousseau, *Social Contract*

1765–1790   Reign of Joseph II in the Holy Roman Empire

1770–1826   Ludwig van Beethoven in Germany

1771–1774   Parlement dissolved in France

1772   First Partition of Poland

1774–1792   Reign of Louis XVI in France

1774   Goethe, *Sorrows of Young Werther*

1775–1783   American Revolution

1776   Smith, *Wealth of Nations*

1781   Kant, *Critique of Pure Reason*

1787   Assembly of Notables in France

1788   Gibbon, *Decline and Fall of the Roman Empire*

1789   Estates General and Fall of the Bastille in France

1789–1797   Presidency of George Washington in the United States

1790–1792   Reign of Leopold II in the Holy Roman Empire

1791	Legislative Assembly in France
1792–1806	Reign of Francis II in the Holy Roman Empire
1792–1797	War of the First Coalition
1792–1795	National Convention in France
1793	Second Partition of Poland
1793–1794	Reign of Terror in France—execution of Louis XVI and Marie Antoinette
1795–1799	Directory in France
1795	Third Partition of Poland
1799	Coup d'état of Bonaparte
1799–1804	Consulate in France
1799–1802	War of the Second Coalition
1801–1825	Reign of Alexander I in Russia
1804–1814	First Empire in France
1805–1807	War of the Second Coalition
1808–1813	Peninsular War
1812–1813	Russian campaign
1814	First exile of Napoleon
1815	Hundred Days and the Battle of Waterloo

Suggested Readings

CHAPTER 1:   The Problem of Divine-Right Monarchy

Europe in General

M. S. Anderson, *War and Society in Europe of the Old Regime 1618–1789*, 2nd ed. (London and Buffalo: McGill-Queen's University Press, 1998). Compact examination of military developments and their wider impact.

Maurice P. Ashley, *The Golden Century* (New York: Praeger, 1969). Valuable introduction.

Raymond Birn, *Crisis, Absolutism, Revolution: Europe 1648–1789*, 2nd ed. (Fort Worth, Tex.: Harcourt Brace Jovanovich, 1992). Well-balanced survey.

Euan Cameron, ed., *Early Modern Europe: An Oxford History* (Oxford: Oxford University Press, 1999). Collection of broadly conceived essays.

D. C. Coleman, ed., *Revisions in Mercantilism* (London: Methuen, 1969). Collection of articles assessing the Heckscher thesis.

Richard Dunn, *The Age of Religious Wars, 1559–1715*, 3rd ed. (New York: W. W. Norton, 1979). Balanced survey.

Eli Heckscher, *Mercantilism*, 2nd ed. (New York: Macmillan, 1962). Classic work arguing for the medieval origins of mercantilism.

Henry Kamen, *European Society 1500–1700* (London: Hutchinson, 1984). Fine survey.

Derek McKay and H. M. Scott, *The Rise of the Great Powers 1648–1815* (London and New York: Longman, 1983). Overview of the ebb and flow of international politics.

Frederick L. Nussbaum, *A History of Economic Institutions in Modern Europe* (New York: Kelley, 1967). An abridgment of Warner Sombart's *Modern Capitalism*, which argues that war is economically creative. The arguments are attacked by John U. Neff in *War and Human Progress* (New York: W. W. Norton, 1968).

David Ogg, *Europe in the Seventeenth Century* (New York: Collier, 1960). Old, but still useful survey.

Geoffrey Parker, *The Military Revolution: Military Innovation and the Rise of the West, 1500–1800*, 2nd ed. (Cambridge and New York: Cambridge University Press, 1996). Argues for a major transformation of military organization and technology that enabled the West to impose itself elsewhere in the world.

Nikolaus Pevsner, *An Outline of European Architecture* (London: Penguin, 1953). Clear, opinionated romp through the whole of Western Europe.

J. G. A. Pocock, *The Machiavellian Moment: Florentine Political Thought and the Atlantic Republican Tradition* (Princeton, N.J.: Princeton University Press, 1975). Magisterial treatment of the counterabsolutist, republican tradition in western Europe.

Perez Zagorin, *Rebels and Rulers 1500–1660*, 2 vols. (Cambridge: Cambridge University Press, 1982). Comparative history of revolts.

France

William Beik, *Absolutism and Society in Seventeenth-Century France: State Power and Provincial Aristocracy in Languedoc* (Cambridge: Cambridge University Press, 1985). Stimulating reassessment of absolutism in practice, showing how the monarchy co-opted elites more than it dominated them.

Peter Burke, *The Fabrication of Louis XIV* (New Haven, Conn., and London: Yale University Press, 1992). Survey of monarchical propaganda under the Sun King.

William F. Church, *Richelieu and Reason of State* (Princeton, N.J.: Princeton University Press, 1972). Underscores the religious basis for Richelieu's policy.

Charles W. Cole, *Colbert and a Century of French Mercantilism* (Hamden, Conn.: Archon, 1964). A solid, detailed study.

James B. Collins, *The State in Early Modern France* (Cambridge: Cambridge University Press, 1995). Excellent general study of state administration.

Ragnhild Hatton, *Europe in the Age of Louis XIV* (New York: W. W. Norton, 1979). Instructive study of the links among, economic, social, and cultural developments.

Nannerl O. Keohane, *Philosophy and the State in France: The Renaissance to the Enlightenment* (Princeton, N.J.: Princeton University Press, 1980). Fine study of French political philosophy from the sixteenth-century through Rousseau.

Sharon Kettering, *Patrons, Brokers, and Clients in Seventeenth-Century France* (New York: Oxford University Press, 1986). One of the first of attempts to the reassess the politics of absolutism, emphasizing patronage networks rather than bureaucracy.

Andrew Lossky, *Louis XIV and the French Monarchy* (New Brunswick, N.J.: Rutgers University Press, 1994). Fresh look at the reign, by one of its outstanding scholars.

A. Lloyd Moote, *Louis XIII, the Just* (Berkeley: University of California Press, 1989). Sympathetic biography, showing that Louis XIII was no mere puppet of Richelieu.

Roland Mousnier, *The Institutions of France under the Absolute Monarchy, 1598–1789,* trans. Brian Pearce, 2 vols. (Chicago: University of Chicago Press, 1979–1984). Somewhat dated, but still fundamental work on the institutional structure of Old Regime France.

Lionel Rothkrug, *Opposition to Louis XIV: The Political and Social Origins of the French Enlightenment* (Princeton, N.J.: Princeton University Press, 1965). Little on the Enlightenment, but a great deal on the ideological background to the defense and critique of French absolutism with particular emphasis on mercantilism.

England

Maurice Ashley, *England in the Seventeenth Century,* 3rd ed (Baltimore: Penguin Books, 1975). Useful survey.

Stephen B. Baxter, *William III and the Defense of European Liberty* (Westport, Conn.: Greenwood, 1976). Clear and sympathetic.

D. C. Coleman, *The Economy of England, 1450–1750* (Oxford: Oxford University Press, 1978). Short, clear look that combines the perspectives of historian and economist.

Godfrey Davies, *The Early Stuarts, 1603–1660,* 2nd ed. (Oxford: Oxford University Press, 1959); and George N. Clark, *The Later Stuarts, 1660–1714,* 2nd ed. (Oxford: Oxford University Press, 1971). Older, detailed scholarly treatments.

Godfrey Davies, *The Restoration of Charles II, 1658–1660* (San Marino, Calif.: The Huntington Library, 1955). Authoritative monograph.

John Dunn, *The Political Thought of John Locke: An Historical Account of the Argument of the Two Treatises of Government* (Cambridge: Cambridge University Press, 1969). Standard general treatment of Locke's political theory.

Christopher Hill, *The Century of Revolution, 1603–1714* (New York: W. W. Norton, 1982). Sound survey.

Stephen Howe, *Ireland and Empire: Colonial Legacies in Irish History and Culture* (Oxford: Oxford University Press, 2000). Excellent analytical study that also reviews the present historiography.

Mark A. Kishlansky, *A Monarchy Transformed: Britain 1603–1714* (London: Penguin Books, 1997). Elegantly written recent survey.

J. G. A. Pocock, *The Ancient Constitution and the Feudal Law: English Historical Thought in the Seventeenth Century*, 2nd ed. (Cambridge: Cambridge University Press, 1987). Path-breaking study of the political uses of history.

Wilfrid Prest, *Albion Ascendent: English History, 1660–1815* (Oxford: Oxford University Press, 1998). Excellent on why England rose to world power.

Lawrence Stone, *The Causes of the English Revolution 1529–1642* (London: Routledge & Kegan Paul, 1972). Analysis of the structural causes and immediate triggers of the English Revolution.

Joseph R. Tanner, *English Constitutional Conflicts of the Seventeenth Century* (Cambridge: Cambridge University Press, 1962). Full and scholarly.

Michael Walzer, *The Revolution of the Saints: A Study of the Origins of Radical Politics* (Cambridge, Mass.: Harvard University Press, 1965). Emphasis on the radical implications of Puritanism.

Cicely V. Wedgewood, *Oliver Cromwell*, 2nd ed. (London: Duckworth, 1973); and Christopher Hill, *God's Englishman* (New York: Harper and Row, 1972). Among the sounder general studies of Cromwell.

Perez Zagorin, *The Court and the Country* (New York: Atheneum, 1971). Among the first studies to emphasize the importance of court/country distinctions in British politics.

Netherlands

Jan De Vries, *The First Modern Economy: Success, Failure, and Perseverance of the Dutch Economy, 1500–1815* (Cambridge: Cambridge University Press, 1997). Monumental reinterpretation of the economic miracle of the Netherlands.

Jonathan Irvine Israel, *The Dutch Republic: Its Rise, Greatness, and Fall, 1477–1806* (Oxford: Clarendon Press, 1995). Splendid overview of the early modern Netherlands.

Simon Schama, *The Embarrassment of Riches: An Interpretation of Dutch Culture in the Golden Ages* (Berkeley: University of California Press, 1987). Brilliant analysis of Dutch culture, in particular its religion and society.

Germany and Sweden

John G. Gagliardo, *Germany under the Old Regime, 1600–1790* (London and New York: Longmans, 1991). Solid survey.

H. G. Hahn, *German Thought and Culture from the Holy Roman Empire to the Present Day* (Manchester: Manchester University Press, 1995). Especially good on effort to define a state demarked by culture.

Charles W. Ingrao, *The Habsburg Monarchy, 1618–1815,* 2nd ed. (Cambridge: Cambridge University Press, 2000). Useful brief traditional overview.

Michael Roberts, *Sweden as a Great Power, 1611–1697* (London: Edward Arnold, 1968). The still-standard account.

Rudolf Vierhaus, *Germany in the Age of Absolutism,* trans. Jonathan B. Knudsen (Cambridge and New York: Cambridge University Press, 1988). Important overview.

Mack Walker, *German Home Towns: Community, State, and General Estate, 1648–1871* (Ithaca, N.Y.: Cornell University Press, 1971). Now classic study of German urban life.

High Culture

Germain Bazin, *The Baroque* (New York: W. W. Norton, 1978). Unsystematic but suggestive assessment. See also his *Baroque and Rococo Art* (New York: Praeger, n.d.).

Anne Goldgar, *Impolite Learning: Conduct and Community in the Republic of Letters, 1680–1750* (New Haven, Conn.: Yale University Press, 1995). Recent analysis of the world of scholarship.

Roger Hahn, *The Anatomy of a Scientific Institution: The Paris Academy of Sciences, 1666–1803* (Berkeley: University of California Press, 1971). Splendid analysis of the mechanics of a critical intellectual body.

Francis Haskell, *Patrons and Painters* (New Haven, Conn.: Yale University Press, 1980). Enlightening examination of the relationship between Italian society and art in the baroque era.

Julius Held and Donald Posner, *Seventeenth- and Eighteenth-Century Art* (Englewood Cliffs, N.J.: Prentice-Hall, 1972). Systematic survey of art, handsomely illustrated.

Robert M. Isherwood, *Music in the Service of the King: France in the Seventeenth Century* (Ithaca, N.Y.: Cornell University Press, 1973). Fine study of the political uses of court music under Louis XIV.

Jonathan Irvine Israel, *Radical Enlightenment: Philosophy and the Making of Modernity, 1650–1750* (Oxford: Oxford University Press, 2001). New interpretation, emphasizing the impact of Spinoza.

Alan Charles Kors, *Atheism in France 1650–1729: I—The Orthodox Sources of Disbelief* (Princeton, N.J.: Princeton University Press, 1990). Intellectual history at its best; a subtle analysis showing how atheism emerged out of disputes among believers.

Alan Charles Kors and Paul J. Korshin, eds., *Anticipations of the Enlightenment in England, France, and Germany* (Philadelphia: University of Pennsylvania Press, 1987). Collection of fine essays addressing the cultural shifts of the late seventeenth century in several national contexts.

Rudolf Wittkower, *Art and Architecture in Italy, 1600–1700* (London: Pelican, 1980); and Anthony Blunt, *Art and Architecture in France, 1500–1700* (London: Penguin, 1977). Two masterful syntheses.

Economics and Society

Roger Chartier, ed., *A History of Private Life,* vol. III: *Passions of the Renaissance,* trans. Arthur Goldhammer (Cambridge, Mass.: Belknap Press, 1989). Essays exploring various aspects of the private sphere through the eighteenth century.

Natalie Zemon Davis and Arlette Farge, eds., *A History of Women in the West,* vol. III: *Renaissance and Enlightenment Paradoxes* (Cambridge, Mass.: Belknap Press, 1993). Valuable series of essays covering a range of topics connected with the role and life of women.

Jan De Vries, *The Economy of Europe in an Age of Crisis, 1600–1750* (Cambridge: Cambridge University Press, 1976). Cogent analysis of major trends arguing against the notion of a seventeenth-century Malthusian crisis.

Beatrice Gottlieb, *The Family in the Western World from the Black Death to the Industrial Age* (New York: Oxford University Press, 1993). Useful survey.

Christopher Hill, *Change and Continuity in Seventeenth-Century England* (Cambridge, Mass.: Harvard University Press, 1975). Stimulating essays on social attitudes.

Joseph Klaits, *Servants of Satan: The Age of the Witch Hunts* (Bloomington: Indiana University Press, 1985). Balanced introduction to a now much-studied phenomenon.

Emmanuel Le Roy Ladurie, *The Peasants of Languedoc*, trans. John Day (Urbana: University of Illinois Press, 1977). Classic study of peasant life and institutions.

W. H. Lewis, *The Splendid Century* (New York: Morrow, 1954). Brilliantly written old-style social history of the world of Louis XIV. See also the lesser-known sequel, *The Sunset of the Splendid Century: The Life and Times of Louis Auguste de Bourbon, Duc de Maine, 1670–1736* (Garden City, N.Y.: Doubleday Anchor, 1963).

Roland Mousnier, *Peasant Uprisings in Seventeenth-Century France, Russia and China*, trans. Brian Pearce (New York: Harper and Row, 1970). Comparative study of peasant revolts.

Lawrence Stone, *The Family, Sex and Marriage in England, 1500–1800* (New York: Harper and Row, 1977). Controversial argument on the evolution of the family.

Keith Thomas, *Religion and the Decline of Magic* (New York: Scribner's, 1971). Deeply researched but now controversial study of popular beliefs in early modern England.

Merry E. Wiesener, *Women and Gender in Early Modern Europe* (Cambridge: Cambridge University Press, 1993). Survey of the role of women in early modern society and culture.

Immanuel Wallerstein, *The Modern World-System*, vol. II: *Mercantilism and the Consolidation of the European World-Economy, 1600–1750* (New York: Academic Press, 1980). Controversial analysis of European capitalism, emphasizing interaction of Europe with the rest of the world.

Sources

William F. Church, ed., *The Impact of Absolutism in France* (New York: Wiley, 1969). Useful selections from source materials from the era of Richelieu and Louis XIV.

E. William Monter, ed., *European Witchcraft* (New York: Wiley, 1969). Short collection of sources.

Owen F. Morshead, ed., *Everybody's Pepys* (New York: Harcourt, 1926). Abridged version of Samuel Pepys's famous diary of the 1660s.

CHAPTER 2:   The Old Regimes

General

M. S. Anderson, *Europe in the Eighteenth Century 1713–1789*, 4th ed. (London: Longman, 2000). Well-informed general survey.

William Doyle, *The Old European Order, 1660–1800*, 2nd ed. (New York: Oxford University Press, 1993). Short overview.

Leonard Krieger, *Kings and Philosophers, 1689–1789* (New York: W. W. Norton, 1970). Challenging, analytical synthesis.

Isser Woloch, *Eighteenth-Century Europe: Tradition and Progress, 1715–1789* (New York and London: W. W. Norton, 1982). Fine general synthesis.

Economics, Society, and Empire

Jerome Blum, *The End of the Old Order in Rural Europe* (Princeton, N.J.: Princeton University Press, 1978). Fine broad history of the relationship between lords and peasants.

Carlo M. Cipolla, *Guns, Sails, and Empires* (New York: Minerva Press, 1965). Essay on technology and the spread of European empires.

Ralph Davis, *The Rise of the Atlantic Economies* (Ithaca, N.Y.: Cornell University Press, 1973). Comparative study of the economic bases of European empires.

Phyllis Deane, *The First Industrial Revolution* (Cambridge: Cambridge University Press, 1980). Excellent introduction and overview of the subject.

Jonathan Dewald, *The European Nobility, 1400–1800* (New York: Cambridge University Press, 1996). Valuable, up-to-date comparative study, showing the viability of the noble order.

David Eltis, *The Rise of African Slavery in the Americas* (Cambridge and New York: Cambridge University Press, 2000). Shows active role of Africans in the creation of the slave trade, reflecting strength rather than weakness.

Roderick Floud and Donald McCloskey, eds., *The Economic History of Britain since 1700,* 2nd ed. (New York: Cambridge University Press, 1994). Excellent summaries of recent views.

Albert Goodwin, ed., *The European Nobility in the Eighteenth Century* (London: Black, 1953). Older, but still valuable essays on the nobility in different national contexts.

H. J. Habbakuk and Michael Postan, eds., *The Cambridge Economic History of Europe,* vol. VI, Parts 1 and 2 (Cambridge: Cambridge University Press, 1965). Scholarly essays.

Olwen H. Hufton, *The Poor of Eighteenth-Century France* (Oxford: Clarendon Press, 1974). Superb study of the condition of the poor.

Neil McKendrick, John Brewer, and J. H. Plumb, eds., *The Birth of a Consumer Society: The Commercialization of Eighteenth-Century England* (Bloomington: Indiana University Press, 1982). Essays on the role of the consumer in eighteenth-century British society and economy.

David Northrup, *Africa's Discovery of Europe, 1450–1850* (New York: Oxford University Press, 2002). On the development of African awareness of Europe and Europeans.

J. H. Parry, *Trade and Dominion: The European Overseas Empires in the Eighteenth Century* (New York: Praeger, 1971). General study of the fate of European empires.

Roy Porter and Lesley Hall, *The Facts of Life: The Creation of Sexual Knowledge in Britain, 1650–1950* (New Haven, Conn.: Yale University Press, 1995). Interesting history of ideas.

Daniel Roche, *The History of Everyday Things: The Birth of Consumption in France, 1600–1800,* trans. Brian Pearce (Cambridge: Cambridge University Press, 2000). Study of changing consumption patterns in eighteenth century.

John Thornton, *Africa and Africans in the Making of the Atlantic World, 1400–1800,* 2nd ed. (Cambridge and New York: Cambridge University Press, 1998). Shows how Africans themselves regulated the slave trade and how Africans coped with the evils of the system.

The Established Powers

J. V. Beckett, *The Aristocracy in England, 1660–1914* (Oxford: Blackwell, 1986). Solid summary of present scholarship.

Catherine B. A. Behrens, *Society, Government, and the Enlightenment: The Experiences of Eighteenth-Century France and Prussia* (New York: Harper and Row, 1986). Comparative study of what went wrong in France and right in Prussia.

David A. Bell, *The Cult of the Nation in France: Inventing Nationalism, 1680–1800* (Cambridge, Mass.: Harvard University Press, 2001). Original argument locating the origin of French nationalism in the eighteenth century.

John Brewer, *The Sinews of Power: War, Money and the English State, 1688–1783* (Cambridge, Mass.: Harvard University Press, 1990). Brilliant analysis of the financial developments that underlay the growth of British power.

Peter R. Campbell, *Power and Politics in Old Regime France 1720–1745* (London and New York: Routledge, 1996). Penetrating examination of the role of political faction in the age of Cardinal Fleury.

Linda Colley, *Britons: Forging the Nation, 1707–1837* (New Haven, Conn., and London: Yale University Press, 1982). Brilliant work on the development of a British national consciousness.

P. G. M. Dickson, *The Financial Revolution in England: A Study in the Development of Public Credit, 1688–1756* (New York: St. Martin's Press, 1967). Fundamental work on the creation of early modern state finances and its political impact.

William Doyle, *The Short Oxford History of France: Old Regime France* (Oxford: Oxford University Press, 2001). Splendid short essays touching on many aspects of the regime.

Isaac Kramnick, *Bolingbroke and His Circle: The Politics of Nostalgia in the Age of Walpole* (Cambridge, Mass.: Harvard University Press, 1968). Study of the opposition to the Walpole Whigs in the early eighteenth century.

Michael Kwass, *Privilege and the Politics of Taxation in Eighteenth-Century France* (Cambridge: Cambridge University Press, 2000). Close analysis of the politics of finance.

J. H. Plumb, *The Growth of Political Stability in England, 1675–1725* (London: Macmillan, 1967). Fine essay on the transformation of British politics in the wake of the Glorious Revolution.

Daniel Roche, *France in the Enlightenment*, trans. Arthur Goldhammer (Cambridge, Mass.: Harvard University Press, 1998). Sprawling survey, emphasizing society and culture.

Lawrence Stone and Jeanne C. Fawtier Stone, *An Open Elite?: England, 1540–1880* (Oxford: Clarendon Press; New York: Oxford University Press, 1984). Revisionist argument holding that the British nobility was not easily penetrated by the middle class.

Dale K. Van Kley, *The Religious Origins of the French Revolution: From Calvin to the Civil Constitution, 1560–1791* (New Haven, Conn., and London: Yale University Press, 1996). Masterful reinterpretation of French politics as a conflict between two kinds of spirituality, with emphasis on the eighteenth century.

Rising Powers in the East

Francis L. Carsten, *The Origins of Prussia* (Westport, Conn.: Greenwood, 1982). Excellent monograph.

Gordon A. Craig, *The Politics of the Prussian Army, 1640–1945* (Oxford: Oxford University Press, 1964). Major contribution to the study of German history.

Christopher Duffy, *Russia's Military Way to the West* (London: Routledge and Kegan Paul, 1982). Careful examination of the rise of Russia to great power status.

Robert R. Ergang, *The Potsdam Fuhrer* (New York: Octagon, 1973). Study of Frederick William I of Prussia.

Richard L. Gawthrop, *Pietism and the Making of Eighteenth-Century Prussia* (Cambridge: Cambridge University Press, 1993). Important argument in favor of the continued importance of religion in the eighteenth century.

Isabel V. Hull, *Sexuality, State, and Civil Society in Germany, 1700–1815* (Ithaca, N.Y.: Cornell University Press, 1996). Innovative gender approach to German politics and society.

V. D. Klyuschevsky, *Peter the Great* (New York: Vintage, 1961). Stirring account.

Robert K. Massie, *Peter the Great, His Life and World* (New York: Knopf, 1980). Sprawling panoramic view of Peter and Russia.

Hans Rosenberg, *Bureaucracy, Aristocracy, Autocracy: The Prussian Experience 1660–1815* (Boston: Beacon, 1958). Controversial study of state institutions.

The International Balance

Jeremy Black, *The Rise of the European Powers, 1679–1793* (London: Edward Arnold, 1990). Effective combination of narrative and analysis.

Reed Browning, *The War of the Austrian Succession* (New York: St. Martin's, 1995). Comprehensive history of the war.

Ludwig Dehio, *The Precarious Balance* (New York: Knopf, 1962). Classic essay on international relations.

John F. C. Fuller, *A Military History of the Western World* (New York: Funk and Wagnalls, 1954–1956). Volume 2 deals with the seventeenth and eighteenth centuries.

Lawrence H. Gipson, *The Great War for the Empire: The Culmination, 1760–1763* (New York: Knopf, 1954). Magisterial history of the war; Volume 8 of a detailed, sustained analysis.

Henry Kamen, *The War of Succession in Spain, 1700–1715* (Bloomington: Indiana University Press, 1969). Detailed study.

K. M. Panikkar, *Asia and Western Dominance* (London: Allen and Unwin, 1965). Strong survey, with emphasis on India.

Paul W. Schroeder, *The Transformation of European Politics, 1763–1848* (Oxford: Clarendon Press, 1994). Penetrating, sweeping study of European international politics.

Albert Sorel, *Europe under the Old Regime* (New York: Harper and Row, 1964). Famous essay by great master of diplomatic relations.

Benedict H. Sumner, *Peter the Great and the Ottoman Empire* (Hampden, Conn.: Shoe String, 1965). Short, meaty monograph.

Leslie C. Tihany, *A History of Middle Europe* (New Brunswick, N.J.: Rutgers University Press, 1976). Straightforward survey.

Sources

Norbert Elias, *The History of Manners*, Vol. 1: *The Civilizing Process*, trans. Edmund Jephcott (New York: Pantheon, 1982). Study of the impact of the royal court on the development of daily etiquette, with substantial primary source readings.

Robert Forster and Elborg Forster, *European Society in the Eighteenth Century* (New York: Walker, 1969). Excellent anthology.

George P. Gooch, *Courts and Cabinets* (New York: Arno, 1972). Introduction to the memoirs of some of the great personages of the era.

Carlile A. Macartney, ed., *The Hapsburg and Hohenzollern Dynasties in the Seventeenth and Eighteenth Centuries* (New York: Harper and Row, 1970). Useful collection of documents on Austria and Prussia.

Lady Mary W. Montagu, *Letters* (Oxford: Clarendon Press, 1965). Influential observations on the Habsburg and Ottoman empires, which helped inspire use of the smallpox vaccine.

Arthur Young, *Tours of England and Wales* (London: Penguin, 1981). Reports of a prolific and perceptive agricultural expert.

CHAPTER 3:   The Enlightenment

General

Ernst Cassirer, *The Philosophy of the Enlightenment,* trans. Fritz C. A. Koelln and James
P. Pettegrove (Princeton, N.J.: Princeton University Press, 1951). Major work
arguing for the philosophical consistency of the Enlightenment.

Lester G. Crocker, *An Age of Crisis* and *Nature and Culture* (Baltimore: Johns Hopkins
University Press, 1959, 1963). Overviews of Enlightenment ideas.

Peter Gay, *The Enlightenment: An Interpretation,* 2 vols. (New York: Alfred A. Knopf,
1966–1969). Synthesis arguing for religious heterodoxy as the major thread of the
Enlightenment.

Jürgen Habermas, *The Structural Transformation of the Public Sphere: An Inquiry into a
Category of Bourgeois Society,* trans. Thomas Burger and Frederick Lawrence
(Cambridge, Mass.: MIT Press, 1991). Highly influential case for the emergence
of a "public sphere" in eighteenth-century Europe.

Norman Hampson, *The Enlightenment* (London: Penguin, 1977). Good, if slightly out-
dated short survey.

James Van Horn Melton, *The Rise of the Public in Enlightenment Europe* (Cambridge:
Cambridge University Press, 2001). Lucid comparative survey of the "public
sphere" in the political culture of eighteenth-century Britain, France, and Germany.

Dorinda Outram, *The Enlightenment* (Cambridge: Cambridge University Press, 1995).
Up-to-date overview, with more questions than answers.

Roy Porter and Mikulàš Teich, eds., *The Enlightenment in National Context* (Cambridge:
Cambridge University Press, 1981). Useful collection of essays on the Enlightenment in different settings.

Ira O. Wade, *The Structure and Form of the French Enlightenment,* 2 vols. (Princeton, N.J.:
Princeton University Press, 1977). Old-style intellectual history of the Enlightenment.

Specialized Studies

Keith Michael Baker, *Condorcet: From Natural Philosophy to Social Mathematics* (Chicago
and London: University of Chicago Press, 1975). Profound study of Condorcet's
ideas and their ideological setting.

Keith Michael Baker, *Inventing the French Revolution: Essays on French Political Culture
in the Eighteenth Century* (Cambridge: Cambridge University Press, 1990). Brilliant essays on the idea of public opinion and other ideological developments
that allowed the French to "invent" the French Revolution.

Roger Chartier, *The Cultural Origins of the French Revolution,* trans. Lydia G. Cochrane
(Durham, N.C.: Duke University Press, 1991). Survey of cultural shifts that prepared the way for the French Revolution.

Robert Darnton, *The Forbidden Best-Sellers of Pre-Revolutionary France* (New York and
London: W. W. Norton, 1995). Intriguing examination of the book trade and the
circulation of political slander. With translated primary sources.

Elizabeth C. Goldsmith and Dena Goodman, eds., *Going Public: Women and Publishing
in Early Modern France* (Ithaca, N.Y., and London: Cornell University Press, 1995).
Valuable essays examining the challenges and initiatives of female writers.

Dena Goodman, *The Republic of Letters: A Cultural History of the French Enlightenment*
(Ithaca, N.Y.: Cornell University Press, 1994). Examination of the French Enlightenment, with a focus on the role of women and the *salons.*

Richard Herr, *The Eighteenth-Century Revolution in Spain* (Princeton, N.J.: Princeton University Press, 1958). Shows political impact of the Enlightenment.

Robert M. Isherwood, *Farce and Fantasy: Popular Entertainment in Eighteenth-Century Paris* (Oxford: Oxford University Press, 1986). Splendid examination of popular culture, emphasizing the mixed social composition of the audience.

Lawrence E. Klein, *Shaftesbury and the Culture of Politeness: Moral Discourse and Cultural Politics in Early Eighteenth-Century England* (Cambridge: Cambridge University Press, 1994). Imaginative study of the moral role of politeness in English culture.

Isabel F. Knight, *The Geometric Spirit: The Abbé de Condillac and the French Enlightenment* (New Haven, Conn.: Yale University Press, 1973). Solid study of a key Enlightenment philosopher.

Joan B. Landes, *Women and the Public Sphere in the Age of the French Revolution* (Ithaca, N.Y.: Cornell University Press, 1988). Controversial book on the increasing exclusion of women from the public sphere.

Sarah Maza, *Private Lives and Public Affairs: The Causes Célèbres of Prerevolutionary France* (Berkeley: University of California Press, 1993). Traces the role of sensational trials in the demise of the Old Regime.

Sara E. Melzer and Kathryn Norberg, eds., *From the Royal to the Republican Body: Incorporating the Political in Seventeenth- and Eighteenth-Century France* (Berkeley: University of California Press, 1998). Collection of articles examining the body metaphor in different forms of political expression.

Sylvia H. Myers, *The Bluestocking Circle: Women, Friendship, and the Life of the Mind in 18th-Century England* (Oxford: Clarendon Press; New York: Oxford University Press, 1990). Study of the cultural position of women.

Robert Shackleton, *Montesquieu, a Critical Biography* (London: Oxford, 1961). Authoritative biography of a critical figure, as well as a key work on the Enlightenment in general.

Lieselotte Steinbrügge, *The Moral Sex: Woman's Nature in the French Enlightenment*, trans. Pamela E. Selwyn (New York: Oxford University Press, 1995). Shows the tendency to distinguish a specifically female mentality.

Franco Venturi, *Italy and the Enlightenment: Studies in a Cosmopolitan Century* (New York: New York University Press, 1972). Essays on various topics by a leading authority on Italy in the eighteenth century.

Arthur M. Wilson, *Diderot* (Oxford: Oxford University Press, 1972). Excellent biographical study that says much about the Enlightenment in general.

The Enlightened Despots

John T. Alexander, *Catherine the Great* (New York: Oxford University Press, 1988). Fine narrative history.

Derek Beales, *Joseph II*, vol. 1 (Cambridge: Cambridge University Press, 1987). Masterful, detailed study of Joseph's early life and career.

T. C. W. Blanning, *Joseph II* (London: Longman, 1994). Good short overview.

John G. Gagliardo, *Enlightened Despotism* (New York: Thomas Y. Cromwell, 1967). Useful introduction to the problem.

Walther Hubatsch, *Frederick the Great: Absolutism and Administration* (London: Thames and Hudson, 1973). Serviceable overview.

Isabel de Madriaga, *Russia in the Age of Catherine the Great* (New Haven, Conn.: Yale University Press, 1981). Excellent general study.

Carlile A. Macartney, *Maria Theresa and the House of Austria* (London: English Universities Press, 1969). Informative and brief.

James Van Horn Melton, *Absolutism and the Eighteenth-Century Origins of Compulsory Schooling in Prussia and Austria* (Cambridge: Cambridge University Press, 1988). Brilliant study showing how compulsory schooling programs derived from transformations in Austrian and Prussian society and politics.

Gerhard Ritter, *Frederick the Great* (Berkeley: University of California Press, 1968). Sympathetic lectures.

H. M. Scott, ed., *Enlightened Absolutism: Reform and Reformers in Later Eighteenth-Century Europe* (Ann Arbor: University of Michigan Press, 1990). Recent essays on various enlightened rulers, showing that the Enlightenment did have an impact.

England and America

Bernard Bailyn, *Ideological Origins of the American Revolution* (Cambridge, Mass.: Harvard University Press, 1968). Major reinterpretation, in its day, with emphasis on the impact of Whig ideology.

John Brewer, *Party Ideology and Popular Politics at the Accession of George III* (Cambridge and London: Cambridge University Press, 1976). Subtle analysis of the changing dynamics of British politics in the later eighteenth century.

H. T. Dickinson, *The Politics of the People in Eighteenth-Century Britain* (New York: St. Martin's Press, 1995). Fine study of popular mobilization.

Theodore Draper, *A Struggle for Power: The American Revolution* (New York: Random House, 1996). A recent revaluation, with emphasis on interests rather than ideology.

J. G. A. Pocock, *Barbarism and Religion: The Enlightenments of Edward Gibbon, 1737–1764,* vol. I (Cambridge: Cambridge University Press, 1999). Challenging reinterpretation of the great historian in his ideological context.

Georges Rudé, *Wilkes and Liberty* (Oxford: Oxford University Press, 1962). Standard history of one of England's greatest trouble-makers.

J. Steven Watson, *The Reign of George III, 1760–1815* (Oxford: Oxford University Press, 1960). Informative and balanced general account.

Gordon S. Wood, *The Creation of the American Republic, 1776–1787* (Chapel Hill, N.C.: University of North Carolina Press, 1969). Sweeping synthesis of American political ideology during the Revolution and after.

The Arts

Frederick Antal, *Hogarth and His Place in European Art* (London: Routledge and Kegan Paul, 1962). Ingenious study stressing parallels with earlier and later artists.

Germaine Bazin, *Baroque and Rococo Art* (Oxford: Oxford University Press, 1964); and A. Charles Sewter, *Baroque and Rococo* (London: Thames and Hudson, 1972). Concise introductions.

Manfred F. Bukofzer, *Music in the Baroque Era* (New York: W. W. Norton, 1971). Survey through 1750.

Thomas E. Crow, *Painters and the Public Life in Eighteenth-Century Paris* (New Haven, Conn., and London: Yale University Press, 1985). Path-breaking study of French painting in relation to the public that consumed it.

Julius Held and Donald Posner, *Seventeenth- and Eighteenth-Century Art* (Englewood Cliffs, N.J.: Prentice-Hall, 1972). Comprehensive survey.

James H. Johnson, *Listening in Paris: A Cultural History* (Berkeley: University of California Press, 1995). Fascinating account of changing behavior of audiences.

James M. Morris, ed., *On Mozart* (New York: Cambridge University Press, 1994). Collection of essays debunking many myths about the composer.

Jeffrey S. Ravel, *The Contested Parterre: Public Theater and French Political Culture, 1680–1791* (Ithaca, N.Y.: Cornell University Press, 1999). Study of policing audiences and their opinions.

Charles Rosen, *The Classical Style* (New York: W. W. Norton, 1971). Major essay interrelating the musical styles of Mozart, Haydn, and Beethoven.

Mary D. Sheriff, *The Exceptional Woman: Elisabeth Vigée-Lebrun and the Cultural Politics of Art* (Chicago: University of Chicago Press, 1996). Places the painter in the culture of court politics.

Mary D. Sheriff, *Fragonard: Art and Eroticism* (Chicago: University of Chicago Press, 1990). Important reevaluation.

Maynard Solomon, *Mozart: A Life* (New York: HarperCollins Publishers, 1995). Biography with emphasis on the psychology of the composer.

Sources

Max Beloff, ed., *The Debate on the American Revolution, 1761–1783* (London: Kaye, 1949). Handy compilation of British speeches and writings for and against the rebels.

Crane Brinton, ed., *The Portable Age of Reason Reader* (New York: Viking, 1956); and Isaiah Berlin, ed., *The Age of Enlightenment: The Eighteenth-Century Philosophers* (Salem, N.H.: Arno Press, 1956). Two valuable anthologies.

Lester G. Crocker, ed., *The Age of Enlightenment* (New York: Walker, 1969). Useful collection.

Peter Gay, *The Enlightenment: A Comprehensive Anthology* (New York: Simon & Schuster, 1985). Fine collection of key documents.

Immanuel Kant, *On History*, ed. Lewis White Beck (Indianapolis: Bobbs-Merrill, 1963). Kant's historical writings, including the classic essay "What Is Enlightenment?"

Isaac Kramnick, ed., *The Portable Enlightenment Reader* (New York: Penguin, 1995). Generous excerpts from the key thinkers.

David Williams, ed. and trans., *Voltaire: Political Writings* (Cambridge: Cambridge University Press, 1994). Useful collection of Voltaire's key political works, with helpful introduction.

CHAPTER 4: The French Revolution and Napoleon

General Surveys

William Doyle, *The Oxford History of the French Revolution* (Oxford: Oxford University Press, 1988). Reliable, but not especially imaginative account of the Revolution.

François Furet and Mona Ozouf, eds., *A Critical Dictionary of the French Revolution*, trans. Arthur Goldhammer (Cambridge, Mass.: Belknap Press, 1989). Collection of essays written from the revisionist perspective.

Patrice Higonnet, *Sister Republics: The Origins of French and American Republicanism* (Cambridge, Mass.: Harvard University Press, 1988). Interesting comparison and contrast of two republican experiments.

Frank A. Kafker, James M. Laux, and Darline Gay Levy, eds., *The French Revolution: Conflicting Interpretations*, 5th ed. (Malabar, Fla.: Krieger, 2002). Useful collection of different viewpoints, both recent and traditional.

Georges Lefebvre, *The French Revolution,* trans. John Hall Stewart and James Friguglietti (New York: Columbia University Press, 1964). Still valuable classic by one of the master historians of the Revolution.

Robert R. Palmer, *The Age of the Democratic Revolution,* 2 vols. (Princeton, N.J.: Princeton University Press, 1969). Dated, but still valuable sweeping examination of the revolutionary age, arguing for a common democratic core.

Jeremy D. Popkin, *A Short History of the French Revolution,* 3rd ed. (Upper Saddle River, N.J.: Prentice-Hall, 2002). Clear, compact survey.

Simon Schama, *Citizens: A Chronicle of the French Revolution* (New York: Knopf, 1989). Readable, if sensationalized, account of the Revolution, emphasizing the role of violence.

D. M. G. Sutherland, *France 1789–1815: Revolution and Counter-Revolution* (New York: Oxford University Press, 1986). Challenging survey, emphasizing resistance to the Revolution.

Specialized Studies

Harriet B. Applewhite and Darline G. Levy, eds., *Women and Politics in the Age of the Democratic Revolution* (Ann Arbor: University of Michigan Press, 1990). Useful collection of readings.

T. C. W. Blanning, *The French Revolutionary Wars 1787–1802* (London: Arnold, 1996). Military history of the Revolution through the early career of Napoleon.

T. C. W. Blanning, *The Origins of the French Revolutionary Wars* (London: Longman, 1986). Succinct analysis of the diplomatic history of the Revolution.

Richard C. Cobb, *The Police and the People* (Oxford: Oxford University Press, 1970). Major study of French popular protest.

William Doyle, *The Origins of the French Revolution,* 3rd ed. (Oxford: Oxford University Press, 1999). Latest version of a now classic refutation of the social interpretation of the French Revolution.

Jacques Godechot, *The Counter-Revolution: Doctrine and Action, 1789–1804,* trans. Salvator Attanasio (Princeton, N.J.: Princeton University Press, 1981). Disappointing but still useful treatment.

Dominique Godineau, *The Women of Paris and Their French Revolution,* trans. Katherine Streip (Berkeley: University of California Press, 1998). Excellent detailed study of the political role of women in the French Revolution.

Norman Hampson, *The Life and Opinions of Maximilien Robespierre* (Oxford: Basil Blackwell, 1988). Witty reassessment.

Olwen H. Hufton, *Women and the Limits of Citizenship in the French Revolution* (Toronto, Buffalo, N.Y., and London: University of Toronto Press, 1992). Lectures, providing a good introduction to the problem.

Lynn Hunt, *Politics, Culture, and Class in the French Revolution* (Berkeley: University of California Press, 1984). Ground-breaking studies of political culture during the Revolution.

Peter M. Jones, *The Peasantry in the French Revolution* (Cambridge: Cambridge University Press, 1988). Excellent overview.

David Jordan, *The King's Trial: The French Revolution vs. Louis XVI* (Berkeley: University of California Press, 1979). Readable account.

Emmet Kennedy, *A Cultural History of the French Revolution* (New Haven, Conn.,: Yale University Press, 1989). Useful survey of different cultural developments.

Georges Lefebvre, *The Coming of the French Revolution,* trans. Robert R. Palmer (Princeton, N.J. Princeton University Press, 1947). Classic presentation of the Revolution as a conflict of social classes.

Martyn Lyons, *France under the Directory* (Cambridge: Cambridge University Press, 1975). Good overview of a neglected period.

John Markoff, *The Abolition of Feudalism: Peasants, Lords, and Legislators in the French Revolution* (University Park: Pennsylvania State University Press, 1996). Exhaustive analysis of peasant politics in the early Revolution, using sophisticated social science analysis.

Mona Ozouf, *Festivals and the French Revolution*, trans. Alan Sheridan (Cambridge, Mass.: Harvard University Press, 1988). Subtle analysis of the political implications of revolutionary festivals.

Robert R. Palmer, *Twelve Who Ruled: The Year of the Terror in the French Revolution* (Princeton, N.J.,: Princeton University Press, 1941). Old, but still unsurpassed examination of the Terror.

Jeremy D. Popkin, *Revolutionary News: The Press in France, 1789–1799* (Durham, N.C.: Duke University Press, 1990). Solid analysis, showing the critical role of the press in the course of the Revolution.

Georges Rudé, *The Crowd in the French Revolution* (Oxford: Oxford University Press, 1959). Now classic study of popular protest, with emphasis on food shortages.

Samuel F. Scott, *The Response of the Royal Army to the French Revolution: The Role and Development of the Line Army 1787–1793* (Oxford: Clarendon Press, 1978). Excellent blend of political and military history.

Bailey Stone, *The Genesis of the French Revolution: A Global-Historical Interpretation* (Cambridge and New York: Cambridge University Press, 1994). Fresh interpretation of the background to the French Revolution, emphasizing the failure of French foreign policy.

Timothy Tackett, *Religion, Revolution, and Regional Culture in Eighteenth-Century France: The Ecclesiastical Oath of 1791* (Princeton, N.J.: Princeton University Press, 1986). Sophisticated analysis of the impact of the oath in different parts of France.

Dale Van Kley, ed., *The French Idea of Freedom: The Old Regime and the Declaration of Rights of 1789* (Stanford, Calif.: Stanford University Press, 1994). Essays focusing on the historical context of the Declaration of Rights.

Isser Woloch, *The New Regime: Transformations of the French Civic Order, 1789–1820s* (New York: W. W. Norton, 1994). Dry but very useful analysis of institutional changes.

Napoleon

Louis Bergeron, *France under Napoleon*, trans. R. R. Palmer (Princeton, N.J.: Princeton University Press, 1971). Focuses on Napoleon's impact and opposition.

David G. Chandler, *The Campaigns of Napoleon* (New York: Macmillan, 1973). Thorough scholarly account.

Owen Connelly, *Blundering to Glory: Napoleon's Military Campaigns* (Wilmington, Del.: Scholarly Resources, 1987). Close examination of Napoleon's strategies, emphasizing his flexibility.

Owen Connelly, *Napoleon's Satellite Kingdoms* (New York: Free Press, 1970). Impact of Napoleonic rule in Spain, Holland, Westphalia, Italy, and Naples.

Index